INTRODUCTION TO
MODERN SPANISH LITERATURE

Introduction to Modern

SPANISH

LITERATURE

An Anthology of Fiction, Poetry and Essay

Edited by
KESSEL SCHWARTZ

TWAYNE PUBLISHERS, INC.
New York

Acknowledgments

Fiction:

The selection by Vicente Blasco-Ibáñez is from *The Four Horsemen of the Apocalypse* from the Spanish of Vicente Blasco-Ibáñez. Authorized translation by Charlotte Brewster Jordan. Copyright, 1918, by E. P. Dutton & Co., Inc. Renewal, 1945, by Mario Blasco-Ibáñez Blasco, Sigfrido Blasco-Ibáñez Blasco, Libertad Blasco-Ibáñez Blasco, Vda. de Llorca. Reprinted by permission of the publishers.

The selection by Miguel de Unamuno is from *San Manuel Bueno, Mártir* and is reprinted by permission of the publishers, George G. Harrap & Co., Ltd. Translated by Francisco de Segovia and Jean Perez.

Ramón Del Valle-Inclán is represented by a selection from *The Pleasant Memoirs of the Marquis de Bradomín* by Ramón Del Valle-Inclán, translated by May Heywood Broun and Thomas Walsh. Reprinted by permission of Harcourt, Brace and World, Inc.

The selection reprinted from *The Restlessness of Shanti Andía and Other Writings* by Pío Baroja, translated by Anthony Kerrigan, is by permission of the University of Michigan Press; copyright © by the University of Michigan, 1959. Library of Congress Catalog Card No. 59–5063. Published in the United States of America by the University of Michigan Press and simultaneously in Toronto, Canada, by Ambassador Books, Ltd. Printed in the United States of America by Vail-Ballou Press, Inc., Binghamton, N. Y.

The selection from *Belarmino and Apolonio* by Ramón Pérez de Ayala is from *European Caravan*, edited and translated by Samuel Putnam. Reprinted by permission of Harcourt, Brace & World, Inc.

The selection by Ramón J. Sender from *A Man's Place*, translated by Oliver La Farge, is reprinted by permission of the author. The selection from *Requiem for a Spanish Peasant* by Ramón J. Sender is reprinted with the permission of the Las Americas Publishing Company. Translated by Elinor Randall.

The selection from *The Cypresses Believe in God* by José María Gironella, translated by Harriet de Onis, is reprinted by permission of Alfred A. Knopf, Inc., the publisher. Copyright © 1955 by Alfred A. Knopf, Inc.

The selection from *Pascal Duarte's Family* by Camilo José Cela is reprinted by permission of the author. Translated by John Marks.

The selection from *The Hive* by Camilo José Cela is reprinted by permission of Farrar, Straus & Giroux, Inc. Copyright, 1953, by Camilo José Cela. Translated by J. M. Cohen.

The selection from *The Young Assassins* by Juan Goytisolo, translated by John Rust, is reprinted by permission of Alfred A. Knopf, Inc. Copyright © 1958 by Alfred A Knopf, Inc.

Poetry:

The poems of Miguel de Unamuno and Juan Ramón Jiménez, translated by E. L. Turnbull, are reprinted from *Ten Centuries of Spanish Po-*

etry © 1955, with permission of the Johns Hopkins Press. The poems of
Pedro Salinas, Jorge Guillén, Federico García Lorca, Vicente Aleixandre,
Rafael Alberti, and Luis Cernuda are all reprinted from the translations of
E. L. Turnbull appearing in *Contemporary Spanish Poetry* © 1945, with
permission of the Johns Hopkins Press.

The selections of Rubén Darío, "Sonatina," translated by John Pierrepont Rice, "Nightfall in the Tropics," "Canción of Autumn in Springtime,"
and "Portico," translated by Thomas Walsh, are from *Hispanic Notes and
Monographs* © 1920, with permission of The Hispanic Society of America. "Symphony in Gray Major" by Rubén Darío, translated by Alice
S. McVan, is reprinted from *Translations from Hispanic Poems* © 1920.

The poems of Antonio Machado are reprinted from *Eighty Poems of
Antonio Machado* with the permission of Las Americas Publishing Company in agreement with Willis Barnstone, translator.

The poems of León Felípe, "Query," "Where Is God?" "First Lesson,"
"I Know Where He Is," "There Is No God!" and "But Who Is the
Bishop?" translated by Willis Knapp Jones, are reprinted with permission
of Poet Lore, a division of Literary Publications, Inc. The poems "Little
Prologues," "What a Pity," and "Drop a Star" are published by permission
of the Losada Publishing Company of Argentina.

The Hispanic Institute in the United States, Columbia University, has
granted permission for the reprinting of four poems by Miguel Hernández.
The poem "Winds of the People" was taken from *And Spain Sings*, published by Vanguard Press. We asked the publisher for permission to re-
print the poem, but were informed that the editor of the book, M. J.
Bernadette, owned the copyright. We made every effort to locate the editor of *And Spain Sings*, but were unable to do so. Translated by Willard
Maas.

José Hierro has granted permission for the reprinting of his poems.

Essays:
Chapter 1 from *The Tragic Sense of Life*, by Miguel de Unamuno,
translated by J. E. Crawford Flitch, is reprinted with the permission of
Macmillan & Co., Ltd.

Passages from *An Hour of Spain* by Azorin (José Martínez Ruiz),
translated by Alice Raleigh, is reprinted with the permission of Routledge
& Kegan Paul Ltd

The selection by Ramiro de Maeztu is from *Authority, Liberty, and
Function* by Ramiro de Maeztu and is reprinted with the permission of
George Allen & Unwin Ltd.

The selection from *The Revolt of the Masses* by José Ortega y Gasset
is reprinted by permission of W. W. Norton & Company, Inc. Copyright,
1932, by W. W. Norton & Company, Inc., and copyright © 1960 by
Teresa Carey.

Julián Marías has granted permission for the reprinting of selections
from his *Reason and Life*, translated by Kenneth Reid and Edward
Sarmiento.

Contents

Contents

Introduction

Spanish literature, which rivals in richness that of France and England, has often been disregarded by the English-speaking world. In the United States, where the Spaniard was considered the arch-defender of a Catholicism against which Cotton Mather thundered, and where the early cultural impetus came from the colonial bulwarks of religious freedom, such neglect may be understood. The successful revolt of the Spanish possessions from what they felt to be the Catholic tyranny of their erstwhile masters contributed to the exaggerations and distortions accepted about Spanish culture, as Spain became a convenient cultural scapegoat. In later years the efforts of brilliant Spanish professors like Henry Wadsworth Longfellow helped reassess the remarkable Spanish heritage of the English-speaking world. Unfortunately, until quite recently, the lack of good translations of Spanish masterpieces has hampered the understanding of the remarkable Spanish mind.

Few are the Western nations which have escaped the influence of Spanish writers. Corneille, Molière, Scarron, Chateaubriand, Rousseau, Hugo, Camus, and Montherlant are but a few French names in the galaxy of those influenced by Spanish models. In Germany, the Schlegel brothers, the Grimm brothers, Goethe, Fichte, Heine, and Schopenhauer embraced the enchantment of Spanish literature and showed its impact in their literary productions. In the English-speaking world Spanish cultural contributions have been continuous. The didactic literature published under the aegis of Alfonso the Learned in the thirteenth century was translated into English by Lord Rivers and others. Juan Manuel's *Book of Examples* was the genesis of Shakespeare's *The Taming of the Shrew*. The *Celestina*, the picaresque and pastoral novels, and Cervantes' works offered a vast storehouse of materials to the English writers. Fletcher depended, for most of his plots, on Cervantes' *Exemplary Tales*. *The Fair Maid of the Inn*, based on *La ilustre fregona*, and *The Chances*, from *La señora Cordelia*, are but two examples. Middleton and Rowley dramatized Cervantes' *La Gitanilla* as *The*

1

Spanish Gipsie. The plots of *Twelfth Night* and *Two Gentlemen of Verona* stemmed from Jorge de Montemayor's *Diana*. Ben Jonson and John Dryden revealed their debt to Spanish classic literature, and Tirso de Molina's *The Trickster of Seville* influenced countless adaptations including those of Lord Byron and George Bernard Shaw. The picaresque tradition in Spain gave many peripatetic models to Fielding, Smollett, Richardson, and Sterne; and one may see, as well, the direct influence of Spain in the plays of Foote and Steele and the entire Restoration Comedy. In the Romantic period Byron translated ballads in addition to utilizing the Don Juan theme; Hazlitt wrote critical evaluations of Spanish works; Keats used Spanish novels of chivalry as partial sources for some of his poetry; Southey translated Spanish works, including the *Amadís de Gaula*; and Shelley beautifully translated Calderonian poetic drama, especially scenes from *The Wonder Working Magician*.

In the United States Alexander Hamilton held literary gatherings where Spanish literature was discussed, and Thomas Jefferson knew Spanish literature well enough to read *Don Quixote* in the original. Washington Irving wrote works on Spanish history and literature and adapted its folklore to his own use. William Cullen Bryant, W. D. Howells, Herman Melville, and Mark Twain all admitted their admiration for and debt to Hispanic literature. In the twentieth century, Ezra Pound, Christopher Morley, John Steinbeck, Ernest Hemingway, and Katherine Anne Porter reveal the impact of Spain and Spanish themes in their works.

One might generalize about Spanish literature that its characteristics include didactic intent, dignity, humor, stoicism, a strong sense of honor, an interest in popular art forms, improvisation, impetuousness, and great individuality. Such generalizations, of course, cannot be scientifically applied to ten centuries of Spanish literature, but they may serve as guidelines. In all probability, however, it is Spain's incredible dualism, inherited in part from the countless invasions of Spanish soil and the fusion of occidental and oriental philosophy, which sets its literature apart. One Spain is the critical, questioning, liberal, democratic Spain of the Erasmist writers of the sixteenth century, the Encyclopedists of the eighteenth, and the disciples of the Institution of Free Learning in the nineteenth and twentieth centuries. The other Spain is the traditional, scholastic, Catholic Spain of Phillip II, of the Counter Reformation, and in more modern times of Menéndez y Pelayo and Ramiro de Maeztu. The forces of progress combat those of tradition, and the constant interplay of the idealism of Don Quixote, who sees giants, with the materialism of Sancho, who sees only windmills, is reflected in countless other works. In the sixteenth century the Italianate poetry is vigorously combated by the traditional ballad form and other national themes. To oppose the idealistic forms of fiction such as the pastoral novel and the novel of chivalry, there appears the rich picaresque tradition. For every hero such as the chivalrous Amadís there arises an antihero such as Lazarillo. In the seventeenth century, the baroque offerings of Quevedo, Lope, Calderón, Góngora and others reveal the tension of the two worlds. Continuing attempts to graft on to the scholastic Middle Ages the humanism and modernism of the Western world have created a constant coalescence of Ahriman and Ormazd as the distinguishing characteristic of Spanish culture.

An exterior explanation, therefore, of the enchantment of Spanish literature proves difficult and deceptive, for Spanish customs and culture are only partly those of our world. Thus, Janus-faced, Spain evokes images in the viewer's mind of the picturesque, the spiritual or the passionate, depending largely on the reader's own orientation, as Spanish belief struggles with European objective thought.

The Middle Ages

Spain's earliest lyric expression stems from the eleventh century. Some fifty little songs or refrains, attached to Hebrew and Arabic poetry known as *muwassahas,* refer without exception to love. These refrains, known as *kharjas,* express with simple sincerity the dual emotions of grief and joy of the ever fresh first love of the adolescent girl. However, the first complete (or nearly complete) Spanish literary work, epic in form, is the *Song of the Cid* which extols the virtues of Spain's national hero, Rodrigo Díaz de Vivar.

The Cid differs from other epic heroes in that he was a historical figure whose poem was written approximately fifty years after his death. In its treatment of real battles, geography, and historical events, it largely excludes the fantastic elements of other epic poems. The standard edition contains 3,735 assonating lines of varying syllable count with those of sixteen predominating. The poem treats of the unjust exile of the Cid, his conquest of Valencia and other battles, the winning of the king's pardon, the marriage and betrayal of the Cid's daughters by the cowardly Princes of Carrión, and the Cid's final vengeance and victory. The epic Cid, however, is not the historical one. The anonymous poet stresses that the Cid is a self-made man, a brave, democratic but loyal Castilian noble who fights against the arrogant Leonese nobility. He is magnanimous, dignified, pious, a good father, a loving husband, and as a paragon of virtue, the perfect hero. The author uses a direct-dialogued style, evocative verb forms, and suggests much through sudden silences. The poem's naturalness and simplicity make it seem more spontaneous than the more contrived and structured French epic.

From the thirteenth century date the great law and historical volumes produced under Alfonso the Learned (1221-84). Known as the "emperor of culture," he gathered around him men of learning in all branches of knowledge, and although he himself may not have written all the works produced at his court, he directed, revised, and served as the guiding light for the literary and cultural endeavors. His most refreshing work is *The Canticles of Saint Mary*, probably the best Marian poetry of the Middle Ages. Of special interest among the some four hundred brief lyric poems accompanied by Christian, Arabic and popular music, is the one preserved Castilian canticle of love. His great historical works earned him the title of "father of Spanish prose." The first complete national history, the *First General Chronicle*, so called to distinguish it from future ones in part based on it, begins with the Flood and ends with the Visigothic reign. The second part, not finished until 1289, brings Spain's history to the death of Alfonso's father, Saint Ferdinand, and uses Spanish epic poems for some of the historical material. *The Seven Parts*, also known simply as *The Parts*, so called because of the seven chapters each of which begins with a letter of Alfonso's name, is more than the first modern code of laws in any country. In addition to the various kinds of moral, philosophical, and political maxims discussed, it reveals the customs and manners of the day. Its legislative and literary value label it as one of the great masterpieces of the Middle Ages. Alfonso was also responsible for the translation of *Calila y Dimna*, the first animal fables and other stories to be based on Oriental sources.

Other samples of narrative prose of the day include the *Book of the Deceits and Wiles of Women*, translated from the Arabic in 1253 by order of Alfonso's brother Prince Fadrique. The framework is that of a wicked queen, rejected by her stepson, who has him condemned to death. The trial is delayed through the telling of stories, and justice finally triumphs. It is one of the first works to deal with the battle of the sexes. *Barlaam and Josaphat*, attributed to St. John of Damascus, is a Christianized version of the legend of Buddha, and its stories served as a plot storehouse for Boccaccio and others.

The Spanish Middle Ages produced two principal poetic forms, the *mester de juglaría,* or minstrel's mode, used by the public entertainer who recited ballads and epic poems, and the *mester de clerecía,* or cleric's mode, a product of ecclesiastical erudition in the monasteries. The clerics counted their syllables and normally employed a stanza known as "Fourfold Way," of four lines of fourteen syllables each, with the same end rhyme, a form that Rubén Darío, king of Modernist poets, called "a primitive box which encaged a divine bird." Among the many thirteenth-century titles in the *juglar* manner we have: *Life of Saint Mary of Egypt,* about a sinful Egyptian magdalen who embraces holy ways; *Dispute of the Soul and the Body;* and the satirical-allegorical *Debate Between Water and Wine* to which is attached the first complete lyric poem in Castilian known as *Story of Love.* It concerns the meeting between a beautiful lady and the disconsolate poet near a refreshing and flower-encircled spring. Among the *clerecía* contributions are: *Book of Alexander,* a lengthy poem of more than 10,000 lines on the life of Alexander the Great; and *Book of Apolonius,* relating the adventures of the King of Tyre and his daughter, which many consider the oldest Spanish source for the Byzantine adventure novel.

Most of the lyric productions between the twelfth and fourteenth centuries were written in Galician-Portuguese and included satirical and bawdy songs, amorous laments and love songs from a loving lady to her "friend." Much of this poetry has been preserved in *cancioneiros* or song books, of which the three principal ones are *Cancioneiro da Vaticana, Cancioneiro Colocci-Brancuti,* and *Cancioneiro da Ajuda.* The first poet known to us by name is the curate Gonzalo de Berceo, born in the late twelfth century. Although he transcribes in erudite form, he stresses his lack of learning. He writes with simplicity, sweetness, freshness, and popular flavor. His nine poems are largely religious and include the *Life of Saint Domingo, Life of Saint Oria,* and especially the allegorical *Miracles of Our Lady,* poetic rephrasings of twenty-five miracles wrought by the Virgin.

Juglaría productions continued in the fourteenth century along with Galician-Portuguese poetry. The outstanding exponent of gnomic literature, Rabbi Sem Tob, composed his *Moral Proverbs* around 1360. Many prose works appeared including titles such as *The Great Conquest of Palestine,* a pseudohistorical version of the Crusades, which offers, among its motifs, that of Lohengrin, the Swan Knight, *Chronicle of the Kings of Castile*, by Pero López de Ayala, and a variety of treatises on classes, arms, hunting, horsemanship, and "engines of war" by Juan Manuel, the greatest master of the brief narrative form in the century.

Juan Manuel (1282-1349), the nephew of Alfonso the Learned, snatched time from his continual battles against the Moors and others to produce some fifty apologues or pseudo-parables, which he calls examples, collected under the title of *Count Lucanor* or the *Book of Patronio*. The moral anecdotes, many based on oriental and Arabic sources, resemble those found in Boccaccio's *Decameron Tales*, written much later, but without the Italian author's sensuality. The author writes in a clear style as he seeks to use "the fewest and most suitable words possible." In his attack on vanity, avarice, hypocrisy, and all the other defects that plague mankind, he seeks to "sugar-coat" his pills of advice to make them more palatable. Among the well-known stories are *The Taming of the Shrew* and *The Emperor's New Clothes*. The Count, constantly plagued by a variety of problems, asks his counselor, Patronio, for advice. Patronio then relates a story involving the same problem so that the Count may draw the obvious moral lesson. The distrustful author deposited signed accurate copies of all his works in the monastery at Peñafiel to insure that posterity would not consult adulterated works, but unfortunately the monastery was destroyed and the certified copies were lost. Certified or not, however, the stories, told with restrained humor and gentle irony, are among the best products of the writings of a long line of soldier-writers who combine the best of "arms and letters."

Novels of chivalry constitute the other important prose fiction of the century. These were largely exotic transplants from France, but the great Spanish knights-errant such as Amadís became so throughly nationalized that they appeared to be native products. The first original full-length Spanish novel of this type, written about 1300, was *The Caballero Cifar*. Its four parts combined the legend of St. Eustace with later Byzantine fiction and magical elements, but in the creation of the proverb-spouting squire, Ribaldo, and in its didactic realism, the novel is typically Spanish. It concerns the adventures and dangers of Cifar who after countless adventures is reunited with his lady fair. Although it is somewhat theologically oriented, the work contains the germs of the later more sophisticated Renaissance novel of Chivalry and marks a great stride forward in the use of stylistic devices and language.

The greatest literary work of the fourteenth century, and among the greatest of all Spanish literature, is the *Book of Good Love* by the archpriest of the little town of Hita, Juan Ruiz, born around 1283. His archbishop imprisoned him for reasons we do not know, and he supposedly wrote his work in jail, the first of a long series of Spanish masterpieces conceived under such unhappy circumstances. *The Book of Good Love* contains 1,723 lyrical and narrative stanzas written in a variety of poetic meters including the *cuaderna vía or* "Fourfold Way," for the poet hoped to enlighten his readers as to the variety of versification to be found in Spanish poetry. The work deals ironically, satirically, sensually, and delicately with love in its many manifestations. The incidents, perhaps partly autobiographical, serve to delineate two types of love, the good love of God and the crazy love of women. Ruiz says he is writing his work to show the dangers of this mundane love of which all living beings, beautiful and ugly, partake. In addition to a great number of humorous and often scandalously funny fables and tales, encounters with mountain girls, apparently sincere sermons and lovely poems to the Virgin Mary and on the Passion of Christ, and an allegorical battle between Lord Flesh and Lady Lent, the former of whom becomes the ally of Lord Love, the main theme concerns the archpriest's love for Doña Endrina. Love encourages him to choose an old woman procuress, Doña Urraca, known as the Convent Trotter, to aid him in his seduction. The work may have served as a generating force for the *Canterbury Tales* of Chaucer, whose visit to Spain has been little publicized. Juan Ruiz is the first great Spanish humorist and realist. Although his purpose may be didactic, he has written a spontaneous social spectacle of throbbing life whose jokes, proverbs, and popular speech, delightful stanzas in praise of little women, songs of the begging scholars and blind men, and other lyrical, satirical, religious, and moral fragments have fused into a classical, ecclesiastical, and oriental masterpiece.

The work's duality is reflected in the Archpriest, a jovial human sinner and yet a religious and tolerant man who believes that one can be both devout and gay. Some may think the content of the work to be somewhat disparate and heterogeneous, but the principal theme of the pious sinner, who in spite of his good intentions succumbs to human temptation and suffers a series of largely unsuccessful amorous adventures, exudes a universal human freshness whose emphasis foreshadows the approaching Renaissance.

The final figure of the fourteenth century, Pero López de Ayala (1332-1407), is called by some Spain's first humanist. He, too,

supposedly wrote his masterpiece, *Rimado de Palacio*, in jail between the years 1380 and 1400. A satirical-moral composition in
cuaderna vía with interspersed poems of other meters, it is more
serious and sober than Ruiz' work. López de Ayala is embittered at
human depravity and at man's inability to improve or reform, and
his shock, dismay, and moralistic attitude differ greatly from the
cheerful, pagan, and gay spirit of Ruiz. In both books the subjects
range from religious topics to social satire, but the later author
cannot tolerate human weakness. Nevertheless, as a sincere, classi-
cally oriented ascetic he stands with Ruiz as a Renaissance precursor.

Semi-dramatic productions, in satirical narrative verse, were
popular in the fifteenth century. *The Dance of Death* in which the
latter calls members from all social levels to account is one of the
most important European versions of the theme. The *Coplas of
Mingo Revulgo,* an allegorical satire of the politics of the day is
another version of this form. The century produced the first collection of biographies written in Spanish, a series of thirty-four
sharply etched portraits in clean, concise, and sober prose, by
Fernán Pérez de Guzmán (1376?-1460?) in the third part of his
work *Sea of Histories.* Hernando del Pulgar (1436?-93?), official
historian of Ferdinand and Isabella, in his *Famous Men of Castile,*
a loosely structured work, gives us further insight into an important
period of Spanish development. The *Book of Apologues* by Clemente
Sanchez de Vercial, Spain's longest collection of medieval tales,
some five hundred in number, and the didactic prose of Enrique de
Villena (1384-1434) who wrote literary criticism, a treatise on
sorcery, and even an *Art of Carving,* are among other noteworthy
productions.

While the powerful favorite of King John II, Don Alvaro de
Luna (d. 1453) wrote a *Book of Famous and Virtuous Women* in
defense of the fairer sex, it is the satirical and realistic anti-feminist,
Alfonso Martínez de Toledo (1398-1470), the Archpriest of Talavera,
who has won the greater fame. His prose work known as *The
Scourge* contains four parts, the second of which attacks the affecta-
tions and excesses of women, their customs, their makeup, their
characters, and their colloquial and somewhat spicy language, and
makes of misogyny a studied art.

Although the novels of chivalry relating the loves and brave
deeds of loyal knights continued, the century was marked by the
development of another idealistc form of fiction, the sentimental
novel, based on Italian sources such as *La Fiammetta* of Boccaccio.
These novels treated love in an allegorical, idealistic and sentimental

fashion, and in addition to works by Juan Rodríguez de la Cámara (d. *ca.* 1450) and Juan de Flores based on Boccaccio's novel, were best represented by *The Prison of Love,* written about 1465 and published in 1492, by Diego de San Pedro. It had some twenty-five editions and was translated into more than twenty languages. These tales of tragic and unhappy loves continued into the Renaissance.

Song books, especially the *Cancionero de Baena,* 576 poems by 54 poets collected by Juan Alfonso de Baena, secretary of Juan II, reflected the religious, allegorical, and amorous writing of several poetic generations, but poetic fame in the century belongs primarily to three men. The first of these, Don Iñigo López de Mendoza, the Marquis of Santillana (1398-1458), perhaps the most complex poet of the day, was a humanist who combined arms and letters. In his propagation of the new culture he translated a series of Greek and Latin, as well as Italian, works into Spanish. His nonpoetic works include one of the oldest samples of literary criticism in Spanish, his famous "Letter and Prologue to the Condestable of Portugal" in 1449, and a collection of popular proverbs. His better known poetry includes the *Comedieta de Ponza,* an elegiac, narrative poem in the allegorical Dantesque style, which describes the naval defeat of the house of Aragon at Ponza in 1435. Its mythological trappings contrast sharply with the *Dialogue of Bias Against Fortune,* which stresses the stoic life and insists that a man of spirit can triumph over life's adversities. *Sonnets Done in the Italian Manner,* reputed to be the first sonnets written in Spanish, reveals another facet of his talent. It is in his songs and ten *serranillas,* relating the rustic encounters of refined cavaliers with shepherdesses, mountain girls or cow girls, that his exquisite, delicate, and graceful verse is most charming.

Juan de Mena (1411-56), often called Spain's first professional man of letters, for he did little else, wrote difficult poetry which borrows from Latin and Italian sources and uses involved syntax, hyperbaton, numerous erudite mythological references, an ornate style, and antedates the later renovation attempted by the Baroque poets of the seventeenth century. Mena also wrote light and musical amorous verse as well as moral and devout poetry, but he is best known for the *Labyrinth of Fortune,* often called *The Three Hundred* because of its some 297 stanzas, an imitation of Dante's *Divine Comedy,* concerning the Palace of Fortune, where guided by Providence, the poet views the past, present, and future wheels of Fortune. In spite of the allegory, the poem contains sincere human emotion and true patriotic fervor in some of its incidents.

The great nephew of the Marquis of Santillana, Jorge Manrique (1440-78) would be unknown today were it not for his creation of one poem, the immortal masterpiece and perhaps the most popular poem in the Spanish language, *On the Death of His Father*. The *coplas*, as they are known, which for Lope de Vega merited being written in letters of gold, consist of forty stanzas written in "limping verse," that is, two lines of eight syllables followed by one of four. An elegiac poem, it reveals more than personal sadness, for it both sums up the philosophy of the Middle Ages that this life is a preparation for the the eternal one beyond, and half glimpses the approach of the Renaissance. The principal but by no means exclusive theme is that of the *ubi sunt*, used by François Villon and others before Manrique, but to the latter belongs the honor of crystallizing the medieval spirit, as in elevated and yet simple style, he meditates on the transitory nature of worldly things, considers the brevity of power, beauty, and nobility, and follows with a eulogy for his father. Tranquillity and repose permeate the poem, which accepts that all lives are like rivers that wind to the sea, which is Death, and the value of virtue and eternal salvation.

The Renaissance

No exact definition of what constitutes the Golden Age of Spanish literature exists. For some it begins in 1492; others argue for 1499, the publication date of the famous *Celestina*; for others it is the period between 1575 and 1681, the date of Calderón's death. In general terms one may say that the Golden Age includes the first Spanish Renaissance of the first half of the sixteenth century; the second Renaissance, which corresponds roughly to the second half of the century; and the Baroque period of the seventeenth century. Spain, of course, had special ties with Italy through the domination of Milan, the Sicilies, and Naples, and many Spaniards studied in Italian universities, especially that of Bologna. Also, as we have seen, Renaissance manifestations may be found in the works of Juan Ruiz, the Marquis of Santillana and other supposed medieval Spanish writers. It was the Spaniards who made full use of new inventions such as the compass, accepted men like Erasmus and Baldassare Castiglione, ambassador to the court of Charles V and author of *The Courtier*, famous Renaissance guidebook of manners. Pedro Ponce founded the first school for deaf-mutes and, by teaching them to communicate, refuted Aristotle's position that they lacked a soul. The Copernican theory was taught in Spain.

The most enterprising humanists of the day were philologists. Antonio de Nebrija (1441-1522) wrote a Spanish grammar, the first in any modern tongue, which promoted that language over Latin as a cultural vehicle and as an instrument for consolidation of conquests, and Juan de Valdés (d. 1541) wrote the first stylistic treatise of the Spanish language. Cardinal Jiménez de Cisneros (1436-1517) supervised the writing of the six volumes of the great Complutensian Bible, and Antonio de Guevara (1481?-1545) and Juan Luis Vives (1492-1540) represented, along with Juan de Valdés and his brother Alfonso, the Erasmist philosophical current so important in the first half of the sixteenth century. Guevara's rhetorical prose, *Dial of Princes*, known as the *Golden Book of Marcus Aurelius*, 1529, achieved an extraordinary popularity at home and abroad, as did his *Scorn of Court and Praise of Rustic Life*, 1539.

Many insist, nevertheless, that the Renaissance never really triumphed in Spain because of the Inquisition, authorized in 1478, with its censorship of freedom of expression, and the later Counter Reformation led by Spanish churchmen. It must be noted that the old traditions continued to exist side by side with the Renaissance spirit. Thus it might be said that the Renaissance, as a transition from the medieval world to the modern one, involving a change in the minds and hearts and spirit of man and a switch from the single scholastic truth to the experimental human truth, achieved a coexistence with national religious and philosophical tenets. Spanish duality continued throughout the Golden Age in a constant interplay between humanists and the Church, Erasmists and the Counter Reformation, and the national religious sentimentality and intellectual curiosity, which explains, in part, the rigid point of honor of the great seventeenth-century drama.

One of the greatest Spanish masterpieces is the *Tragicomedy of Calisto and Melibea*, usually known simply as *The Celestina* after its colorful central character. Appearing at the end of the fifteenth century, in its fusion of the medieval spirit with that of the Renaissance in a new manner, it marks the appearance of the first really modern and classic work of Spanish literature. The hero and heroine symbolize the interplay of divine and human love; and the true protagonist, the procuress, Celestina, a direct descendant of the Convent Trotter in *The Book of Good Love*, is one of the truly great character creations in all literature. Although the work is presented in dialogue and semitheatrical form (it has no stage directions) and exhibits a decided dramatic intensity, it should probably be studied as fiction or as a work without genre. Controversy exists as to its composition and authorship. The first known version, in sixteen acts, appeared in 1499, but many critics feel it was written earlier. The third edition added five acts to the original sixteen. Some literary historians claim that Fernando de Rojas, a converted Jew, wrote the entire work. Others insist that he wrote all but the first act.

The plot itself is incidental, as it relates the love of Calisto and Melibea, brought together by Celestina, the falling out of the latter with her henchmen, her death, that of Calisto and his servants, and Melibea's suicide. Its prose is both richly classic and popular, in keeping with its fusion of humor and tragedy, profound idealism and crude naturalism; the description, dialogue, and action convey the idea of a world in transition. Melibea, the poetic lady, is contrasted with the witchlike Celestina, the noble Calisto with his greedy servants, the elevated language of the lovers with the racy dialect of the others, and all the characters take on an individual life and spirit unknown previously in Spanish literature. The lovers come to a tragic end, as the author perhaps intended, and the theme of moral retribution once more reveals how Spanish literature, even in the Renaissance, continued to utilize medieval motifs.

The ballads, which had existed in the fifteenth century (and even, some say, in the fourteenth), began to be published in the sixteenth century as a kind of popular refutation of the Italian metrical forms. Although countless theories exist about the origin of the ballads, their probable beginnings stem from "purple passages" torn from epics and sung to musical accompaniment. One theory, accounting for the slight variations found in any given ballad, holds that the people remembered favorite passages, which they had repeated for them, but which they remembered imperfectly. Later, of course, certain versions became fixed as the most popular ones. The ballads, orally transmitted from one generation to another, treat of historical, traditional, legendary, personal, and artistic themes. In older versions they were arranged in sixteen-syllable lines, all assonated. In modern form the ballads appear in lines of eight syllables, with even lines assonating. Varying in length from eight to about two hundred lines of verse, often fragmentary in nature, the ballads exhibit both epic and lyrical elements in a rapid narrative normally concerning a single incident or episode.

The ballads reflect the dignity and national spirit of Spain and have had a remarkable influence, even in the twentieth century.

The greatest poet of the first half of the sixteenth century was Garcilaso de la Vega (1503-36), the peerless soldier-poet, who through his friend Juan Boscán and his own diplomatic and military missions, learned Italian literature. Married unhappily, this refined Renaissance courtier, who possessed all the virtues of the day, became enamoured of the Portuguese Isabel Freyre,.a lovely lady who married another man, died in childbirth, and served as the heroine of Garcilaso's most successful eclogue. Garcilaso wrote only about 4,500 lines in all, published by Boscán's widow in 1543, but his sonnets, epistles, and eclogues reveal an accomplished artistry and quest for perfection. Garcilaso's bucolic and amorous poetry is important, for with him there begins a poetic revolution based on classic and Italian forms but fused with Spanish tradition, which was to leave its mark on following poetic generations such as those of Luis de León and Fernando de Herrera. The pastoral themes of which he was so fond are no longer in vogue, but no poet has surpassed him to this day in harmony, melody, and musicality; and he may number among his disciples some of the best poets of the twentieth century. In his famous first eclogue, two shepherds, representing Garcilaso in two time periods, lament the faithlessness and death of Elisa and Galatea (both Isabel Freyre). His sonnets and fifth song, where he gives birth to the Spanish *lira*, must also be noted. Garcilaso creates an ideal world of poetic imagination in adoration and exaltation of beauty and love. His nature is full of color, clarity, rhythm and sound, and a melancholy love that will have appeal as long as all the world loves a lover.

Gutierre de Cetina composed melodious and charming love lyrics, including the best known madrigal in the Spanish language, *Clear and Serene Eyes*. Other poets, led by Cristóbal de Castillejo (1490-1550), defended the traditional Spanish forms against the Italian imports.

In the second half of the century Fernando de Herrera (1534-97) represented the exuberant poetry of the so-called School of Seville. He, like an earlier poet in the century, Francisco de Figueroa, was granted the sobriquet *El Divino* (the divine). He wrote amorous elegies and songs under the inspiration of a lovely lady, but he also initiated an emphatic nationalization of Italian forms. He tried to be Spain's patriotic and epic poet, as his most celebrated poem, "On the Victory of Lepanto," in praise of the Spanish victory and

Don Juan of Austria, shows. His grandiloquent, noble style, full of majesty and rich metaphors, contrasts strongly with the gentle, graceful poetry of Garcilaso on whom he wrote a critical study in 1580, as he sought to establish the theoretical base for the classical Renaissance forms.

Spaniards of the sixteenth century went wild over Amadís de Gaula, the knight, whose adventures, publicized in a 1508 edition by Garci-Rodríguez de Montalvo, gained an unheard-of popularity. This series reached some two dozen books in all, and in spite of the prohibition on exporting them to the New World, they were read by almost everyone, including the conquistadors, St. Theresa, and St. Ignacio de Loyola. As with most novels of this type, Amadís, the illegitimate hero, fights giants, loves his lady fair, is both helped and hindered by magic, and finally triumphs over all. Although it is little read today because of its artificial prose and fantastic episodes, this form of idealistic fiction teaches bravery, sacrifice, the protection of the weak, and fair play.

Another type of idealistic fiction flourished around the middle of the century. The pastoral, whose origin can be traced to L'Ameto of Boccaccio, offered as its most famous Spanish sample The Seven Books of Diana, in mixed prose and verse, which appeared around 1559. Its false idealization of country living appealed to aristocratic readers, who identified themselves with the amorous laments and complicated loves of the false shepherds, who, like the knight-errant, had to contend with enchantment in order to win their lovely ladies.

Standing between the pastoral and the novel of chivalry in its mixture of realistic and idealistic fiction, the Moorish novel, a native Spanish form, extolled the virtues of gallant Moors and Christians, each outdoing the other in nobility and generosity. The first example, the simple and touching El Abencerraje, was included in the fourth book of the second edition of Diana and also appeared in 1565 in a miscellany called El Inventario by Antonio de Villegas. It is a typical Renaissance tale and one of the first truly artistic Spanish stories in the modern sense, in spite of its sometimes cloying sentimentality. The other work that may pass as a Moorish novel is The Civil Wars of Granada, in two parts. The first part, published in 1595, is almost a historical novel. Its author, Ginés Pérez de Hita (1544-1610), called it History of the Factions of the Zegríes and Abencerrajes. The work was universally acclaimed and copied by Mme de Scudéry, Madame de Lafayette, Cervantes, Chateaubriand, Washington Irving, and many others. It is a highly fictionalized account of the discovery of Granada, its kings, their histories, the battles of Christians and Moors, and, as background, the constant struggles between the two rival jealous Moorish bands, the Zegríes and the Abencerrajes. Supposedly, the false accusation and assassination of thirty-six leading Abencerraje nobles contributed to the fall of Granada to the Spaniards. The descriptions of the opulent Moorish society created a false but lasting image in Europe of that period and may have contributed to the concept of the Noble Savage of Rousseau.

As was to be expected in this land of contrasts, the idealistic forms of fiction conflicted with a new kind of novel based on the troubled life of the day, the deeply realistic picaresque form. Honor and glory gave way to the realities of hunger, cruelty, and crime, and instead of fighting monsters for the lady fair, the new protagonist fought society for his stomach's sake. The *pícaro* or rogue became a kind of antihero who reflected, not the false vision of a triumphant nation, but the real one of a land that wasted its gold for luxuries, a country where only Moors and Jews worked with their hands, and where returning conquerors and poor knights, too proud to beg, starved alongside the thousands of poor beggars in the city.

The picaresque novel, in spite of its humorous incidents, provides the tragic background of a nation in decay, as is amply illustrated by the first such novel, *The Life of Lazarillo de Tormes and of His Fortunes and Adversities,* which had three editions in 1554. The plot, based on folklore elements in a series of seven episodes connected by the protagonist, concerns the adventures of the illegitimate little Lazarillo in his service to a blind beggar, a curate, an impoverished hidalgo, and a variety of other masters. In this anonymous little work the several episodes allow the author to satirize various segments of society and present us with a gallery of human types, as each master opens, a little more, the innocent eyes of the goodhearted little ragamuffin to the realities of the day. Especially symbolic of sixteenth-century Spain is the starving hidalgo whose false pride and silly aristocratic airs keep him in his condition. Well dressed outwardly with cloak and sword, this perfect gentleman suffers inwardly and is content to live off the begged bread of his servant, Lazarillo, who cannot afford the false pride and fine sentiments of his master. *Lazarillo de Tormes* was forbidden, put on the Index, but was eventually published in expurgated form.

The other picaresque novels, published after a hiatus of some forty years, were longer and more complete documents of the

dilemmas of the day. They contained a cruder language, more
bitterness as well as moralizing, as they attacked the conditions
which had spawned economic chaos and crime in Spain. Among
the best of these was that of Mateo Alemán (1547-1614?), *Life of
the Rogue Guzmán de Alfarache,* published in two parts in 1599
and 1604. Subtitled "a watchtower to view human life," it told a
tale of bad companions, crooked shopkeepers, thieving monasteries,
and a corrupt government. The grace, simplicity, subtlety, and warm
humor of Lazarillo gave way to a caustic exposure of a society
where life belonged to the swift and the strong. Other picaresque
novels include: *Paul, the Spanish Sharper,* by Francisco de Quevedo
y Villegas (1580-1645); *Life of the Squire Marcos de Obregón,*
by Vicente Espinel (1550-1624); *The Book of Entertainment of
the Rogue Justina* (1605), a kind of rough and ready Moll Flanders,
attributed to Francisco López de Ubeda; and *The Limping Devil*
(1640) by Luis Vélez de Guevara (1579-1644). Most of the *picaros*
are old when they relate their autobiographies, which may logically
account for the cynical tone. In a sense the picaresque novel, given
its almost too vivid adventures, reflects the deformation of reality
rather than reality in an absolute sense, but its intent is to portray
accurately the essence of the times.

The sixteenth-century drama had nothing to compare with the
great works of genius of the following century. The so-called father
of the Spanish theater, Juan del Encina (1463?-1529) composed
some 170 works before the age of thirty. Most of his eclogues, as
he called his dramatic pieces, dealt with the rustic reaction to a
religious event, and his crude types, who often spoke amusing
gibberish, became almost standard creations in the drama of the
day. In his later work he showed marked improvement in dramatic
form as a love theme complemented the comic-lyrical elements
normally part of his work. Of much greater importance, Gil Vicente
(1469?-1536?), known better today as a lyric poet, wrote forty-three
dramas, of which twenty are a combination of Spanish and Portuguese and eleven are entirely in Spanish. His *autos,* such as *The
Sibyl Cassandra,* combine pagan mythology with Biblical elements;
his allegorical trilogy, *Ship of Glory,* contributes an important *Dance
of Death* version; and his *Comedia de Rubena* (1521) is the first
comedy of magic. All his works contain a poetic, evocative language
and musical expression.

The first author to exhibit a complete dramatic technique, however, was Bartolomé Torres Naharro (d. 1531). He divided his
works, published under the title *Propalladia* ("The first fruits of

Pallas"), in 1517 into *a noticia* (realistic) and *a fantasía* (imaginary) types, an early division into tragedy and comedy not observed by later authors. He used other dramatic rules based on classical models, such as the limitation of characters, insistence on decorum, and five acts. He contributed excellent character portrayals as well as the first real cape-and-sword play, *Comedia Himenea,* a tale of frustrated lovers which involves the use of the *gracioso,* or comic foil for the hero, as well as the Spanish concept of honor. Lope de Rueda (1510?-65), actor, manager, and author, brought the people a kind of repertory theater and the creation of types such as the cleric, the soldier, and the fool. In his longer works, such as *Comedia Armelina* and his best known, *Comedia Eufemia,* he employs Italian-based formulas, but it is for his *pasos,* one-act farces based on the foibles of humble folk, that he is remembered today. The ten extant lively, realistic, and humorous playlets satirize, with fidelity and naturalness, the customs and manners of his time. Juan de la Cueva (1550?-1610?), the first to dramatize national themes such as the Cid, insisted on many innovations such as the mixing of tragedy and comedy, the portrayal of violence on stage, the disregarding of the unities, and the use of four acts instead of five.

Spanish mysticism appeared late in terms of Western tradition; Italian influences and popular tradition had already prepared the necessary metaphors and symbols for a more complicated language, and this fusion of realism and idealism can clearly be seen in the lives and works of the mystics. They explained a series of steps along a mystic way through which one might reach God, including a desire for God, purification through penitence and prayer, and the final dark rapture of the spiritual union of the soul with God. Many mystics contributed eloquent expressions of faith, but it was St. Theresa (1515-82), a mystic who wrote familiarly and unpretentiously, who symbolized the best of the movement, as can be seen in *Book of Her Life,* where she describes her mystic experiences, and in *Book of Foundations,* the history of her struggles to establish her new Carmelite Order. Her capacity to combine religious contemplation and mystic rapture with human struggle reveals itself most perfectly in her masterpiece, *The Inner Citadel* or *The Mansions of the Soul,* 1588: One must pass through seven rooms, the several stages necessary to reach God.

Luis de León (1527-91), scholar, theologian, and philosopher, persecuted as were most of the mystics by the Inquisition, wrote a number of prose works such as *The Names of Christ,* a meditation on the meaning of sobriquets in the Bible, and *The Perfect Wife*, a somewhat conservative guide for married women, both published in 1583. We remember him today, however, for his poetry, published by Francisco de Quevedo in 1631, which establishes him as one of the half-dozen great poets of the language. In his work one finds the perfect mixture of the Christian and Platonic ideal, of mystical aspiration and Renaissance spirit, of the divine and human. In his forty poems he sometimes surpasses Garcilaso in form, as he meditates harmoniously on the somewhat Horatian message that one should lead a simple life and appreciate the joys of nature and the handiwork of God, freed from love and hate. He combined beauty and morality with technical perfection and profundity in the *lira* form of which he is the supreme master. In addition to his many moving original poems such as "Withdrawn Life" and "Calm Night," he produced lovely translations of Biblical verses. Saint John of the Cross (1542-91), the Carmelite disciple of St. Theresa, is the most complex, abstract, metaphysical, and perhaps lyrical mystic of the sixteenth century. His sensory imagery seeks to express his anguished longing and superhuman love. In his work there is almost a complete separation from the real world, although to express himself he is forced to use the vocabulary of human love and tenderness, as well as a nature of fields and animals. In his "Dark Night of the Soul," "Spiritual Canticle," and "Living Flame of Love," he conveys his desire for an ineffable union with the Almighty and seeks through his own interior light and rapturous spiritual joy to illuminate the "dark night of his soul."

The Baroque Period

The greatest figure of Spanish literature is Miguel de Cervantes (1547-1616). An ordinary man, plagued by the problems which beset us all, he represents the supreme combination of arms and letters on which he discourses in his immortal *Don Quixote*. He appeared at the perfect moment, when Erasmus and the Protestant Reformation had left their mark, when Spain was a unified world power, and when all types of novel had already become known. Like his immortal Don Quixote he was an hidalgo, that is, of a family which had held property and could date its Catholicism to the ninth century. His soldiering, wounds, ransom, and countless other experiences appear in one form or another in his works, which include some twenty or thirty dramas, as he states in the prologue of his 1615 collection of dramas, of which *Numancia,* written between 1582 and 1587, is the best known extant one. His *entremeses* or Interludes, one-act farces published in 1615, contain an interplay of the real and the ideal, universal values and the human spirit. Although they are hilarious, in his best ones, such as *The Altarpiece of Marvels,* he exposes the hypocritical aspects of racial superiority or explains some human virtue or vice in a new light. Among his novels are the pastoral *La Galatea,* 1585, inferior only to the *Diana,* and *The Trials of Persiles y Sigismunda,* a Byzantine novel, published posthumously in 1617, and involving a romantic description of fearful adventures, which stylistically almost equals his famous masterpiece.

His twelve *Exemplary Tales,* intended for the refreshment of the spirit, also convey a moral lesson. He paints vice and brutality along with delicate fantasy, but always with a richness of style and with philosophical overtones such as the importance of true honor or the meaning of pride. He stresses that moral and spiritual values and bravery, honesty, and truth will triumph over adversity, as purity and beauty will overcome sensuality and ugliness, but he is too good a psychologist to falsify the apparent nature of human beings. He conveys also a rollicking humor which involves insight into what it means to be a human being. *The Colloquy of the Dogs* and *The Licentiate Made of Glass* demonstrate profound truths about people through the mouths of dogs and a madman. *The Little Gypsy Girl* and *Rinconete and Cortadillo,* a study of two little rogues who join a thieves' union to live, convey other striking portraits.

Don Quixote de la Mancha, in two volumes (1605 and 1615), possibly the world's greatest novel, has gone through about six hundred editions. From the title itself, a mixture of known and unknown elements, to the end of the work, the author never precisely describes anything but uses general terms which give a universal and almost timeless quality to the work. Thus the housekeeper was a lady who "kept on passing forty," much as Quixote "was flirting with fifty." Written in a rhythmical and poetic style, the novel obviously follows the form of the novel of chivalry, although it contains many insert stories based on the Moorish, Picaresque, Pastoral, and Italianate novels formerly in vogue. The work is much more, however, than a parody of chivalric romance or even a masterful portrait of Spanish society. Cervantes seeks the beautiful in the ugly, the poetic in the materialistic. It is significant that, for whatever reason, those who mock the knight enter his idealistic frame of reference, however briefly, and that he does not descend to theirs. In the final analysis Don Quixote, the idealist who wants to redress wrongs, and Sancho Panza, his credulous and good-hearted squire who half-accepts a mysterious unmaterialistic world, represent, not two sides of a coin, but a humanity which struggles to raise itself and reaffirm the highest values man possesses. Although every reader will interpret meanings for himself, and some will still read the work for entertainment and appreciation of its humor, *Don Quixote* reflects on the meaning of reality, the meaning of life, good and evil, the relativity of truth, the meaning of creative imagination, and the concept of good works. This poor devil, crazed, according to the "normal" members of society, by too much reading of novels of chivalry, enters the world to combat for his faith and his ideal. In spite of the humor inherent in converting windmills into giants, a barber's basin into the enchanted helmet of Mambrino, and prostitutes into ladies, one cannot claim that Quixote has failed spiritually. In the brief space of three or four months, while traveling over a relatively small geographical entity, Quixote and Sancho savor life's entire gamut of experiences and give us an almost universally applicable philosophy of life, based not on the differences between the two as much as on their identity as human beings. In the end it is as Alonso Quijano, *the Good,* a man who followed the Golden Rule, that he dies. Flaubert, Dostoevski, and others have paid moving tributes to Cervantes' creation, but it is the author himself, through the words of Sampson Carrasco in the third chapter of the second part, who realized he had created a work for all ages and for all time.

Seventeenth-century Spanish literature, in its preoccupation with an ornate style and in its reflection of the doubts and tensions of the age, is clearly baroque. Of the two baroque literary forms of the day, culteranism and conceptism, the former is an artificial exaggeration of language in order to create esoteric beauty, whereas the latter operates on a level of abstract thought. Both represent a distortion of proportion. The century reflects the antithetical and paradoxical combination of the scholastic philosophy of the Middle Ages and the humanism of the Renaissance.

Luis de Góngora (1561-1627), whose name became synonymous with the baroque movement known as Gongorism, wrote subtly, though not unintelligibly, and he elevated poetry to a new level with his sophisticated form. Góngora also wrote countless simple and lyric ballads, songs and sonnets, along with works such as the unfinished polyphonic pastoral, *Solitudes* (1613), the extravagant *Fable of Polyphemus and Galatea* (1612), and the Fable of *Pyramus and Thisbe* (1618). If, as some say, he lacked ideas and real emotion, he succeeded esthetically in fusing the popular and cultured forms, and few have equalled his superlative lyrics in colorful image, harmonious rhythms, or daring metaphors.

Dozens of good dramatists held the stage in the seventeenth century including Francisco de Rojas Zorrilla (1607-48), author of one of the most perfect honor plays, *None Below the King* and Guillén de Castro (1569-1630), whose *Youthful Exploits of the Cid* inspired Corneille's work. Four names, however, undoubtedly stand out from the galaxy of stars: Lope de Vega, Tirso de Molina, Juan Ruiz de Alarcón, and Calderón de la Barca.

Lope Félix de Vega Carpio (1562-1635), called by Cervantes the "Monster of Nature," like the other great writers of his day expressed the baroque Spanish duality in his life and works. Although he composed short stories, pastoral novels, a dialogued novel, religious works, and epic and didactic poetry, his genius was essentially lyric. His melodious and delicate poetry, much of it published separately, adds great luster to his reputation. His poetic dramas of varied types are basically historically and popularly oriented and draw their themes from collections of ballads, legends, and national traditions. His eighteen hundred dramas, of which almost five hundred have survived, contain complicated intrigue, duels, and rivalries; but the principal elements are the point of honor, love, defense of the monacrhy, and orthodox Catholic faith. In these dramas Lope brings the *gracioso* to his highest development as a comic foil. Cervantes and Góngora synthesized the modern Spanish novel and poetry, respectively, much as Lope created modern Spanish drama.

To please the public, which almost deliriously demanded his productions, Lope composed too rapidly to maintain a consistent high level, but even in his worst dramas there occur marvelous poetic lines, and his versatility, grace, and facility help disguise his improvisations. Among his best works are the semihistorical *Fuenteovejuna*, about the revolt of an entire village against a corrupt and villainous nobleman; *The Best Magistrate the King*, where the king takes the side of the peasant against an unworthy nobleman; *Peribáñez and the Comendador of Ocaña*, another honor play in which the commoner asserts his right to dignity; and *The Star of Seville*, which some deny he wrote, a drama which examines the intricate relationships of the honor code, between a king and his subjects and between men and women.

Tirso de Molina (1584-1648), a follower of Lope's new *comedia*, exhibits greater character portrayal, expository clarity, sharper satire, and better comic sense than the master. He wrote historical plays such as *The Prudence of Women*, about an early fourteenth-century queen; one of the great religious dramas, *Doubter Damned*, on the problem of salvation and God's grace; and complicated cape-and-sword plays such as *Don Gil of the Green Breeches*; but of his four hundred dramas, of which seventy have survived, the most famous is *The Trickster of Seville*, which gave to the world the figure of Don Juan. The principal idea expressed by Tirso is that man must answer for his conduct to God, and Don Juan, for all his positive qualities of rank and bravery, so important in his time, must suffer the consequence of his folly in choosing the pleasures of the flesh over the possibility of salvation. It is from Tirso's creation that all future Don Juans receive their impetus, although some of the modern versions would hardly be recognizable by their origi-nator. As with Don Quixote, each generation interprets and defines the great seducer in accordance with its own esthetic and philo-sophical norms.

Juan Ruiz de Alarcón (1581-1639), of Mexican origin, most nearly represents the modern drama as we understand it. An ugly little red-bearded hunchback whose infirmities caused him to be the butt of Lope, Góngora, and other wits of the period, he wrote only some thirty dramas, but all are polished and stylized works that disclose his disciplined craftmanship. Lacking in the action, life, and rich invention of those of Tirso, these dramas represent the first Spanish comedies of manners. Alarcón picks a vice from which to draw a moral point and with dry dignity promotes courtesy, chivalry, discretion, and sincerity. *The Suspicious Truth* shows how a compulsive liar suffers the consequences of his own deceit, and *The Walls Have Ears* reveals the evils of slander.

Pedro Calderón de la Barca (1600-1681), author of magnificent *autos sacramentales*, allegorical, religious dramas concerning a sacrament of the Church, is equally famous for his honor plays and philosophical and religious dramas. His plays are more com-plicated and almost mathematically arranged, although he uses the standard paraphernalia of disguises, the honor code with its demands on all male members to defend the family name, the gallant, and the lady. Calderón subjected himself to a technical rigor unknown to Lope, and his court connections enabled him to employ elaborate and expensive stage machinery unavailable to others. Perhaps his most famous honor play is *The Mayor of Zalamea*, an improved version of a Lope play by the same name, which mirrors brutal, pathetic, noble, and tragic emotions as it presents us with the magnificent portrait of the equalitarian, avenging peasant mayor, Pedro Crespo. His many philosophical and theological dramas include such important pieces as *The Wonder Working Magician*, based on the legend of St. Cyprian, and his masterpiece, *Life is a Dream*, overflowing with baroque ornamentation and theological musings on the doctrine of free will and the concept of good works. As the protagonist, Segismundo, reflects on man's final destiny, he reaches an orthodox Catholic answer that only eternal life matters. Calderón's intellectual, symbolical, and abstract plays, in spite of their sparkling repartee, appear less spontaneous and human than those of Lope, but though they are more perfect, stylized, and intense and are often profoundly philosophical, like Lope's dramas they reflect perfectly the exaggerated religiosity, point of honor, and Catholic sacramental view of life.

The two principal *conceptistas* of the seventeenth century were Francisco Gómez de Quevedo y Villegas (1580-1645) and Baltasar Gracián (1601-58). The former, one of the great neglected geniuses of Spanish literature, lived a life of intrigue and politics and yet managed to create enduring literary works. He wrote theological, ascetic, philosophical, moralistic, political, and satirical works as well as literary criticism, novels, poetry, and drama. He saw clearly the decadence into which his country had fallen, and he pitilessly dissected the weak kings, corrupt favorites, and hypocritical subjects who had contributed to it. His most important political work, *Politics of God and Government of Christ* (1626-55), promotes a political system based on Christian doctrine, loyalty, and justice. His nine hundred poems treat satirical, heroic, jocose, tender, amorous, religious, and humorous themes in diverse meters and stanza forms. His picaresque novel, *Paul the Sharper*, is a bitter, almost grotesque, analysis of Spanish life and crime. Its cruelty, crudeness, and misanthropy are offset by its vigor and brilliance. His most important and enduring work, a great moral satirization of society, is *The Visions* (1627), a collection of five fantasies on the last judgment, hell, and salvation, viewed secularly rather than apocalyptically. He condemns false preachers, doctors, dentists, lawyers, women, poets and, pointedly, hypocrites of all conditions. Quevedo was a paradoxical man, a sarcastic stoic and moral idealist who believed in living according to the tenets of Christ but who could not accept the vice and corruption he saw around him and despaired completely of bringing man out of his corrupt state.

Gracián, who like Quevedo scorned fools, published several moral treatises such as the anti-Machiavellian *The Heroe* (1637), in praise of Phillip IV, and *The Politician, King Ferdinand the Catholic* (1640), whom he viewed as the model ruler. In 1648 he published *Cleverness and the Art of Wit,* an anthology of conceit writers of the day. His *Oracular Manual and Art of Prudence* (1647), a collection of some three hundred philosophical maxims and pungent advice on the problems of life, influenced La Rochefoucauld and Schopenhauer. In his masterpiece, *El criticón* (1651-53-57), an allegorical novel about human existence, Andrenio, the natural man, and Critilo, the man of reason, travel through the world and observe man's struggle against himself. It is a severe indictment of human folly. Gracián, along with Quevedo and Diego de Saavedra Fajardo (1584-1648), who also contributed an anti-Machiavellian analysis of government, *Idea of a Political Prince* (1640), completes the triumvirate of Christian political moralists who painted the most pessimistic pictures while stressing Christian virtues.

The Eighteenth Century

The Neo-Classic eighteenth century reacted adversely to the Baroque period and concentrated on rules and rule-giving bodies such as the Royal Academy of Language founded in 1714. Countless literary polemics took place between the supporters of Neo-Classic drama and the proponents of a national drama. While some continued to view Lope and Calderón as symbols of Spain's greatness, others attacked them for what they considered Gongoristic excesses. Most of the writing was didactic and dealt with history, biography, literary criticism, and scholarship. No worthy fiction existed, although Diego de Torres Villarroel (1693-1770), prolific author held to be a magician by the superstitious, wrote a kind of hybrid, autobiographical picaresque novel, *Life and Adventures of Dr. Diego de Torres Villarroel* (1743), and José Francisco de Isla (1703-81) wrote *Fray Gerundio* in two parts, 1758 and 1768, satirizing the pedantic, baroque sermons of the times.

Many tried to imitate Góngora but managed only his distortions and exaggerations and not his genius. Most of the Neo-Classic imitators of French writing who rejected what they termed turgid and obscure national authors, produced correct but prosaic verse of little merit. The fabulist Tomás de Iriarte (1750-91) wrote seventy-six *Literary Fables* satirizing the literary defects of the day, which brought him into conflict with critics such as Juan Pablo Forner and Félix María Samaniego (1745-1801), Iriarte's literary enemy, whose *Moral Fables*, modeled on those of Aesop, ridicule human defects. Nicolás Fernández de Moratín (1737-80) wrote a few inspired odes and what many consider to be the best poem of the eighteenth century, "Feast of Bulls in Madrid"; José Cadalso Vázquez de Andrade (1741-82), more famous as an essayist; Fray Diego Tadeo González (1733-94) who sought to re-establish the Salamancan School of poetry previously headed by Fray Luis de León; Gaspar Melchor de Jovellanos (1744-1811), primarily an austere statesman, educator, and devoted public servant; Nicasio Alvarez Cienfuegos (1764-1809); and Alberto Lista y Aragón (1775-1848), more widely regarded as a teacher and critic, are other worthy poets. The two most famous, however, are Juan Meléndez Valdés (1754-1817) and Manuel José Quintana (1772-1857). The former wrote ballads, odes, epistles, anacreontic verse, and bucolic poems of great artistry. He wrote sweet poetry as well as philosophical and melancholy themes of great descriptive power and poetic sensibility. The latter, an important political figure who wrote some interesting dramas, was primarily a patriotic poet who incidentally sang of love and nature. Among his best known works are his odes to the fatherland, *To the Combat of Trafalgar*, 1805, and *To Spain After the Revolution of March*, 1808. He was classical in form but romantic in emotion and spirit.

The Neo-Classic drama in Spain followed the precepts and doctrines of critics such as Ignacio de Luzán (1702-54) whose *Poética*, 1737, based on French and Italian models, contained the essence of the Spanish Neo-Classic movement. He deplored the excesses of the Baroque, although he did not completely condemn Calderón and Lope, as did his more rabid followers, and recommended reforms that included the observance of the three unities, verisimilitude, utilitarian justification, and clarity of style. These rules proved too restrictive for the romantic Spanish genius. Vicente García de la Huerta (1734-87) managed to breathe life into the drama, in spite of classical molds, through nationalistic emphasis, but only two dramatists produced enduring works.

Ramón de la Cruz (1731-94) rejected the coldness of Neo-Classic drama, as he emphasized realism and nationalism, especially in his *sainetes*, or one-act farces, which portrayed picturesque and popular types, dances, pilgrimages, and street quarrels. Ramón de la Cruz parodied the heroic drama of the day as he satirized the social abuses and vices in a colorful, colloquial, and animated language. He did for the Spanish theater what Goya did for painting.

Leandro Fernández de Moratín (1760-1828), the son of Nicolás, commented on the decadence of poetry in his *Rout of the Pedants* (1789) and hack writers in *The New Comedy*, subtitled *The Café* (1792). Of his five original plays *The Consent of the Girls* (1806) has best stood the test of time. Moratín believed in Luzán's utilitarian principles and sought to expose some social evil or exalt some virtue. In this thesis play he objects to interference by parents in their children's marriages. Although he observes the unities, his brilliant and forceful dialogue and warm characterization breathe life into his drama. If he lacks depth, he merits attention as the only author of his time who combines good taste with artistic values and dignity.

The most important eighteenth-century writing occurred in the fields of scholarship and literary criticism. Gaspar Melchor de Jovellanos (1744-1811) wrote on agriculture, economics, education, fine arts, history, and language. José Cadalso (1741-82), in his *Eruditos a la violeta* (*False Wise Men*), 1772, attacked poetasters, and in *Moroccan Letters* (1789), his didactic masterpiece supposedly inspired by Montesquieu's *Lettres persanes*, assailed Spanish selfishness, vanity, and ignorance. Lorenzo Hervás y Panduro (1735-1809) fathered comparative philology; Fray Martín Sarmiento (1694-1771) composed works of literary criticism; and Gregorio Mayáns y Siscar (1699-1781) edited many classic works.

Undoubtedly the most renowned writer of the century was Benito Jerónimo Feijóo y Montenegro (1676-1764), a Benedictine monk who managed to reintroduce European culture into Spain. Between 1726 and 1739 he wrote eight volumes of essays under the title of *Critical Universal Theater* and five volumes of *Curious and Erudite Letters* (1742-60). He discussed science, philosophy, language, law, education, literature, and almost every other branch of knowledge. A devout Catholic, although some challenged his orthodoxy because of his attacks on false miracles and superstition, he sought to free Spanish letters from the stranglehold of scholasticism and to explore the scientific method. As the outstanding exponent of the Spanish Enlightenment he fought narrow-mindedness and bigotry and became the "first contemporary Spanish essayist."

The Romantic Period

The nineteenth-century Romantic Movement, which one critic labeled both a revival and a revolt, in a sense, re-created Golden Age drama. Nicolás Böhl von Faber (1770-1836) and Agustín Durán (1793-1862), among others, extolled the merits of Calderonian drama. At the same time the novels of Sir Walter Scott and the French drama exerted an influence. Spanish Romanticism emphasized the exotic, the Middle Ages, national spirit, special vocabulary such as cadavers, chains, and tombs, and a literary orientalism of caravans, pirates, and harems. Most of the early Romantics, such as Martínez de la Rosa (1787-1862), whose *The Conspiracy of Venice* (1834) initiated Spanish Romantic drama, and Antonio Alcalá Galiano (1789-1865), whose prologue to *The Foundling Moor* by the Duke of Rivas (1791-1865) was considered a romantic manifesto, thought of themselves as men of the golden mean. *The Foundling Moor*, a romantic epic poem in twelve cantos, treats the well-known story of the seven sons of Lara. His *Historical Ballads* (1841), inspired by an admiration for great Spanish deeds, reveal a painter's eye and a fine use of color. *Don Alvaro* (1835), in spite of its use of local color and customs, is one of the most extravagant Romantic dramas with its melodramatic coincidences, mysterious hero of unknown birth, unfortunate love affair, and the destruction of the innocent heroine and the dashing hero.

José de Espronceda (1808-42), known to many as "the Spanish Byron," served as a catalytic agent for all the poetic tendencies of his time, and proved to be the most highly personal, subjective, and Romantic lyric poet in Spain. Most of his short lyrics, done in a variety of experimental meters, were collected in a volume published in 1840. His themes include an insistence on love of liberty, concern for the social outcast, doubt, and a philosophy that pleasure and happiness are illusions to which only death can bring a successful conclusion. "Song of the Pirate," "To Jarifa in an Orgy," and "The Executioner" are representative. *The Student of Salamanca* (1836) and *The Devil World* (1841) were his most ambitious undertakings. The first, a *leyenda* or semi-epic-narrative poem overlaid with an imaginative and colorful lyricism, is a burlesque, satirical, and Romantic revival of the Don Juan theme. The protagonist, Félix de Montemar, a blasphemous and cynical young man, deliriously chases love but finds only death. The second, never completed, relates man's spiritual aging, ideal dreams, and dismal grief at the realization that all is illusion and that virtue is impossible in an evil world. Inserted as a second canto is the famous "Song to Teresa," inspired by his unhappy love affair with and death of Teresa Mancha, which contains the typical themes of dreams of glory and despair. The impetuous and passionate Espronceda reflects both the negative destructive elements of the revolutionary and cynic and the constructive values of the frustrated idealist who loves the individual and society. In essence, Espronceda's brilliant and personal style, harmony, musical variety, and occasional artificial trickery fail to disguise his existential longing.

José Zorrilla (1817-93), "the spoiled darling of Romanticism," represented national spirit. His lyric, epic, and dramatic productions, often marred by sensational imagery, bombast and prolixity, are saved by an inspired emotion and feeling for beauty. His works include an unfinished epic poem, *Granada* (1852), many short lyric poems, *leyendas* such as "A Good Judge and Better Witness," and a series of plays on national themes of which the best are *The Shoemaker and the King* (1840), and *Traitor, Unconfessed and Martyr* (1849). His most famous work, *Don Juan Tenorio* (1844), full of fantastic and religious elements as well as spirited action and sonorous verse, involves the salvation of the protagonist.

Among other worthy Romantic dramatists are Juan Eugenio Hartzenbusch (1806-80), whose *The Lovers of Teruel* revived an old Spanish legend, and Antonio García Gutiérrez (1813-84), whose *The Troubador* (1836) and *Simón Bocanegra* (1843) served as models for Verdi operas. Gutiérrez emphasized historical and legendary themes and sought startling dramatic effects in his eighty dramas. Noteworthy lyric poets include Juan Arolas (1805-49), who wrote amatory poetry against an oriental and voluptuous background, as well as fervent religious poems, Gertrudis Gómez de Avellaneda (1814-73), and Nicomedes Pastor Díaz (1811-63), a melancholy, delicate, and dreamy Romantic.

The literary sketch of local color or social commentary that flourished during the Romantic period was extremely influential. Serafín Estébanez Calderón (1799-1867) damaged his work by exaggerated attempts at archaic flavor in his sketches of Andalusian scenes. Ramón Mesonero Romanos (1803-82), a kind of chronicler of Madrid, concerned himself largely with trivial foibles, but his humor and moral and humanitarian purpose helped disguise his lack of creativity. The most important essayist and satirical writer of the century was the sad, bitter, and frustrated idealist, Mariano José de Larra (1809-37), whose suicide summed up the conflict of his age between the classical and romantic spirit and between liberalism and conservatism. Larra wrote articles on Madrid society, current events, the theater, politics, and national foibles. He loved his country but cruelly chastised Spanish ignorance and decadence. His amusing wit, elegant prose style, and clear vision made him the precursor of the "Generation of ninety-eight" writers of the twentieth century who accepted him as a great non-fiction writer who embodied their ideals.

Three poets, at times classified as post-Romantics, greatly influenced, both negatively and positively, the poetry of the twentieth century. Ramón de Campoamor (1817-1901) enjoyed a tremendous popularity. Modern critics, in trying to assess his worth, often accept him as the perfect reflection of a prosaic age but also as a poet of merit. Others find him vulgar and superficial. A paradoxical man, both liberal and reactionary, heretical and religious, he wrote many long philosophical poems. His reputation, however, depends on shorter works, *Doloras* (1846), *Small Poems* (1872), and *Humoradas* (1886). The *Doloras* sentimentally exemplify an eternal or philosophical truth in ironic fashion; the *Small Poems* are elaborated *doloras*; and the *humoradas* express, in two or three chiseled lines, the "comic in its smallest dimension." Essentially, the three forms are the same. Skeptical, ironical, and at times bitter, they reflect Campoamor's feelings about human problems and reveal him as an experimenter who attempted to revolutionize verse form.

The sad, sweet, and highly Romantic Gustavo Adolfo Bécquer (1836-70) wrote musical, colorful, subjective lyrics of frustrated love. His *Rhymes*, which consists of some seventy-five or eighty poems, deals with interior soul states, in delicate and deceptively simple verse. It is difficult to come to grips with the fugitive experiences and the impalpable and intangible world he creates, for, as one critic said, he "creates subtle vibrations of an ethereal music." For him the rustle of a dry leaf replaces the howling storm wind found in Espronceda. In his other works, especially in his twenty prose legends, there exists the same supernatural, impressionistic, melancholy, subtle, fugitive, dreamy, and elusive atmosphere of his poetry.

Rosalía de Castro (1837-85) also endured a sorrowful and unhappy existence and died tragically of cancer. She wrote unrhetorical, tender, musical, vague, and melancholy poems. In her early work she interpreted Galician folklore. In her Spanish masterpiece, *Beside the River Sar* (1884), we can glimpse her nostalgia for her native land and her longing for eternal rest and surcease from pain.

Nineteenth-Century Realism

Nineteenth-century dramatists cultivated a realistic theater of various types. Some retained the passionate tone of the Romantic drama but concentrated on the problems and tensions of the middle class. Others, like Manuel Bretón de los Herreros (1796-1873), an eclectic writer, Moratinian in tone, was at his best in the satirical comedy of manners. Manuel Tamayo y Baus (1829-98) wrote sentimental and passionate theater as well as one of social content. His most original play, A New Drama (1867), involves a play within a play as it recounts the story of Yorick, the Shakespearean clown who plays on the stage a part he must also play in real life. Adelardo López de Ayala (1828-79), the Ruiz de Alarcón of his day, attempted didactic and moralistic works such as A Certain Percent (1861) where true love triumphs over money. José Echegaray (1832-1916), a Nobel Prize winner, replaced the exotic Romantic themes with those of home and hearth, but his dramas of tragedy, pain, and death continue the Romantic tradition. His principal themes are those of fate, duty, passion, and love. His best thesis plays are probably Folly or Saintliness (1877), about a man whose sense of duty forces him to try to return property he has discovered is not rightfully his, and The Great Galeoto (1881), about the power of slander and gossip. His plays contain melodramatic outbursts, and the latter drama contains a duel, clandestine visits, and coincidences.

The inherent dichotomy and ideological conflict of the two Spains, the orthodox, Catholic one and the liberal, rationalist one continued throughout the century. Jaime Balmes (1810-48), a Catalan priest, Juan Donoso Cortés (1809-53), the great orator, and Marcelino Menéndez y Pelayo (1856-1912), the most famous literary critic, defended in varying degree Catholic orthodoxy, Spanish tradition, and Spanish Manifest Destiny. In opposition to these tendencies as the spiritual heirs of Erasmism and the Enlightenment, the Krausists, reflecting a philosophy brought to Spain by Julián Sanz del Río (1817-69), based on the teachings of a student of Kant, stressed religious tolerance, logic, and reason. They provided the impetus for educational reform and for the founding by Spain's greatest educator, Francisco Giner de los Ríos (1839-1915), of the Free Institute of Teaching (1876) where some of the greatest names of early twentieth-century literature studied and received their philosophical orientation from teachers such as the reformer and historian, Joaquín Costa (1866-1911).

The regionalistic novel, which portrayed in realistic fashion the life and customs of Spain, was initiated by Cecilia Böhl von Faber (1796-1877) who wrote under the pseudonym, Fernán Caballero. Her novel, *The Sea Gull* (1849), presenting traditionalism, moralizing, and picturesque and accurately drawn Andalusian popular types, concerns the somewhat romantic social transformation of a peasant girl with a beautiful voice and her eventual return to her peasant status. Pedro Antonio de Alarcón (1833-91), a great humorist ·and short-story writer, also wrote of Andalusia. He considered *The Scandal* (1875), a strong defense of Catholic orthodoxy, his major work, but his fame rests on the humorous, fast-paced, folkloric "king of Spanish tales," *The Three Cornered Hat* (1874). The charm and wit of the story of the official who fails in his attempted seduction of the miller's wife appeal to modern audiences. Juan Valera (1827-1905), an aristocratic Andalusian, wrote good literary criticism and a great number of novels. *Doña Luz* (1879), about the love of a girl for a priest, *El comendador Mendoza* (1877), and *Pepita Jiménez* (1874) are representative. The last-named, his most famous, is written in epistolary form and relates the struggle in a young seminary student's soul between a false mysticism and vocation on the one hand and his love for the beautiful young widow, Pepita, on the other. Valera believed in art for art's sake and wrote in a refined, ironic, somewhat cold but beautiful, classic style. Although he was a master of the *mot juste* and a good psychologist, his optimistic temperament led him to overvalue beauty and entertainment to the exclusion of the real problems of life. José María de Pereda (1833-1906), the most regional and reactionary of the Spanish novelists, wrote largely about Santander. His two outstanding novels were *Sotileza* (1884), about the sea, an orphan girl, and her suitors, and *Up the Crag* (1895), about a city man who finally realizes the positive virtues country life has to offer and decides to accept his patriarchal inheritance. The conservative Pereda stressed Catholic orthodoxy, traditionalism, and national pride; he painted beautiful nature descriptions of the country he loved and the joy and peace he found there.

The greatest nineteenth-century novelist and one who merits a ranking with Balzac or Dickens, Benito Pérez Galdós (1843-1920), exemplifies the best of the Erasmist-Cervantine tradition. Galdós defies accurate classification, for he wrote novels of every type, including forty-six *National Episodes,* historical novels of nineteenth-century Spain. Among the novels of his so-called first period are *Doña Perfecta* (1876), a somewhat melodramatic but effective novel about religious fanaticism, bigotry, and the struggle of modern science and progress, in which he believed, against Spain's traditional and conservative forces; *Gloria* (1877), about the tragic love of a Catholic girl and Jewish boy, the nature of intolerance, and mankind's hope in the elimination of false barriers; and *Marianela* (1878), an idyllic and pathetic story of an ugly girl and her love for the young blind boy she served as a guide. Later novels include *Angel Guerra* (1890-91), which examines the concept of humility and true Christianity; *Misericordia* (1897), which concerns the meaning of true Christian charity; and *Fortunata y Jacinta* (1886-87), his four-volume masterpiece, full of a gallery of types, good and bad, sane and mad, which discusses the rivalry of two women, the wife and the mistress, for the love of a man. In most of his novels Galdós stresses Christian love, scientific progress, harmony, spiritual and ethical values, and the union of various classes.

Spanish naturalists, while technically following Zola's school, were unable, as good Catholics, to accept completely his deterministic philosophy. Also as subjective Spaniards they found it difficult to maintain the scientific objectivity of the "experimental novel." Leopoldo Alas (1852-1901), usually called by his pseudonym, *Clarín,* in his masterpiece, *The Judge's Wife* (1884-1885), dissects the sexual, political, and religious mores of a provincial town, and excoriates the envy and gossip to which its human residents are prone. The heroine, Ana Ozores, a victim of psychological and mystical urges who finally succumbs to the blandishments of a seducer, is one of the great feminine creations of the nineteenth century. Clarín, one of the good literary critics of his generation, was, along with Emilia Pardo Bazán, a supreme master of the short story. Armando Palacio Valdés (1853-1938), like Clarín an Asturian, was too optimistic and pleasant a writer to dwell long on the sordid and pathological. His best-known work, *Sister San Sulpicio* (1889), is a warm and picturesque portrayal of Seville and substantiates the claim that he excels at portraying feminine characters. The leader of the Naturalistic school, Emilia Pardo Bazán (1851-1920), a Galician, was both an ardent feminist and Catholic. Of her novels, the best known are *The Manor Houses of Ulloa* (1886) and its sequel, *Mother Nature* (1887). The former concerns the violence of nature and man, political intrigues and decaying feudalism in Galicia; the latter chronicles the continuing decadence of the Marquis' family, which culminates in the incestuous love of his illegitimate son for the latter's half sister.

The Twentieth Century

The "Generation of ninety-eight" writers, not in a strict sense either a school or movement, demonstrated a religious restlessness, love of countryside, evocation of past spiritual and cultural glories and the need for Europeanization of Spain. Whatever their practical or spiritual tendencies, they sought for Spanish identity in a new and troubled world. Some see unity in the Generation's skepticism and pessimism, but few can really agree on the authors who constitute the Generation. Some of the members of the so-called group deny that it exists, and a continuing polemic exists about the difference between the ninety-eighters and the Modernists. Azorín coined the title Generation of 1896 in 1910 but changed it to 1898 in 1913 because of the symbolism involved in that date. He stressed a love for old towns and the countryside, a love for the spirit of El Greco and Larra, and the re-creation of Spanish tradition as the principal components of the writings. Others viewed the productions as a protest against the moribund past. Esthetic, philosophical, idealistic, historical, and scholarly themes marked the writing. In their soul-searching the authors sought salvation for their country, and in their search for identity, insistence on will, action, and individualistic attempts to overcome life's boundary situations, revealed themselves as an existential generation. The primary vehicle of expression was the personalized essay, for it lent itself to the discussion of the "Spanish problem," but dramatists such as Benavente and novelists like Pío Baroja belonged to the group. Modern Spanish literature does not lend itself to easy classification into genres, however useful such classification may be for reader orientation.

Angel Ganivet (1865-98), although not precisely a member of the Generation, had identical ideas. He believed in engaging in life, and in his often contradictory, confusing, but nevertheless moving *Idearium Español* (1897), he views Spanish paralysis of will or *abulia,* the loss of her superior culture, which stemmed from her synthesis of East and West, through dispersing her energies in war rather than concentrating on spirit, and hopes for the purification and re-creation of the spiritual Spaniard. Miguel de Unamuno (1864-1936), philosopher, essayist, dramatist, poet, and novelist, seeks the eternal tradition of Spain. He feels existential anguish at the impossibility of obtaining personal immortality. José Martínez Ruiz (1873-1967), who writes under the pseudonym, Azorín, offers what one critic calls "little albums of Spanish life." In his lyrical evocation of Spain he tries to define the essence of the Spanish soul and sees eternal verities in the tiny and repetitive details of everyday life. Ramón Menéndez Pidal (b. 1869) re-creates the historical and national treasures of Spain through scientific and philological scholarship.

The following generation, more intellectual in its approach, was best represented by José Ortega y Gasset (1883-1955), in his vital-ism, existentialism, and new theories of depersonalized art. He sought Spanish salvation through the creation of a civilized select minority. Other essayists of his generation and later ones contrib-buted significant works in all intellectual fields. Among the out-standing contemporaries are Pedro Laín Entralgo (b. 1908), a Catholic intellectual of the modern stripe, and Julián Marías (1914), a historical philosopher who was one of Ortega's favorite disciples.

Modernism, which manifests the influence of Bécquer and others, was largely promoted by Rubén Darío (1867-1916), a Nicaraguan poet who was himself the synthesizer of a previous generation of poets. The Modernists, who wrote primarily although not exclusively in poetry, reacted against bourgeois values and outworn esthetic codes. They emphasized the importance of language and the value of words and subtle nuances and, in general, provided a revolution in technique much as the "Generation of ninety-eight" provided one in ideology. Darío, in *Blue* (1888) and *Profane Prose* (1896), reno-vated meters and rhymes and rhythms, as he assimilated the contri-butions of French Symbolists and medieval and Renaissance Spanish poets. A generation of poets followed him, but they also soon reacted away from his exotic creations and perfect form in the direction of more eternal themes. Antonio Machado (1875-1939), one of Spain's greatest all-time poets, best represents these eternal values in his examination of the Castilian landscape and the mean-ing of life and death. Unamuno's religious and unmusical poetry desires answers to fundamental universal questions of faith and human destiny, and Juan Ramón Jiménez (1881-1958), a poet of changing moods, stresses beauty, impeccable form, a kind of panthe-ism, and a search for God.

The next generation of poets, called post-modernists by some critics, represents the consolidation of the modernist innovations, but poetic themes revolve around the constants of love, death, and

God. The unclassifiable León Felipe (b. 1884), a kind of Biblical prophet, concerns himself with human sorrows and man's inhumanity to man. After the First World War Spain shared in the various vanguard movements. The Creationists talked of creating a poem as nature creates a tree; the Ultraists identified with Futurism; and the Surrealists emphasized dreams and the unconscious. The poets who started writing in the 1920's represent one of the great poetic generations of Spain, and their individualized poetry transcends all definitions. Pedro Salinas (1891-1951) writes pure, intellectual and contemplative poetry as he searches for reason in a loveless world; Jorge Guillén (b. 1893) defends "pure poetry" and sings about the natural beauty of the world and the joy of living. Federico García Lorca (1898-1936), the purest lyric voice since Lope de Vega, re-creates popular poetry with new and daring imagery, a surprising surrealism, magic metaphors, and a realization of the antithetical elements of modern civilization. Vicente Aleixandre (b. 1898) concentrates on surrealistic, erotic themes. Rafael Alberti (b. 1902) follows the folklore tradition of Lorca, but shares also in the Gongoristic revival of the late 1920's and in the surrealistic movement, as he searches for values in an absurd world. In the next generation, Miguel Hernández (1910-42) fuses the popular and baroque. The 1930's also produced a revival of classic influence, especially that of Luis de León and Garcilaso de la Vega, as poets stressed stylized and graceful poetry. The newer poets identify themselves with the Spanish people and talk of religion, the hearth, the home, and remembrance of things past. Some prefer social and existential preoccupations.

Drama went through the same Modernist re-creation and succession of "isms" which affected other genres. Jacinto Benavente (1866-1954) freed the drama from the melodramatic tenets established by Echegaray, and in an elegant style and with subtle irony, satirized Spanish aristocratic society. Ramón María del Valle-Inclán (1866-1936) concentrated on the dehumanized drama of the *esperpento*, based on a grotesque deformation of reality. Jacinto Grau (1877-1959) combated the overcommercialization of the Spanish stage with his existential dramas and the Don Juan theme. The poetic drama of García Lorca concentrated on a life-death symbolism and elementary passions and on themes such as motherhood, virginity, and passionate love. Alejandro Casona (1903-65) combined realistic and fantastic elements in optimistic works on the joy of living and duty to the world. Antonio Buero Vallejo (b. 1916), a tragic dramatist of "hope" who examines humble lives in an anguished world in his philosophical, fantastic, realistic, psychological, and mythological and historical dramas, and Alfonso Sastre (b. 1926), who writes social drama and of man tortured and trapped by his own weakness, are the two best dramatists writing today.

The novel, too, has shown the spirit of the new age. Unamuno wrote existential novels about obsessed and often grotesque heroes. Ramón María del Valle-Inclán composed sensual, esoteric, erotic, and esthetically refined novels in a musical style about Galician superstitions and a deformed and grotesque world. Pío Baroja (1872-1956), whom many consider to be the outstanding novelist of the century, portrayed picaresque vagabonds and men of action, as he attacked civilization's institutions and shibboleths. Ramón Pérez de Ayala (1880-1962), lyrical, tragic, symbolic, ironic, humorous, and intellectual, contrasted Dionysian and introspective life and re-created the honor theme of the Golden Age. Gabriel Miró (1879-1930) contributed poetic, impressionistic works; Concha Espina (1877-1955) and Ricardo León (1877-1943) stressed tradition and Catholic orthodoxy. Ramón Gómez de la Serna (1888-1963) fully implemented Ortega's critical view of the depersonalized novel in his gloomy, grotesque, and absurd creations, and Benjamín Jarnés (1888-1949) created a surrealistic vogue.

Among living novelists Ramón Sender (b. 1902) reveals his faith in humanity and a true Christian ethic in warm, tolerant, symbolic, and idealistic novels. Camilo José Cela (b. 1916), a master of the vernacular, travel literature and an exponent of the *tremendista* novel with its emphasis on horrible and bloody environmental factors in an existentialist framework, has helped invigorate the post Civil War novel. His works are at times depersonalized by a baroque humor. A host of newer novelists reveal the sordid, hopeless, and gray lives of the modern Spaniard in an imprisoned society. José María Gironella (b. 1917) attempts to give perspective to the Spanish Civil War, and Juan Goytisolo (b. 1931) examines the lost generation of Spanish youth and their rebellion against life. Many women novelists such as Carmen Laforet (b. 1921), Elena Quiroga (b. 1921), and Ana María Matute (b. 1926) contribute richly to the philosophical, social, and psychological analysis of the day.

In the brief pages allotted an introduction, one can only hint at the provocative bouillabaisse of an entire literary creation. The task of the anthologist is equally complicated and unsatisfying by its very nature, for one can never be sure that he has included the "right" selections or rejected the "wrong" ones. This is especially true in a compilation of modern literature where it is difficult to view in proper perspective the works of living or recently departed authors. While an attempt has been made to give representative works of the important writers, personal favorites have been included. In all cases, however, the fragments selected, despite distortions which limited selections may convey, are intended to give the nonspecialist and the intelligent browser a glimpse of one of the world's most fascinating cultures while allowing him to assess the indeterminate but considerable stature that culture enjoys.

PART I

Fiction

Vicente Blasco Ibáñez

(1867-1928)

Many describe Blasco Ibáñez as a nineteenth-century Naturalist writer, but he followed, also, Flaubert's dictum that the novel is "reality seen through temperament." Valencian by birth, he was brought up as a devout Catholic, but an uncle won him over to revolutionary principles. His revolutionary reputation and his political activities in support of liberal causes resulted in his exile and imprisonment on several occasions. He published a socialist newspaper, became a book publisher, traveled around the world, won and lost money in many ventures, including one in Latin America, and finally became wealthy through his international best sellers. Exiled once more by the dictator Primo de Rivera in 1924, he died in France. His whole life was devoted to the cause of progress, idealism, and liberty.

In his first period of writing he published regional novels, which painted the light and shadow, vivid colors, and elemental passions of his native province. His best novel of this group is *The Cabin* (1898), about the sufferings and persecution of peasant farmers, their prejudices and superstitions, against the lush and picturesque Valencian backdrop. His second period produced thesis novels, which pleaded for social justice. Of these, *The Cathedral* (1903), set in Toledo, and *The Intruder* (1904), set in Bilbao, analyze Spanish religious fanaticism and Jesuit tyranny, respectively. Blasco Ibáñez wrote a number of psychological novels, studies of passion and love, and in the last years of his life, antifeminist and pseudo-historical novels, which added little to his reputation.

The novels that brought him fame in the United States were *Blood and Sand* (1908) and *The Four Horsemen of the Apocalypse* (1916). The former, a study of the national pastime of bullfighting, presents the Spanish public as the real animal. The latter novel, partially based on his experiences as a war correspondent for the Allies in the First World War, gives us an almost photographic reproduction of war and the suffering it causes.

Blasco improvised a great deal and sometimes wrote impulsively and carelessly, which caused some to call him a "gifted vulgarian." His rich and exuberant imagination and his warmth, strength, sincerity, passion and creative power belie that label. Upon adding to these his keen observation, colorful and brilliant descriptions of nature, and a great feeling for humanity, one realizes that he may merit his status as one of the masters of Spanish realism.

The selection given is the complete fourth chapter of Part III of *The Four Horsemen of the Apocalypse.*

The Four Horsemen of the Apocalypse

CHAPTER 4

NO ONE WILL KILL HIM

Four months later, Don Marcelo's confidence received a rude shock. Julio was wounded. But at the same time that Lacour bought him this news, lamentably delayed, he tranquilized him with the result of his investigations in the war ministry. Sergeant Desnoyers was now a sub-lieutenant, his wound was almost healed and, thanks, to the wire-pulling of the senator, he was coming to pass a fortnight with his family while convalescing.

"An exceptionally brave fellow," concluded the influential man. "I have read what his chiefs say about him. At the head of his platoon, he attacked a German company; he killed the captain with his own hand; he did I don't know how many more brave things besides. . . . They have presented him with the military medal and have made him an officer. . . . A regular hero!"

And the rapidly aging father, weeping with emotion, but with increasing enthusiasm, shook his head and trembled. He repented now of his momentary lack of faith when the first news of his wounded boy reached him. How absurd! . . . No one would kill Julio; his heart told him so.

Soon after, he saw him coming home amid the cries and delighted exclamations of the women. Poor Doña Luisa wept as she embraced him, hanging on his neck with sobs of emotion. Chichí contemplated him with grave reflection, putting half of her mind on the recent arrival while the rest flew far away in search of the other warrior. The dusky, South American maids fought each other for the opening in the curtains, peering through the crack with the gaze of an antelope.

The father admired the little scrap of gold on the sleeve of the gray cloak, with the skirts buttoning behind, examining afterwards the dark blue cap with its low brim, adopted by the French for the war in the trenches. The traditional kepi had disappeared. A suitable visor, like that of the men in the Spanish infantry, now shadowed Julio's face. Don Marcelo noted, too, the short and well-cared-for beard, very different from the one he had seen in the trenches. The boy was coming home, groomed and polished from his recent stay in the hospital.

"Isn't it true that he looks like me?" queried the old man proudly.

Doña Luisa responded with the inconsequence that mothers always show in matters of resemblance.

"He has always been the living image of you!"

Having made sure that he was well and happy, the entire family suddenly felt a certain disquietude. They wished to examine his wound so as to convince themselves that he was completely out of danger.

"Oh, it's nothing at all," protested the sub-lieutenant. "A bullet wound in the shoulder. The doctor feared at first that I might lose my left arm, but it has healed well and it isn't worth while to think any more about it."

Chichí's appraising glance swept Julio from head to foot; taking in all the details of his military elegance. His cloak was worn thin and dirty; the leggings were spatter-dashed with mud; he smelled of leather, sweaty cloth and strong tobacco; but on one wrist he was wearing a watch, and on the other, his identity medal fastened with a gold chain. She had always admired her brother for his natural good taste, so she stowed away all these little details in her memory in order to pass them on to René. Then she surprised her mother with a demand for a loan that she might send a little gift to her artilleryman.

Don Marcelo gloated over the fifteen days of satisfaction ahead of him. Sub-lieutenant Desnoyers found it impossible to go out alone, for his father was always pacing up and down the reception hall before the military cap which was shedding modest splendor and glory upon the hat rack. Scarcely had Julio put it on his head before his sire appeared, also with hat and cane, ready to sally forth.

"Will you permit me to accompany you? . . . I will not bother you."

This would be said so humbly, with such an evident desire to

have his request granted, that his son had not the heart to refuse
him. In order to take a walk with Argensola, he had to scurry down
the back stairs, or resort to other schoolboy tricks.

Never had the elder Desnoyers promenaded the streets of Paris
with such solid satisfaction as by the side of this muscular youth in
his gloriously worn cloak, on whose breast were glistening his two
decorations—the cross of war and the military medal. He was a
hero, and this hero was his son. He accepted as homage to them
both the sympathetic glances of the public in the street cars and
subways. The interest with which the women regarded the fine-
looking youth tickled him immensely. All the other military men
that they met, no matter how many bands and crosses they dis-
played, appeared to the doting father mere *embusqués*,[1] unworthy
of comparison with his Julio . . . . The wounded men who got out
of the coaches by the aid of staffs and crutches inspired him with
the greatest pity. Poor fellows! . . . They did not bear the charmed
life of his son. Nobody could kill him; and when, by chance, he had
received a wound, the scars had immediately disappeared without
detriment to his handsome person.

Sometimes, especially at night, Desnoyers senior would show an
unexpected magnanimity, letting Julio fare forth alone. Since before
the war, his son had led a life filled with triumphant love-affairs,
what might he not achieve now with the added prestige of a dis-
tinguished officer! . . . Passing through his room on his way to bed,
the father imagined the hero in the charming company of some
aristocratic lady. None but a feminine celebrity was worthy of him;
his paternal pride could accept nothing less. . . . And it never
occurred to him that Julio might be with Argensola in a music-hall
or in a moving-picture show, enjoying the simple and monotonous
diversions of a Paris sobered by war, with the homely tastes of a
sub-lieutenant whose amorous conquests were no more than the
renewal of some old friendships.

One evening as Don Marcelo was accompanying his son down
the *Champs Elysées*, he started at recognizing a lady approaching
from the opposite direction. It was Madame Laurier. . . . Would
she recognize Julio? He noted that the youth turned pale and began
looking at the other people with feigned interest. She continued
straight ahead, erect, unseeing. The old gentleman was almost

---

1. *Embusqués* literally means "the hidden ones." It was applied by the
French in the First World War to the stay-at-homes who did not fight at
the war front. (*Editor's note.*)

irritated at such coldness. To pass by his son without feeling his presence instinctively! Ah, these women! . . . He turned his head involuntarily to look after her, but had to avert his inquisitive glance immediately. He had surprised Marguerite motionless behind them, pallid with surprise, and fixing her gaze earnestly on the soldier who was separating himself from her. Don Marcelo read in her eyes admiration, love, all of the past that was suddenly surging up in her memory. Poor woman! . . . He felt for her a paternal affection as though she were the wife of Julio. His friend Lacour had again spoken to him about the Lauriers. He knew that Marguerite was going to become a mother, and the old man, without taking into account the reconciliation nor the passage of time, felt as much moved at the thought of this approaching maternity as though the child were going to be Julio's.

Meanwhile Julio was marching right on, without turning his head, without being conscious of the burning gaze fixed upon him, colorless, but humming a tune to hide his emotion. He always believed that Marguerite had passed near him without recognizing him, since his father did not betray her.

One of Don Marcelo's pet occupations was to make his son tell about the encounter in which he had been hurt. No visitor ever came to see the sub-lieutenant but the father always made the same petition.

"Tell us how you were wounded. . . . Explain how you killed that German captain."

Julio tried to excuse himself with visible annoyance. He was already surfeited with his own history. To please his father, he had related the facts to the senator, to Argensola and to Tchernoff in his studio, and to other family friends. . . . He simply could not do it again.

So the father began the narration on his own account, giving the relief and details of the deed as though seen with his own eyes. . . .

He had to take possession of the ruins of a sugar refinery in front of the trench. The Germans had been expelled by the French cannon. A reconnoitering survey under the charge of a trusty man was then necessary. And the heads, as usual, had selected Sergeant Desnoyers.

At daybreak, the platoon had advanced stealthily without encountering any difficulty. The soldiers scattered among the ruins. Julio then went on alone, examining the positions of the enemy; on turning around a corner of the wall, he had the most unexpected

of encounters. A German captain was standing in front of him.
They had almost bumped into each other. They looked into each
other's eyes with more suspense than hate, yet at the same time,
they were trying instinctively to kill each other, each one trying to
get the advantage by his swiftness. The captain had dropped the
map that he was carrying. His right hand sought his revolver,
trying to draw it from its case without once taking his eyes off his
enemy. Then he had to give this up as useless—it was too late.
With his eyes distended by the proximity of death, he kept his
gaze fixed upon the Frenchman who had raised his gun to his face.
A shot, from a barrel almost touching him . . . and the German fell
dead.

Not till then did the victor notice the captain's orderly who was
but a few steps behind. He shot Desnoyers, wounding him in the
shoulder. The French hurried to the spot, killing the corporal. Then
there was a sharp cross-fire with the enemy's company which had
halted a little ways off while their commander was exploring the
ground. Julio, in spite of his wound, continued at the head of his
section, defending the factory against superior forces until supports
arrived, and the land remained definitely in the power of the French.

"Wasn't that about the way of it?" Don Marcelo would always
wind up.

The son assented, desirous that his annoyance with the persistent
story should come to an end as soon as possible. Yes, that was the
way of it. But what the father didn't know, what Julio would never
tell, was the discovery that he had made after killing the captain.

The two men, during the interminable second in which they had
confronted each other, had showed in their eyes something more
than the surprise of an encounter, and the wish to overcome the
other. Desnoyers knew that man. The captain knew him, too. He
guessed it from his expression. . . . But self-preservation was more
insistent than recollection and prevented them both from co-ordinat-
ing their thoughts.

Desnoyers had fired with the certainty that he was killing someone that he knew. Afterwards, while directing the defense of the
position and guarding against the approach of reinforcements, he
had a suspicion that the enemy whose corpse was lying a few feet
away might possibly be a member of the von Hartrott family. No,
he looked much older than his cousins, yet younger than his Uncle
Karl who at his age, would be no mere captain of infantry.

When, weakened by the loss of blood, they were about to carry
him to the trenches, the sergeant expressed a wish to see again the

body of his victim. His doubt continued before the face blanched by death. The wide-open eyes still seemed to retain their startled expression. The man had undoubtedly recognized him. His face was familiar. Who was he? . . . Suddenly in his mind's eye, Julio saw the heaving ocean, a great steamer, a tall, blonde woman looking at him with half-closed eyes of invitation, a corpulent, moustached man making speeches in the style of the Kaiser. "Rest in peace, Captain Erckmann!" . . . Thus culminated in a corner of France the discussions started at table in mid-ocean.

He excused himself mentally as though he were in the presence of the sweet Bertha. He had had to kill, in order not to be killed. Such is war. He tried to console himself by thinking that Erckmann, perhaps, had failed to identify him, without realizing that his slayer was the shipmate of the summer. . . . And he kept carefully hidden in the depths of his memory this encounter arranged by Fate. He did not even tell Argensola who knew of the incidents of the transatlantic passage.

When he least expected it, Don Marcelo found himself at the end of that delightful and proud existence which his son's presence had brought him. The fortnight had flown by so swiftly! The sublieutenant had returned to his post, and all the family, after this period of reality, had had to fall back on the fond illusions of hope, watching again for the arrival of his letters, making conjectures about the silence of the absent one, sending him packet after packet of everything that the market was offering for the soldiery—for the most part, useless and absurd things.

The mother became very despondent. Julio's visit home but made her feel his absence with greater intensity. Seeing him, hearing those tales of death that her husband was so fond of repeating, made her realize all the more clearly the dangers constantly surrounding her son. Fatality appeared to be warning her with funereal presentiments.

"They are going to kill him," she kept saying to Desnoyers. "That wound was a forewarning from heaven."

When passing through the streets, she trembled with emotion at sight of the invalid soldiers. The convalescents of energetic appearance filled her with the greatest pity. They made her think of a certain trip with her husband to San Sebastian where a bull fight had made her cry out with indignation and compassion, pitying the fate of the poor, gored horses. With entrails hanging, they were taken to the corrals, and submitted to a hurried adjustment in order that they might return to the arena stimulated by a false energy.

Again and again they were reduced to this makeshift cobbling until finally a fatal goring finished them. . . . These recently cured men continually brought to her mind those poor beasts. Some had been wounded three times since the beginning of the war, and were returning surgically patched together and re-galvanized to take another chance in the lottery of Fate, always in the expectation of the supreme blow. . . . Ay, her son!

Desnoyers waxed very indignant over his wife's low spirits, retorting:

"But I tell you that Nobody will kill Julio! . . . He is my son. In my youth I, too, passed through great dangers. They wounded me, too, in the wars in the other world, and nevertheless, here I am at a ripe old age."

Events seemed to reinforce his blind faith. Calamities were raining around the family and saddening his relatives, yet not one grazed the intrepid sub-lieutenant who was persisting in his daring deeds with the heroic nerve of a musketeer.

Doña Luisa received a letter from Germany. Her sister wrote from Berlin, transmitting her letters through the kindness of a South American in Switzerland. This time, the good lady wept for some one besides her son; she wept for Elena and the enemies. In Germany there were mothers, too, and she put the sentiment of maternity above all patriotic differences.

Poor Frau von Hartrott! Her letter written a month before, had contained nothing but death notices and words of despair. Captain Otto was dead. Dead, too, was one of his younger brothers. The fact that the latter had fallen in a territory dominated by their nation, at least gave the mother the sad comfort of being able to weep near his grave. But the Captain was buried on French soil, nobody knew where, and she would never be able to find his remains, mingled with hundreds of others. A third son was wounded in Poland. Her two daughters had lost their promised lovers, and the sight of their silent grief, was intensifying the mother's suffering. Von Hartrott continued presiding over patriotic societies and making plans of expansion after the near victory, but he had aged greatly in the last few months. The "sage" was the only one still holding his own. The family afflictions were aggravating the ferocity of Professor Julius von Hartrott. He was calculating, in a book he was writing, the hundreds of thousands of millions that Germany must exact after her triumph, and the various nations that she would have to annex to the Fatherland.

Doña Luisa imagined that in the *avenue Victor Hugo,* she could hear the mother's tears falling in her home in Berlin. "You will understand, Luisa, my despair. . . . We were all so happy! May God punish those who have brought such sorrow on the world! The Emperor is innocent. His adversaries are to blame for it all . . ."

Don Marcelo was silent about the letter in his wife's presence. He pitied Elena for her losses, so he overlooked her political connections. He was touched, too, at Doña Luisa's distress about Otto. She had been his godmother and Desnoyers his godfather. That was so—Don Marcelo had forgotten all about it; and the fact recalled to his mental vision the placid life of the ranch, and the play of the blonde children that he had petted behind their grandfather's back, before Julio was born. For many years, he had lavished great affection on these youngsters, when dismayed at Julio's delayed arrival. He was really affected at thinking of what must be Karl's despair.

But then, as soon as he was alone, a selfish coldness would blot out this compassion. War was war, and the Germans had sought it. France had to defend herself, and the more enemies fell the better. . . . The only soldier who interested him now was Julio. And his faith in the destiny of his son made him feel a brutal joy, a paternal satisfaction almost amounting to ferocity.

"No one will kill *him!* . . . My heart tells me so."

A nearer trouble shook his peace of mind. When he returned to his home one evening, he found Doña Luisa with a terrified aspect holding her hands to her head.

"The daughter, Marcelo . . . our daughter!"

Chichí was stretched out on a sofa in the salon, pale, with an olive tinge, looking fixedly ahead of her as if she could see somebody in the empty air. She was not crying, but a slight palpitation was making her swollen eyes tremble spasmodically.

"I want to see him," she was saying hoarsely. "I must see him!"

The father conjectured that something terrible must have happened to Lacour's son. That was the only thing that could make Chichí show such desperation. His wife was telling him the sad news. René was wounded, very seriously wounded. A shell had exploded over his battery, killing many of his comrades. The young officer had been dragged out from a mountain of dead, one hand was gone, he had injuries in the legs, chest and head.

"I've got to see him!" reiterated Chichí.

And Don Marcelo had to concentrate all his efforts in making his daughter give up this dolorous insistence which made her exact an immediate journey to the front, trampling down all obstacles, in order to reach her wounded lover. The senator finally convinced her of the uselessness of it all. She would simply have to wait; he, the father, had to be patient. He was negotiating for René to be transferred to a hospital in Paris.

The great man moved Desnoyers to pity. He was making such heroic efforts to preserve the stoic serenity of ancient days by recalling his glorious ancestors and all the illustrious figures of the Roman Republic. But these oratorical illusions had suddenly fallen flat, and his old friend surprised him weeping more than once. An only child, and he might have to lose him! . . . Chichí's dumb woe made him feel even greater commiseration. Her grief was without tears or faintings. Her sallow face, the feverish brilliancy of her eyes, and the rigidity that made her move like an automaton were the only signs of her emotion. She was living with her thoughts far away, with no knowledge of what was going on around her.

When the patient arrived in Paris, his father and fiancée were transfigured. They were going to see him, and that was enough to make them imagine that he was already recuperated.

Chichí hastened to the hospital with her mother and the senator. Then she went alone and insisted on remaining there, on living at the wounded man's side, waging war on all regulations and clashing with Sisters of Charity, trained nurses, and all who roused in her the hatred of rivalry. Soon realizing that all her violence accomplished nothing, she humiliated herself and became suddenly very submissive, trying with her wiles, to win the women over one by one. Finally, she was permitted to spend the greater part of the day with René.

When Desnoyers first saw the wounded artilleryman in bed, he had to make a great effort to keep the tears back. . . . Ay, his son, too, might be brought to this sad pass! . . . The man looked to him like an Egyptian mummy, because of his complete envelopment in tight bandage wrappings. The sharp hulls of the shell had fairly riddled him. There could only be seen a pair of sweet eyes and a blond bit of moustache sticking up between white bands. The poor fellow was trying to smile at Chichí, who was hovering around him with a certain authority as though she were in her own home.

Two months rolled by. René was better, almost well. His betrothed had never doubted his recovery from the moment that they permitted her to remain with him.

"No one that I love, ever dies," she asserted with a ring of her father's self-confidence. "As if I would ever permit the Boches to leave me without a husband!"

She had her little sugar soldier back again, but, oh, in what a lamentable state! . . . Never had Don Marcelo realized the depersonalizing horrors of war as when he saw entering his home this convalescent whom he had known months before—elegant and slender, with a delicate and somewhat feminine beauty. His face was now furrowed by a network of scars that had transformed it into a purplish arabesque. Within his body were hidden many such. His left hand had disappeared with a part of the forearm, the empty sleeve hanging over the remainder. The other hand was supported on a cane, a necessary aid in order to be able to move a leg that would never recover its elasticity.

But Chichí was content. She surveyed her dear little soldier with more enthusiasm than ever—a little deformed, perhaps, but very interesting. With her mother, she accompanied the convalescent in his constitutionals through the *Bois de Boulogne*. When, in crossing a street, automobilists or coachmen failed to stop their vehicles in order to give the invalid the right of way, her eyes shot lightning shafts, as she thundered, "Shameless *embusqués!*" . . . She was now feeling the same fiery resentment as those women of former days who used to insult her René when he was well and happy. She trembled with satisfaction and pride when returning the greetings of her friends. Her eloquent eyes seemed to be saying, "Yes, he is my betrothed . . . a hero!" She was constantly arranging the war cross on his blouse of "horizon blue," taking pains to place it as conspicuously as possible. She also spent much time in prolonging the life of his shabby uniform—always the same one, the old one which he was wearing when wounded. A new one would give him the officery look of the soldiers who never left Paris.

As he grew stronger, René vainly tried to emancipate himself from her dominant supervision. It was simply useless to try to walk with more celerity or freedom.

"Lean on me!"

And he had to take his fiancées's arm. All her plans for the future were based on the devotion with which she was going to protect her husband, on the solicitude that she was going to dedicate to his crippled condition.

"My poor, dear invalid," she would murmur lovingly. "So ugly and so helpless those blackguards have left you! . . . But luckily you have me, and I adore you! . . . It makes no difference to me that one of your hands is gone. I will care for you; you shall be my little son. You will just see, after we are married, how elegant and stylish I am going to keep you. But don't you dare to look at any of the other women! The very first moment that you do, my precious little invalid, I'll leave you alone in your helplessness!"

Desnoyers and the senator were also concerned about their future, but in a very definite way. They must be married as soon as possible. What was the use of waiting? . . . The war was no longer an obstacle. They would be married as quietly as possible. This was no time for wedding pomp.

So René Lacour remained permanently in the house on the *avenida Victor Hugo,* after the nuptial ceremony witnessed by a dozen people.

Don Marcelo had had dreams of other things for his daughter —a grand wedding to which the daily papers would devote much space, a son-in-law with a brilliant future . . . but ay, this war! Everybody was having his fondest hopes dashed to pieces every few hours.

He took what comfort he could out of the situation. What more did they want? Chichí was happy—with a rollicking and selfish happiness which took no interest in anything but her own love-affairs. The Desnoyers business returns could not be improved upon; —after the first crisis had passed, the necessities of the belligerents had begun utilizing the output of his ranches, and never before had meat brought such high prices. Money was flowing in with greater volume than formerly, while the expenses were diminishing. . . . Julio was in daily danger of death, but the old ranchman was buoyed up by his conviction that his son led a charmed life—no harm could touch him. His chief preoccupation, therefore, was to keep himself tranquil, avoiding all emotional storms. He had been reading with considerable alarm of the frequency with which well-known persons, politicians, artists and writers, were dying in Paris. War was not doing all its killing at the front; its shocks were falling like arrows over the land, causing the fall of the weak, the crushed and the exhausted who, in normal times, would probably have lived to a far greater age.

"Attention, Marcelo!" he said to himself with grim humor. "Keep cool now! . . . You must avoid Friend Tchernoff's four horsemen, you know!"[1]

He spent an afternoon in the studio going over the war news in the papers. The French had begun an offensive in Champagne with great advances and many prisoners.

---

1. An elaborated description of the horses described in The Revelation to John. (*Editor's note.*)

Desnoyers could not but think of the loss of life that this must represent. Julio's fate, however, gave him no uneasiness, for his son was not in that part of the front. But yesterday he had received a letter from him, dated the week before; they all took about that length of time to reach him. Sub-lieutenant Desnoyers was as blithe and reckless as ever. They were going to promote him again—he was among those proposed for the *Legion d'Honneur*. These facts intensified Don Marcelo's vision of himself as the father of a general as young as those of the Revolution; and as he contemplated the daubs and sketches around him, he marvelled at the extraordinary way in which the war had twisted his son's career.

On his way home, he passed Marguerite Laurier dressed in mourning. The senator had told him a few days before that her brother, the artilleryman, had just been killed at Verdun.

"How many are falling!" he said mournfully to himself. "How hard it will be for his poor mother!"

But he smiled immediately after at the thought of those to be born. Never before had the people been so occupied in accelerating their reproduction. Even Madame Laurier now showed with pride the very visible curves of her approaching maternity, and Desnoyers noted sympathetically the vital volume apparent beneath her long mourning veil. Again he thought of Julio, without taking into account the flight of time. He felt as interested in the little newcomer as though he were in some way related to it, and he promised himself to aid generously the Laurier baby if he ever had the opportunity.

On entering his house, he was met in the hall by Doña Luisa, who told him that Lacour was waiting for him.

"Very good!" he responded gaily. "Let us see what our illustrious father-in-law has to say."

His good wife was uneasy. She had felt alarmed without knowing exactly why at the senator's solemn appearance; with that feminine instinct which perforates all masculine precautions, she surmised some hidden mission. She had noticed, too, that René and his father were talking together in a low tone, with repressed emotion.

Moved by an irresistible impulse, she hovered near the closed door, hoping to hear something definite. Her wait was not long.

Suddenly a cry . . . a groan . . . the groan that can come only from a body from which all vitality is escaping.

And Doña Luisa rushed in just in time to support her husband as he was falling to the floor.

The senator was excusing himself confusedly to the walls, the furniture, and turning his back in his agitation on the dismayed René, the only one who could have listened to him.

"He did not let me finish. . . . He guessed from the very first word. . . ."

Hearing the outcry, Chichí hastened in in time to see her father slipping from his wife's arms to the sofa, and from there to the floor, with glassy, staring eyes, and foaming at the mouth.

From the luxurious rooms came forth the world-old cry, always the same from the humblest home to the highest and loneliest:—

"Oh, Julio! . . . Oh, my son, my son!" . . .

Translated by Charlotte Brewster Jordan

Miguel De Unamuno

(1864-1936)

Born into a traditional Catholic family, Unamuno struggled throughout his life to find belief and in the process created a series of paradoxical qualities which make it extremely difficult to define what he is and what he represents. He became a professor of Greek and Latin at the University of Salamanca in 1891 and Rector in 1901. He lost his position in 1914 because of his opposition to the German cause. He continued to fight against restrictions and was imprisoned and exiled in 1924 by Primo de Rivera. He returned to Spain and to his position in 1930. He supported the Second Spanish Republic and later opposed it, but he also fought against the anti-intellectualism of the Franco position.

Unamuno excelled in all literary genres and produced noteworthy essays, dramas, short stories, and poetry. In 1895 he wrote five important essays on the meaning of Spanish culture and what he called the eternal tradition. *Life of Don Quixote and Sancho* (1905), a gloss of Cervantes' work, represents Quixote as a symbol of life who through action may triumph over death. *The Tragic Sense of Life* (1913) concerns the man of flesh and bone who despairs at his inability to prove God's existence and personal immortality but believes in salvation through faith. His dramas, such as *The Other* (1932) and *Brother John* (1934), contain the same tragic themes. His characters agonize existentially as they seek to express their essence.

Unamuno published his first novel, *Peace in War*, in 1897. Treating of the Carlist war and the siege of Bilbao, his birthplace, it was his only novel in the realistic tradition of the nineteenth century. His other novels, beginning with *Love and Pedagogy* (1902), represent human passions, abstractions, humor, and existential philosophy and do not rely on description or coherently developed plots. In response to negative criticism Unamuno said he would call his works *nivolas* instead of *novelas* and defined them as "panting narratives of intimate realities." *Love and Pedagogy* attacks the scientific spirit and reinforces man's existential struggle, in depicting the failure of a father to help create a genius son. *Mist* (1914) antedates Pirandello's *Six Characters in Search of an Author* in stressing the independence of his fictional creations as they interact with the author himself. Life is a fog, says Unamuno, which love may help clarify. *Abel Sánchez* (1917) analyzes jealousy and man's struggle to overcome his passion, in a Cain and Abel framework. In his many other novels Unamuno insists that one creates life through anguish the quest for immortality, and the wish to believe. One of his most strik ing novels is *Saint Manuel Bueno, Martyr,* about a kindly priest who i tormented by inability to believe in immortality but yet professes faith in order to bring happiness to his simple parishioners.

Unamuno claimed that in these works he was dealing with "agonist instead of protagonists." His tense and dynamic style helps set off hi personified ideas and tortured human beings who seek to survive, and a with almost all his works, these novels may be classified as a form o Unamuno's own spiritual autobiography.

The selection starts with an excerpt from the middle of Chapter and includes Chapters 5 and 6 about halfway through the novel.

Saint Manuel Bueno, Martyr

My brother ended by always going to Mass, to hear Don Manuel and when it was said that he would do his duty by the parish, tha he would take communion when the others did, an intimate feelin of rejoicing ran through the whole village, which believed it ha recovered him. But it was such a rejoicing, so clean, that Lázaro fel neither defeated nor belittled.

The day of his communion arrived, before the whole village with the whole village. When my brother's turn came, I could se that Don Manuel, as white as the January snow upon the mountai and trembling as the lake trembles when the north wind whips it approached him with the Sacred Host in his hand, which tremble so as he put it to Lázaro's lips, that, overcome by faintness, h dropped the Host. It was my brother himself who picked up th Host and put it in his mouth. The people, seeing Don Manuel weep wept, saying to each other: "How he loves him!" And then, as i was early morning, a cock crowed.

When I had returned home and was alone with my brother, threw my arms round his neck and kissing him said:

"Ah, Lázaro, Lázaro, what joy you have given to us all, to th whole village, to the living and the dead and especially to Mama to our mother. Did you see? Poor Don Manuel wept for joy. Wha joy you have given us all!"

"I have done it because of that," he answered.

"Because of that? To give us joy? You will have done it firs and foremost because of yourself, because of your conversion."

Then Lázaro, my brother, as pale and trembling as Don Manue

when he gave him communion, made me sit down, in the very armchair where our mother used to sit, took a deep breath, and then, as if making an intimate confession of a domestic and family nature, he said to me:

"Look, Angelita, the moment has come to tell you the truth, the whole truth, and I am going to tell it you, because I must; because I cannot and must not keep it from you and because moreover you would, sooner or later, have to guess at it and only guess half the truth, which is worst of all."

And then, serenely and quietly, in a low voice, he told me a story which plunged me into a lake of sadness. How Don Manuel had been working on him, particularly during those walks to the ruins of the old Cistercian abbey, begging him not to give offence, to set a good example, to join in the religious life of the village, to pretend to believe if he did not believe, to conceal his ideas on the subject, but without even trying to catechise him, or to convert him in any other way.

"But is it possible?" I exclaimed, in consternation.

"It is indeed, sister! And when I said to him: 'But is it you, you the priest, who are advising me to pretend?' he replied, stammering: 'Pretend? Not pretend! Take holy water, as someone once said, and you will end by believing.' And as I, looking him in the eye, said: 'And you, by celebrating Mass, have you ended by believing?', he looked down at the lake and his eyes filled with tears. And that is how I wrenched his secret from him."

"Lázaro!" I groaned.

At that moment daft Blasillo passed down the street, calling out his "My God, my God! Why hast Thou forsaken Me?", and Lázaro shuddered thinking he heard Don Manuel's voice, perhaps that of Our Lord Jesus Christ.

"Then," my brother went on, "I understood his motives and with them his saintliness; because he is a saint, sister, a true saint. When he undertook the task, he did not try to win me for his holy cause—because it is a holy cause, most holy—to take credit for a triumph, but he did it for the sake of the peace, the happiness, the illusion, if you like, of those entrusted to him. I realised that if he deceives them like that—if it is deception—it is not for his own benefit. I surrendered to his reasoning, and that is my conversion. I shall never forget the day when I said to him: 'But, Don Manuel, the truth, the truth before all else,' and he, trembling, whispered in my ear—and this in spite of our being alone in the heart of the country—'The truth? The truth, Lázaro, is perhaps something terrible, something intolerable, something deadly; simple people could not live with it.' 'And why do you let me glimpse it here and now, as at confession?' I said to him. And he answered: 'Because if I didn't, it would torment me so much, that I would end by shouting it in the middle of the market-place, and that must never happen, never, never. I am here to make the souls of my parishioners live, to make them happy, to make them dream they are immortal, and not to kill them. What is needed here is that they should live healthy lives, that they should live unanimous in feeling, and with the truth, with my truth, they would not live. Let them live. That is what the Church does, it makes them live. True religion? All religions are true, in so far as they make the people who profess them live spiritually, in so far as they console them for having had to be born only to die; and for each people the truest religion is their own, that which has made them. And mine? Mine is to console myself by consoling others, although the consolation I give them may not be mine.' I shall never forget these words of his."

"But your communion has been a sacrilege!" I dared to insinuate, promptly feeling sorry for having insinuated it.

"Sacrilege? And he who gave it to me? And his Masses?"

"What torture!" I exclaimed.

"And now," added my brother, "there is one more to console the people."

"To deceive them?" I said.

"To deceive them, no," he replied, "but to corroborate them in their faith."

"And they, the people," I said, "do they really believe?"

"How am I to know? They believe involuntarily, from habit, from tradition. What is necessary is not to waken them. Let them live in their spiritual poverty, so that they may be kept from the torments of luxury. 'Blessed are the poor in spirit!' "

"You have learnt that, brother, from Don Manuel. And now, tell me, have you kept that promise that you made to our mother when she was about to die, that you would pray for her?"

"As if I shouldn't keep it! But what do you take me for, sister? Do you believe me capable of breaking my word, a solemn promise, a promise made to a mother on her death-bed?"

"How do I know! . . . You might have meant to deceive her, so that she might die with that consolation."

"If I had not kept the promise I should live unconsoled."

"And so?"

"I kept the promise and I have not ceased to pray for her a single day."

"Only for her?"

"For whom else, then?"

"For yourself! And from now on, for Don Manuel."

We parted to go each one to his own room, I to weep all night, to pray for the conversion of my brother and Don Manuel, and he, Lázaro, I don't quite know what he did.

CHAPTER 5

From that day on I trembled at the thought of finding myself alone with Don Manuel, whom I continued to assist in his errands of mercy. He appeared to notice my innermost state of mind and guess the reason, and when at last I approached him in the confessional—who was the judge and who the offender?—both of us, he and I, bowed our heads in silence and began to weep. It was Don Manuel who broke the tremendous silence, to say to me in a voice which seemed to come from the tomb:

"But you, Angelina, you believe as you did when you were ten years old, don't you? You do believe?"

"Yes, I believe, father."

"Then go on believing. If any doubts arise, keep them from yourself. We must live . . ."

I became bold, and trembling all over I said:

"But you, father, do you believe?"

He hesitated a moment and, recovering himself, said:

"I believe."

"But in what exactly, father? Do you believe in the other life? Do you believe that on our death we do not wholly die? Do you believe we shall see each other and love each other again in another world to come? Do you believe in the other life?"

The poor saint was sobbing.

"Come, child, let us leave this!"

And now, as I write this record, I say to myself: "Why did he not deceive me? Why did he not deceive me then as he deceived the others? Why was he distressed? Because he could not deceive himself, or because he could not deceive me? I want to believe that he was distressed because he could not deceive himself in order to deceive me."

"And now," he added, "pray for me, for your brother, for yourself, for everyone. We must live. And we must give life."

And after a pause:

"And why don't you get married, Angelina?"

"You already know why, father."

"But no, no; you must get married. Between Lázaro and me we'll find you a bridegroom, because it is in your interest to marry, so that those worries may be dispelled."

"Worries, Don Manuel?"

"I know what I am saying. Don't distress yourself too much over others, for everyone has enough to do to have to answer for himself."

"That you should be the one, Don Manuel, to say that to me! To advise me to marry so as to answer for myself and not care about others! That you should be the one!"

"You are right, Angelina, I don't know what I am saying; I don't know what I have been saying since I have been confessing myself to you. Yes, yes, we must live."

When I was about to get up and leave the church, he said to me:

"And now, Angelina, in the people's name, do you absolve me?"

I felt as if I were permeated with a mysterious priesthood and said: "In the name of God the Father, the Son and the Holy Ghost, I absolve you, father."

We left the church, and as we left, my maternal instincts welled up within me.

CHAPTER 6

My brother, now entirely at the service of Don Manuel in his work, was his most assiduous collaborator and companion. They were bound together, moreover, by their mutual secret. He accompanied him on his visits to the sick and to the schools, and put his money at the saintly man's disposition. He very nearly learned to assist him at Mass. And he penetrated more and more deeply into Don Manuel's unfathomable soul.

"What a man!" he would say to me. "Why, yesterday, while walking along the shores of the lake, he said to me: 'This is my greatest temptation.' And as I looked at him enquiringly, he added: 'My poor father, who died when he was almost ninety, spent his life, as he confessed to me, tortured by the temptation to commit suicide, which he had felt as long as he could remember. "I was born with it," he would say, in his own defence. And this defence was his life. So as not to yield to such temptation he went to extremes in the care he took to safeguard his life. He told me of terrible scenes. It seemed like madness. And I have inherited it. How this water calls me, as with its apparent calm—the current runs below the surface—it mirrors the sky! My life, Lázaro, is a sort of continuous suicide, a struggle against suicide, which is the same; but let them live, let our people live!' And then he added: 'Here the course of the river is slowed down and forms a lake, and afterwards, descending to the plateau, it rushes in cascades, waterfalls and torrents, through chasms and gullies, close by the city, and thus life is checked, here, in the village. But the temptation to commit suicide is greater here, beside the backwater which mirrors the stars at night, than it is beside the frightening cascades. You see, Lázaro, I have attended poor, ignorant, illiterate villagers at their death, people who had scarcely ever left the village, and I have been able to learn from their lips, and if not, guess, the real cause of their mortal illness, and I have been able to see, there, at their deathbed, all the blackness of the abyss of boredom with life. A thousand times worse than hunger! Let us go on then, Lázaro, committing suicide in our work and in our village, and let the village dream its life as the lake dreams the sky.'"

"Another time," my brother also said to me, "when we were coming back here, we saw a lass, a goatherd, who, standing on a spur of rock on the mountain slope, in sight of the lake, was singing in a voice fresher than its waters. Don Manuel stopped me and, pointing to her, said: 'Look, it seems as if time had come to an end, as if this girl had always been there, just as she is, singing as she does, and as if she must go on being like that for ever, as she was before my consciousness began, as she will be when it has ceased. Along with the rocks, the clouds, the trees, the waters, this girl is part of nature and not of history.' How Don Manuel feels nature and gives it life! I shall never forget the day of the snowfall when he said to me: 'Have you seen, Lázaro, a greater mystery than that of the snow falling on the lake and dying in it, while it covers the mountain with its cloak?'"

Don Manuel had to restrain my brother in his zeal and in his inexperience as a neophyte. As he knew that Lázaro was preaching against certain popular superstitions, he had to say:

"Leave them alone! It is so difficult to make them understand where orthodox belief ends and superstition begins. And more so for us. Leave them alone then, so long as they find consolation. It is better that they should believe everything, even things which contradict each other, than that they should believe nothing. That those who believe too much end by believing nothing is a Protestant idea. Let us not protest. Protest kills contentment."

One night when the moon was full—my brother also told me—they were returning to the village along the shore of the lake, whose surface was then ruffled by the mountain breeze, and on the ripples frolicked the shafts of light from the full moon, and Don Manuel said to Lázaro:

"Look, the water is reciting the Litany, and now it says *'ianua caeli, ora pro nobis,* gate of heaven, pray for us!' "

And there fell trembling from his eyelashes to the grass two fleeting tears which, like the dew, caught the quivering light of the full moon.

Translated by Francisco de Segovia and Jean Perez

Ramón María Del Valle Inclán

(1866-1936)

Descendant of an aristocratic Galician family, the author never forgot the mysticism, superstition, and legends of his native province, even though he lived elsewhere during most of his life. He abandoned his law studies at the University of Santiago in 1890 and worked as a newspaperman and free-lance writer in Madrid. He lived in Mexico, the setting of some of his novels, and back in Spain, became a professor of esthetics, held various government offices, and carried out a variety of cultural duties under the Spanish Republic. His long, scraggly beard and lame arm, as well as his tendency to elaborate wild tales about his background, created legends about him which were never clearly dispelled.

Valle-Inclán was an exponent of the regional Galician novel, but he also wrote poetry, of which the Baroque and somewhat grotesque *The Pipe of Kif* (1919) is his best known, and a series of plays including some he labeled *esperpentos* (side show mirrors), which reflect the absurd and grotesque aspects of life. Perhaps his two most famous *esperpentos* are *The Horns of Don Friolera* (1921), a parody of the Calderonian code of honor and a commentary on the defects to be found in Spanish character, and *Lights of Bohemia* (1924), which also reduces human beings to the category of deformed or grotesque spiritual puppets, distorted reflections of an imperfect mirror. But just as it is hard to know the reality of his life because of his deliberately invented mythology, it is difficult to distinguish genres in his work, which conveys great dramatic tension and an exquisitely artistic and poetic technique.

Among his best-known novels are his four *Sonatas, Autumn* (1902), *Summer* (1903), *Spring* (1904), and *Winter* (1905). Subtitled the *Memoirs of the Marquis of Bradomín,* they concern the amorous adventures of a kind of narcissistic Don Juan who describes himself as "ugly, Catholic and sentimental." The four seasons, representing the four stages of man's existence from youth to old age, reveal an exaltation of the flesh, mystic overtones, and a musical style that fits the season being described. Thus, *Spring* is filled with the fragrance of roses, *Summer* with voluptuous passion, *Autumn* with languid memories, and *Winter* with cold rain and death. His other fiction includes: *Shady Garden* (1903), full of mystery and magic, a collection of short stories which the author calls "histories of saints, souls in pain, spirits and thieves"; *Flower of Holiness* (1904), about a peasant girl who superstitiously

63

thinks she has had an affair with the Saviour; *Barbarous Comedies*, which some call dialogued novels, especially *Ballad of Wolves* (1908) whose protagonist is a relative of the Marquis of Bradomín; a trilogy on the Carlist War in which the Marquis is again a character; *The Tyrant* (1926), a strangely deformed caricature of a Spanish American country; and some historical novels about the reign of Isabel II, especially *Court of Miracles* (1927).

Valle-Inclán, an impressionistic prose stylist, used musical, elegant, and artificial language, but he also wrote popular, regional, and historical works. He never fully abandoned his sensuality, refinement, and symbolism, but he combined these and his themes of terror, death, and superstition in his most enduring works, grotesque, baroque, and bitter visions of Spanish reality.

The excerpt begins in the middle of Chapter 22 and includes Chapters 23 through 27, the concluding pages of the novel.

Sonata of Autumn

Taking the two children by the hand, she left the room with them. Concha and I were alone. She moved languidly over to her chair and sat down. She sighed heavily, as she often did, and told me she was dying. I went up to her laughing and she became indignant. "Laugh! You do well to leave me alone. Go with Isabel."

I took up one of her hands, bunched the fingers into a pale little rose, and with closed eyes kissed them.

"Don't make me suffer, Concha."

She dropped her lids over tear-filled eyes and said, in a low penitent voice: "Why do you want to leave me alone? It's not your fault, I know. It is she who is mad about you and runs after you."

I dried her tears: "Concha dear, it is you who are mad and nobody else, but it is such a charming madness that I would never wish to see it cured."

"I am not mad."

"Indeed you are—mad about me."

"No, no, no!" she repeated in pretty vexation.

"Yes."

"Conceited!"

"Why then do you want to keep me beside you?"

Concha threw her arms about my neck, kissed me and exclaimed laughing: "The truth is, if you are so vain of my affection, it must be because it is so valuable."

"Of priceless value."

Concha passed her hands over my hair in a lingering caress: "Let them go without you, Xavier. You see, I care more for you than for my own children."

Yielding like a submissive child, I pressed my head against her breast and closed my eyes. With rapturous ecstasy that yet was sorrow I breathed the perfume of that drooping flower.

"I will do whatever you wish. You know that."

Looking me in the eyes and lowering her voice, Concha murmured: "Then you won't go to Lantañon?"

"No."

"Are you annoyed?"

"No. I am only sorry on the children's account. They were told they could go."

"They can go with Isabel—the major-domo can accompany them."

At that moment a sudden shower lashed the window panes and deluged the green garden; clouds obscured the sun; and the October afternoon took on a soft, sad light that seemed the very spirit of autumn.

Maria Fernanda entered much distressed: "Have you seen what bad luck we are having, Xavier? It is raining."

Then Maria Isabel came in: "May we go if it clears, Mamma?"

"Yes, if it clears," Concha answered.

The two children stationed themselves at the window and with faces glued against the glass watched the rain. Dark, lead-coloured clouds were gathering over La Sierra de Céltigos on a watery horizon; shepherds, calling their sheep, hurried down the road enveloped in capes of frieze; a rainbow spanned the garden; the dark cypress-trees and rain-washed myrtle trembled in rays of orange light. Candelaria, with skirts tucked up above clumping wooden shoes, went about, under a big blue umbrella, gathering roses for the chapel altar.

CHAPTER 23

The chapel was dark, damp, resounding. Above the altar hung a shield of sixteen quarterings, enamelled in colour, gules and azure, sable and sinople, gold and silver—the arms granted by writ of Their Catholic Majesties to Captain Alonzo Bendaña, founder of the house of Brandeso.

There is a wild legend recounted of this same Captain in the nobiliary accounts of Galicia. The tale goes that having taken prisoner his enemy, the Abbot of Mos, while on a hunting party, he dressed the abbot in a wolf-skin and turned him loose on the mountain, where his enemy was torn to pieces by the teeth of the dogs. Candelaria, Concha's old nurse, like all ancient servants, was intimately familiar with the history and genealogy of the house she served. And in the old days, she used to relate to us this legend of Captain Alonzo Bendaña, as it is given in those old accounts which no one now reads. But Candelaria knew futhermore that two black dwarfs had carried the Captain's body to hell. It was a tradition of the house of Bradomín that the men of the race were cruel and the women pious. I well remember the time when there was a chaplain attached to the Palace and my Aunt Agueda, following a noble old custom, used to hear mass from a small gallery near the pulpit, surrounded by all her daughters. In this gallery was a bench of crimson velvet, its high back crowned with two escutcheons, but only my Aunt Agueda, because of her age and failing health, enjoyed the privilege of being seated there.

At the right of the altar was interred Captain Alonzo Bendaña with other caballeros of his line. A statue of a praying warrior guarded the sepulchre. At the left of the altar was interred Doña Beatriz de Montenegro with other ladies of various lineage. The sepulchre was adorned by the statue of a praying nun, robed in the white habit of the Comendadoras de Santiago. The chancel lamp burned day and night before an altar-piece as finely wrought as the jewel of a queen. An evangelic vine laden with golden fruit framed the guardian saint, pious King Mago, as he offered myrrh to the Infant Jesus. His gold-embroidered, silken tunic shone with the splendour of an oriental miracle. The light of the lamp, between silver chains, had the timid flutter of a prisoned bird struggling to fly upward to the Saint.

That afternoon Concha desired to place with her own hands the rose-laden vases at the feet of King Mago as an offering of her devout spirit. Afterwards, accompanied by the children, she knelt before the altar. To me, in the gallery, Concha's voice was only a murmur as she recited the Ave Marias, but when it came to the children to respond I could hear every word of the ritual. At the end of the prayer, Concha kissed the rosary, got up and traversed the chancel, making the sign of the cross. She called the children to pray before the sepulchre of the warrior, where Don Miguel Bendaña, Concha's grandfather, was also buried. This Señor of Brandeso was in the act of dying at the time when my mother brought me to the Palace for the first time. Don Miguel Bendaña was an aristocrat, despotic, generous, faithful to the traditions of his house. Upright as a lance, he passed through the world with no unbending to the common touch. Beautiful and noble eccentricity! When he died, at eighty years, his spirit was still valiant, proud and finely tempered as an ancient sword. For five days he lay at the point of death refusing to confess himself. My mother asseverated that she had never seen the like. That old hidalgo was a heretic. One night, a short while after his death, I heard it related, in a hollow whisper, that Don Miguel Bendaña had murdered one of his own servants. Well might Concha pray for his soul!

The afternoon was dying; the prayers reverberated through the quiet dark of the chapel, solemnly sad like an echo of the Passion. I drowsed in the gallery. The children seated themselves on the steps before the altar. Their dresses were as purely white as the liturgic linen. I could just distinguish a shadow that prayed under the chancel lamp. It was Concha. She had an open book between her hands and read with head devoutly bent. Now and then, as the wind stirred the draperies of the great, high window, I could see the moon's pale, supernatural face gazing from the now darkened sky, like some goddess looking to her altars in wood and lake.

Concha closed the book with a sigh and called again to the children. I saw their white shadows flit across the chancel and I knew that they knelt beside their mother. The trembling lamplight shed a pale glory over Concha's hands as they supported the open book. In the silence her voice read slowly and devoutly. The children listened. I divined their bright hair flowing over the pure whiteness of their garments. Concha read.

CHAPTER 24

It was the middle of the night. I was writing when Concha softly entered my room, wrapped in her nun-like gown. "To whom are you writing?" she asked.

"To Doña Margarita's secretary."

"What are you saying to him?"

"Giving an account of a donation for missions which I have made in the Queen's name."

There was a moment of silence. Concha stood, leaning her hands on my shoulders. As she bent over me her hair brushed my forehead. "Are you writing to her secretary or are you writing to the Queen herself?"

I turned with deliberate coldness: "I am writing to the secretary. Surely you are not jealous of the Queen?"

"No, no," she protested eagerly.

I took her upon my knee and said, caressing her: "Doña Margarita is not like the other, you know. . . ."

"A great many things that were said of the other were calumny. My mother, who was her lady-in-waiting, always maintained so."

Seeing that I smiled, poor Concha dropped her eyes in adorable embarrassment.

"Men always believe the evil that is spoken of women. . . . And a queen has so many enemies!"

She saw the smile still on my lips and twisted my black moustache with her white fingers: "Naughty mouth!"

She stood up with the intention of going. With one hand, I detained her.

"Stay, Concha."

"It cannot be, Xavier. You know that."

"Stay," I repeated.

"No, no. . . . I want to confess to-morrow. . . . It frightens me to offend God like this."

I stood up, courteously, icily disdainful. "It appears, then, that I have a rival?"

Concha looked at me with supplication in her eyes: "Xavier, don't hurt me so."

"I have no wish to hurt you. I leave the Palace to-morrow."

Tearful, angry, she exclaimed: "You shall not leave to-morrow!"

Almost tearing off the clinging white gown, she stood naked, trembling.

I held out my arms: "My poor love!"

She looked at me through her tears, pale and changed:

"How cruel you are. . . . Now I cannot confess to-morrow."

I kissed her and said to console her: "We will both confess the day I leave."

I saw a fugitive smile pass in her eyes: "If you hope to gain your liberty with that promise you will not succeed."

"Why?"

"Because you are my prisoner for life."

Circling my neck with her arms she laughed. The black knot of her hair came down; she lifted the dusky perfumed flood in her white hands and whipped me with it.

"The lash of God!" I sighed, with eyes half closed.

"Be still, heretic!"

"Do you remember how this used to make me all but swoon?"

"I remember every bit of your mad behaviour."

"Whip me now, Concha. . . . Whip me as though I were the Divine Nazarene. . . . Whip me to death. . . ."

"Be still, be still."

With wild eyes and hands that trembled, she commenced to gather up the dark, perfumed mass. "You fill me with terror when you say such impious things. Yes, terror . . . because it is not you who speaks. It is Satan. Even to your voice you are different. It is Satan."

In extreme agitation she closed her eyes as my arms sheltered her lovingly. It seemed to me that a prayer strayed on her lips. Laughing, I sealed the lips with mine. "Amen. . . . Amen. . . . Amen!" I murmured.

There was a silence. Suddenly I felt her mouth moan under my mouth. "I am dying."

Her body, clasped in my arms, trembled as if shaken by a mortal chill. Her livid head rolled on the pillow in a faint. Her eyelids half opened, sluggishly; I saw her eyes, dulled, anguished.

"Concha. . . . Concha. . . ."

I sat up against the pillow. Instantly cool and prudent I freed the hands that were still clasped around my neck. They were like wax.

I stood irresolute, not daring to move.

"Concha. . . . Concha. . . ."

Far off, I heard the howl of a dog. I slid to the floor without a sound. Seizing the light I gazed at the changed face. I touched the forehead with a trembling hand. The chill repose of death appalled me. No, I could not depend upon myself. I thought of fleeing and cautiously opened a window. With my hair standing on end I gazed out into the blackness, while inside the room the curtains of my bed fluttered and the flames of the candles in the silver stands wavered sickeningly. The dog's howl still came from very far away; the wind went through the labyrinth complaining like a soul in pain; clouds passed over the moon and quenched the burning stars as death snuffs out poor human lives.

CHAPTER 25

I left the window open and, moving without a sound, as if I feared my footsteps might waken the pallid spectre on the bed, I crossed to the door which, but a moment before, had been closed by hands tremulous with passion that now were motionless. Fearfully I looked down the black corridor and adventured into its dark. Everything in the Palace seemed to sleep. My footsteps scarcely made a sound, but they rang in my imagination with a fearful resonance. Far ahead, in the ante-chamber, a pale light trembled from the lamp that burned before the image of Jesus of Nazareth. That holy face, livid and discomposed, inspired a greater fear than the dead face of Concha. With trembling limbs I reached Concha's bedroom and stopped at the door to watch a streak of light, far down the corridor, which marked on the blackness of the floor the bedroom where my cousin Isabel was sleeping. I feared to see her appear, aghast and terrified at the sound of my footsteps. I feared her cries would alarm the Palace. I resolved to go in to her and tell her everything. I moved stealthily to her door. Opening it softly, I called in a muffled voice: "Isabel. . . . Isabel. . . ."

I waited. Nothing disturbed the silence. I took a few steps forward and called again: "Isabel. . . . Isabel. . . ."

Still no response. My voice died away in the vast chamber, as if too terrified to sound. Isabel was asleep. In the faint glow of the night-light that flickered in a crystal vase, my eyes made out the wooden bed. In the silence, my cousin Isabel's breathing rose and fell with a slow regular rhythm. Beneath the damask coverlet her body showed softly indefinite; her loose hair lay like a dark veil spread over the white pillows. I called again: "Isabel. . . . Isabel. . . ."

I had reached the bedside and stretched out my hand. By chance it rested on my cousin's bare, warm shoulder. I felt a quiver. In a low voice I spoke again: "Isabel. . . . Isabel. . . ."

Isabel sat up with a start: "Don't call. Concha can hear you."

My eyes filled with tears. Bending down I murmured: "Poor Concha cannot hear us."

One of Isabel's soft tempting curls touched my lips. I believe I kissed it. As with the saints, my heart is at its tenderest when touched with grief. Concha in heaven will have pardoned my weakness, for here on earth she knew it well. Isabel, breathing excitedly, whispered: "Had I suspected this I would have turned the key."

"Which way, Isabel?"

"To lock you out, bandit. To lock you out!"

I had not the heart to contravert my cousin Isabel's suspicions. To prove her mistaken would have been so ungallant and so painful. Isabel was pious and the knowledge that she had calumniated me would have caused her suffering. Ah me! All the saintly martyrs gone before me, monks, and patriarchs and holy fathers, were in better case than I to triumph over sin. The lovely women who tempted them were not their cousins. Life plays some cruel jests. When destiny smiles on me, it is always as it was that night, with the leering grimace of a bow-legged dwarf capering on castle chimney-tops by moonlight.

Suffocated by my kisses, Isabel stammered: "I'm afraid Concha may come."

A shudder of horror ran through my body. Isabel thought it was the ecstasy of love. She never knew why I had gone to her.

CHAPTER 26

When my mortal eyes again beheld Concha's yellow disfigured face; when my feverish hands again touched her stiff hands, the terror that I felt was such that I began to pray, and again the temptation came to flee by the window which stood open to the dark, mysterious garden. The silent breeze of night fluttered the curtains and lifted the hair on my head. The stars were paling in the livid sky and the wind had visited the silver candelabra, extinguishing the flames till only one remained. The ancient cypresses, standing erect below the window, slowly bowed their melancholy tops and the moon passed fugitive and white between them like a soul in torment. In the silence the distant crow of a cock announced the imminent dawn. A shudder passed through my frame and I gazed with horror at the inanimate body of Concha stretched upon my bed. Then, suddenly recovering my senses, I lighted all the candles of the branching candlestick and placed it in the doorway to illuminate the corridor. I went back; my arms grasped with terror the ghastly phantom that had so often slept in them. I walked out with the funereal burden. As we crossed the threshold, an inert hand swung itself slowly through the burning candle-flames and knocked over the candelabrum. On the floor the candles continued to burn where they fell with a sickly, flickering light. For an instant I stood petrified and listened. All that I heard was the murmur of the fountain in the labyrinth. I went on. Ahead of me, in the vast ante-chamber, shone the lamp of the Nazarene; I was afraid to pass before that livid, dishevelled image. I feared its dead gaze. I went back.

To reach Concha's bedroom without going through the ante-chamber it was necessary to traverse the entire Palace. I did not hesitate. One after the other I passed through huge salons and shadowy corridors. At times the light of the moon reached into the deserted depths of the apartments. I moved like a shadow before the long succession of gloomy, leaded windows standing sombrely closed, in crumbling, blackened frames. When I crossed before a mirror I closed my eyes so as not to see myself. Cold sweat stood on my forehead. At times the darkness was so dense that I went astray and was forced to adventure at random—rigid, anguished —supporting the body with only one arm, the other stretched out before me to prevent a stumble. As we passed through a doorway, a waving strand of the tragic hair caught and held fast. I groped about in the blackness trying to loosen it. I could not. It became more entangled every moment. My hand, stupid with terror, trembled over it and the door pulled slowly open and closed, creaking lengthily. To my horror, I saw that day was dawning. Giddiness seized me and I pulled . . . the body seemed trying to escape my arms. In desperation, I clasped it more tightly. Under the forehead, tight-drawn and dark, the waxen eyelids slowly opened. I pressed them shut and pulled brutally until the beloved, perfumed hair broke. . . . With the body grappled in my arms I fled.

I reached the open door of Concha's bedroom. The warm perfumed dark beyond breathed mystery as if it still guarded the tender secret of our amorous hours. What a tragic secret it must guard henceforth!

Carefully, cautiously, I left Concha's body stretched upon the bed and moved away without a sound. At the door I stopped, irresolute, and drew a long breath. I was uncertain whether to go back and place a last kiss upon those icy lips. I resisted the temptation. An almost religious scruple constrained me. I feared there might be something sacrilegious in the sensuous grief that possessed me. The warm fragrance of the bedroom kindled voluptuous memories of the senses that were a torture to me. I fervently desired to feel pure and sweet, but could not control my wild imaginings. It has happened at times even to the mystics that sacred things have suggested to them monstrous diabolisms. To this day there is a touch of subtle depravity in the sorrow that the

memory of Concha's death brings to me. It claws at my heart like
a lean cat with glittering eyes. It twists my heart till it bleeds
in agony, yet all the while, deep down, the devil in me, who can
change all grief to glee, laughs and laughs.

My memories, lost glories of my soul, are like burning music,
cruel and sad, to whose strange rhythm dances the weeping phantom
that was my love. Poor white phantom! Worms have eaten the eyes;
tears roll from the sockets as it dances in the ring of my youthful
memories; never touching earth, it floats upward on a wave of
perfume, the scent of her sweet hair which lives on after she has
gone. Poor Concha! Her passage through the world left behind no
more than a wake of perfumes. But it may be that she, the whitest
and chastest of my loves, was never more than an exquisite incarna-
tion of the sensuous perfumes of Aphrodite.

CHAPTER 27

Maria Isabel and Maria Fernanda first announced themselves
by knocking with childish hands upon my door. Then came their
fresh voices, crystal clear, like the voice of a mountain spring as
it talks with the birds and the flowers. "May we come in, Xavier?"

"Yes, children, come in."

The morning was well advanced and they had come to inquire,
in Isabel's name, how I had passed the night—a gentle question that
filled my heart with remorse. The children stood beside me, in the
window, looking out into garden. The frowning green branches of
a yew tree brushed mournfully against the panes. Under the wind
from the mountains the yew felt shiverings of cold, and the touch of
its green branches on the panes seemed like an appeal from the
dark old garden for the children to come out and play. Deep in the
labyrinth, a band of doves circled about close to the ground, and
from the cold blue sky above a keen-eyed hawk swooped down on
long, black wings. "Oh, Xavier, kill it! . . . Kill it!" the children
cried.

I went for the gun which slept, dust-covered, in a corner of my
room and came back to the balcony. The children clapped their
hands: "Kill it! Kill it!"

At that moment the hawk fell upon the doves which flew about
terror-stricken. I put the gun to my cheek and, when an opening
came, fired. Some dogs barked in the fields near by. The doves

wheeled about in the smoke and the hawk, with wings outstretched, fell dead. The children ran down and picked it up by the tips of the wings. Bright blood trickled from the plumage of the breast. They started off carrying the hawk triumphantly between them. A new anxiety awoke in me.

"Where are you going?" I called to them.

They turned in the doorway, smiling delightedly. "Wait and see how we will frighten mother when she wakes up."

"No, no, no!"

"Oh, just a make-believe fright."

I did not dare to stop them. I stayed and waited, sick at heart. Bitter suspense! Waiting on that radiant morning of sunlight for the fatal moment when the cries of the innocent should ring through the chambers of the Palace! Heartbroken moans and violent sobbings. . . .

I felt the dull anguish of despair in the presence of that mute, cold phantom, Death, who reaped the dreams in the garden of my heart . . . beautiful dreams conjured up by the magic of love! An extraordinary sadness fell upon me; as if the twilight were closing in upon my life; as if my life like a dreary day of winter were drawing to a close, to begin anew, to-morrow, with a sunless dawn. Poor Concha was dead! Dead, that flower of my dreams to whom all my words seemed beautiful! That flower of my dreams to whom my every gesture seemed sublime! . . . Would I ever again encounter a pale princess with enchanting, sorrowful eyes who would see me always magnificent? In the face of this doubt I wept. Wept like an outworn god of antiquity, lamenting the extinction of his cult.

Translated by M. H. Broun and Thomas Walsh

Pío Baroja

(1872-1956)

Born in San Sebastián, he lived a kind of nomad existence, as his father, an engineer, took him along on his many trips. His life as a wanderer influenced many of his later plots whose heroes, often the author himself, are vagabonds. He studied medicine and practiced for a while as a village doctor. He worked for a time with his brother, Richard, in a bakery owned by his aunt. After a series of financial speculations, he earned enough money to be able to dedicate himself exclusively to writing and traveling.

Baroja, who became a member of the Royal Academy in 1935, wrote more than a hundred volumes of essay, criticism, travel literature, and especially fiction. In his efforts to obtain simplicity in his novels he sacrificed much of the stylistic structure that most critics felt was necessary. He claimed that as a realistic novelist he should include all of life with its inconsistencies, illogical happenings, frustrations, and futilities. Thus, most of his novels seem to be a series of episodes connected by a central character, often a *pícaro*. Although he employed a picaresque framework, Baroja denied all technique or formulas, for he felt the novel was a "multiformed and protean" genre, which each person had to develop in his own manner. His ideas about the novel influenced many contemporary novelists, especially Camilo José Cela.

Baroja wrote nine trilogies, one tetralogy, and a series of twenty-two novels under the general title of *Memoirs of a Man of Action* (1913-35), whose central hero is Eugenio de Aviraneta, an energetic extrovert. He also produced pathological novels, adventure novels, and psychological novels. Among his many titles are *Road of Perfection* (1902), about the defeat of an idealistic reformer who becomes an aimless wanderer; *The Quest* (1904), about Madrid low life and a juvenile delinquent who lives off the streets; *Paradox, King* (1906), a sarcastic evaluation of civilized man and his ridiculous institutions; *Zalacaín, the Adventurer* (1909), about a hero who becomes a smuggler and dies in the Carlist War; *Caesar or Nothing* (1910), whose Nietzschean hero fruitlessly seeks political success; and *The Tree of Knowledge* (1911), whose frustrated hero voices most of Baroja's ideas about Spain and the futility of life. Baroja continued to write novels into the 1950's.

Baroja views man as a cruel, egotistical, and unjust being, and he expects nothing from him or from his institutions. Life is stupid, empty, and evil. Many of these ideas were based on an imperfect digestion of his reading of Nietzsche and Schopenhauer, and he offered no real solutions, philosophical or scientific. At first reading, then, these novels seem to be antisocial, for the author attacks all government systems, social institutions, and religious morality. His protagonists almost always fail, since they exhibit a lack of will power or action. Yet this cynical and pessimistic man's novels are marked by humor, lyric force, and great sincerity, and, reading between the lines, by a desire for justice and a wish to believe in a world of positive values, of freedom for the individual, and dignity for mankind.

The selections are taken from *Paradox, King* Chapters 1 and 2 of Part III, and Chapters 10, 11, 12, the concluding chapters of the novel, and from *The Restlessness of Shanti Andía* (1911), Chapters 7, 8 and the Epilogue of Book 7, the final pages of the novel.

Paradox, King

PART THREE

I

The Conspirators

A party of negroes is coming up the slope of the island, to the music of drums. All the inhabitants of Fortunate House are looking out from the wall.

PARADOX

What can this mean? Are they coming to attack us again?

UGU

No, certainly not that.

DIZ

What's that they're carrying on that spear head?

SIMPSON, *who has brought his telescope, and is looking through it.*

It's a human head.

BEATRICE

Oh, how awful!

The party approaches to within a few yards of the fortress.

UGU, *advancing on the wall*

What do you want?

A REBEL

We wish to speak with the foreigners. We have risen against King Kiri and cut off his head. We are coming to offer it to you and to ask you to govern us yourselves from this day forth.

On UGU *communicating his countrymen's wishes to* PARADOX *and* SIMPSON, *they both cross the drawbridge and leave the fort. The rebels bow before them, and offer them the bloody remains of King Kiri.*

PARADOX

Throw this into the river, and afterwards we will start the discussion. What have you done?

THE REBEL

Tired of this man's oppression and crimes, some of us conspired together; this morning at dawn we entered his palace and killed him. The entire people, as soon as they knew what had happened, joined us and all rejoiced that the reign of this monster had come to an end; but afterwards . . .

PARADOX

You were sorry for what you had done.

THE REBEL

No; what happened was that we did not know what to do next or whom to name king, and then we thought of you.

SIMPSON

And what do you want us to do?

THE REBEL

You are wiser than we are and know many things of which we are utterly ignorant. We want a just and good king; we ask you to find him for us.

SIMPSON

You set us a difficult task. Give us at any rate a little time in which to choose.

THE REBEL

Take the day, but no more. The people cannot be long without a king. One party will fight another and civil war will break out.

PARADOX

All the same, you must understand that it is very little time which you give us. Afterwards you may blame us and protest against our decision.

THE REBEL

We will not complain; he whom you elect is well chosen. Decide without delay; we will wait your choice. See: the whole people, knowing our proposal, is coming to the island.

*In fact: more canoes are seen coming, and quantities of negroes
assembling on the low ground.*

SIMPSON

Agreed. Before night comes, we will tell you who is to be your
king.

II

The Constitution of Uganga

*All the Europeans have assembled in the big hall at Fortunate
House, and also* UGU, *who has been specially admitted to the de-
liberations.* PARADOX *is presiding.*

GANEREAU

I ask permission to ask a preliminary question.

PARADOX

I call on Ganereau.

GANEREAU

Gentlemen; I do not see any necessity to interpret the rebels'
petition too literally.

In asking us for a king, what they mean is that they need a
government; and in my opinion a personal government is inferior to
a republic.

GOIZUETA

My view is just the opposite.

HARDIBRAS

And mine too.

SIMPSON

Besides, their request was quite definite; they want a king.

GANEREAU

A king! What's the use of a king?

PARADOX

Well, he fulfils much the same duties as the president in a republic; he shoots rabbits, kills pigeons, and in some cases, it is
said, has been useful in governing the country.

GANEREAU

For my part, my dignity does not allow me to obey a king.

PARADOX

As if a king ever was obeyed in any country! One obeys a collection of laws. There's no question of one's dignity being affected.

In every country in Europe we have as head of the state a sort of military gentleman dressed in uniform, wearing a regular ironmonger's shop of crosses and medals on his chest, while you have a sort of legal gentleman, wearing a morning coat and a top hat, with a ribbon in his buttonhole.

GANEREAU

I don't agree.

PARADOX

It is so, all the same.

SIMPSON

In any case, what has this to do with the matter in hand?

GANEREAU

My point is that the inhabitants of Uganda don't realise that their country could be governed in any different way.

SIMPSON

And how are we going to convince them of the contrary in the space of a few hours? (*Aside.*) He's already got it into his head that he's in Montrouge.

PARADOX

I don't think we ought to impose a government on European lines upon the Mandingoes.

THONELGEBEN

I entirely agree.

GANEREAU

If we give them an absolute monarch, they will run the danger of finding themselves the slaves of a new tyrant as abominable as the former.

PARADOX

What shall we do then? Shall we try a Constitution, or simply choose some individual to be their king?

GANEREAU

I think the idea of a Constitution has great merits, and I propose that we formulate two or three projects, and submit them for discussion.

PARADOX

Is Ganereau's idea approved?

ALL

Approved. We'll see if it gives any practical result.

GANEREAU *goes to one end of the table, and* DIZ *to the other; both start to write rapidly. After half an hour both rise with sheets of paper in their hands.*

PARADOX

Have you finished already?

GANEREAU *and* DIZ

Yes.

PARADOX

Good; let us hear the drafts.

GANEREAU

I have omitted all explanations in order to make the writing as short as possible. The chief articles of the Constitution are these:

First: All the inhabitants of Uganda shall be free.

PARADOX, *aside, to* LA MOME FROMAGE

Free to eat, if there is anything to eat; free to scratch, pick off fleas, or go for a stroll: but not free to annoy the others.

GANEREAU

Second: All the inhabitants of Uganda shall be equal.

PARADOX, *to* LA MOME FROMAGE

They will remain unequal in height, shape of the nose, and other gifts of Nature. I don't think it should be permitted to cut down large noses to make them equal to flat noses.

GANEREAU

Third: All the inhabitants of Uganda shall be considered brothers.

PARADOX

It being understood all the same that the brother who bites may be muzzled.

GANEREAU

Fourth: The Government will be organised on a representative system, with the proportional vote.

THONELGEBEN

Stop! I don't think we ought to establish the parliamentary system as it is practised in Europe.

DIZ

Nor do I.

PARADOX

I am opposed to the representative system in itself. I don't see the sublimity of a proceeding which implies that the majority is always right.

GANEREAU

Well then, how is the country to be governed?

PARADOX

I think Uganda would be best with a paternal government.

THONELGEBEN

In my opinion the best method is a socialist dictatorship, renewable as the dictator becomes tired or ceases to fulfil his duties in a satisfactory manner. I think in the first place we should declare that the soil of Bu-Tata shall belong to all; that there shall be a common stock of tools, and that each one shall be supplied according to his necessities.

PARADOX

I think, my friend, that your plan supposes the Mandingoes on a higher cultural level than they really are.

THONELGEBEN

No; why should you say so? Communism is nature's plan. Further, it is sound economically. European civilisation is the more artificial because it has departed from reality.

PARADOX

It seems to me that we might discuss this point for ever, and that even to settle it one way or another would not help us in the least.

THONELGEBEN

Surely you all agree that the great thing is to safeguard the happiness of the people?

PARADOX

Yes, we are all agreed in that. But we disagree as to the best method of bringing about this happiness.

GOIZUETA

What about religion? I suppose we shall try to make the negroes Christians?

SIMPSON

Why? Let everyone have the religion which he likes. There is not complete unanimity among ourselves, you know; I am a Pantheist.

DIZ

I am a follower of Haeckel.

THONELGEBEN

So am I.

GANEREAU

I am a Voltairian Deist.

PARADOX

And you, Simpson?

SIMPSON

I'm Church of England. Though to tell the truth, I don't often go to church.

PARADOX

And you, Thady Bray.

THADY BRAY

Presbyterian.

DORA

Well, I'm a Catholic.

BEATRICE

So am I.

GOIZUETA

And I. And we have the certainty of holding the true faith.

HAJJI OMAR

The only true faith is, that there is no God but God, and Mohammed is his prophet.

GOIZUETA

Silence, you Moorish dog. Mohammed was a scoundrel.

HAJJI OMAR *pulls out a rosary, and starts to pray under his breath.*

PARADOX

And you, Piperazzini, what is your religion?

PIPERAZZINI

Corpo di Bacco! I think I'm really a pagan.

PARADOX

And you, Ugu?

UGU

I still believe in dung-balls.

PARADOX

And you, Beppo?

BEPPO

I'm only a cook, Sir.

PARADOX

And you, Hardibras?

HARDIBRAS

I have no religion beyond military discipline and honour.

PARADOX

So, sir, our unanimity is truly delightful. Between Beppo, who believes in nothing but cookery books, to those who rise to the heights of the Koran and the Bible, what a gulf is fixed!

The discussion continues in a violent manner. DORA *requests that no man shall be allowed to have more than one wife, being supported by* BEATRICE *in this demand;* GANEREAU *wants a declaration of the rights of man and a Chamber of Deputies.* DIZ *and* THONEL-

GEBEN *maintain that the first thing necessary is the distribution of the land.*

While they are discussing the afternoon passes without any agreement being reached. SIMPSON, *who keeps going out, observes the agitation of the negroes. He enters the Council chamber and approaches* THONELGEBEN.

SIMPSON

We're wasting time pitifully. The negroes are getting impatient.

THONELGEBEN

What are we to do?

SIMPSON

I have a plan.

THONELGEBEN

What?

SIMPSON

Make Paradox king. What d'you think of it?

THONELGEBEN

It seems to me excellent.

SIMPSON

You don't foresee any difficulties? Do you think anybody would be offended at his election?

THONELGEBEN

I don't think so. Except possibly himself.

SIMPSON

We'll get to work, then. You must help me. Tell Paradox that we have something to show him from the wall.

THONELGEBEN

Very good.

THONELGEBEN *speaks to* PARADOX *mysteriously, and the pair of them go out.*

PARADOX

What can he want? What plan has he got?

PARADOX *and* THONELGEBEN *climb on to the wall.* SIMPSON *stretches out his arms and shows* PARADOX *to the multitude.*

SIMPSON

People of Bu-Tata, behold your King!

All the negroes approach the wall, and break into shouts of approbation.

PARADOX, *indignant, trying to descend from the wall*

What are you doing? You've deceived me. I don't want to be king.

SIMPSON, not allowing him to get down

The will of the people has decided. The people wishes Paradox to be its king. Long live King Paradox!

Within and without Fortunate House

Long live the King!

PARADOX

In this matter, my will comes before that of the people; I don't wish to be king. Let Don Avelino be appointed.

ALL

Long live King Paradox!

HAJJI

Long live Muley Paradox!

ALL

Long live the King!

SIMPSON

Long live the dynasty of the Paradoxides!

ALL

Long live the King!

THONELGEBEN

Long live Sylvester I!

ALL

Long live the King!

PARADOX

Gentlemen, gentlemen, I fear you are presuming upon my royal benevolence. Let us finish quickly, for if not I abdicate on the spot, and the Paradoxides come to a sudden end.

PARADOX gets down from the wall.

A REBEL, approaching

Sire and great King, the virgins of Bu-Tata ask leave to greet you at this solemn moment.

PARADOX

Let the worthy ladies approach.

A multitude of horrible negresses enter, and carry out grotesque ceremonies in the king's presence. They are followed by a deputation of warriors and priests, who invite KING PARADOX to go to Bu-Tata for the coronation ceremonies . . .

X

In the French Chamber of Deputies

The Minister for War mounts the tribune.

THE MINISTER

Gentlemen: the despatch which I am about to read you will convince the honourable deputies of the Right of the futility of certain reports to the effect that the French expeditionary force operating in the Gulf of Guinea had been inactive, on account of the diplomatic interposition of certain foreign powers. It says as follows:

General Headquarters, Bu-Tata. To the Minister for War.

After four days' march the expeditionary force which I have the honour to command reached the neighbourhood of the City of Bu-Tata. The enemy had entrenched himself in the city, to the number of ten thousand, with guns and ammunition. After a day's bombardment, the troops under the command of Major Gauguin attacked the city by the left flank, dislodging the enemy immediately from their positions. Their losses were 500 dead and 3,000 captured. Several Europeans are included in the latter number, English and German, who had organised the resistance.

Barland, Colonel, Commanding-in-Chief, the Expeditionary Force.

DEROULEDE, *rising*

Three cheers for the army! Three cheers for France! (*Wild applause and cheering from the Right.*)

A few hours later, all the bloodthirsty ragtag and bobtail of Paris are marching down the Boulevards with a tricolour flag, cheering the Army and DEROULEDE.

XI

Three Years Later

In the office of the Medical Officer of the day, the Hospital, Bu-Tata.

THE DOCTOR

Any new cases?

THE ASSISTANT

Ten smallpox cases admitted yesterday.

THE DOCTOR

Ten?

THE ASSISTANT

Ten. Also five syphilis, six infectious influenza, eight tuberculous, two delirium tremens . . .

THE DOCTOR

Phew! That's bad.

THE ASSISTANT

And a woman whose husband stabbed her out of jealousy and who died within a few hours.

THE DOCTOR

If we go on like this, there won't be enough beds in the hospital. Never trust experts on hygiene.

THE ASSISTANT

Why?

THE DOCTOR

Because there's a report of Lanessan saying that Uganda is a very healthy country.

THE ASSISTANT

It was.

THE DOCTOR

You think it's changed?

THE ASSISTANT

Yes, Sir.

THE DOCTOR

Why?

THE ASSISTANT

Civilisation.

THE DOCTOR

What's civilisation got to do with it?

THE ASSISTANT

A great deal. There usen't to be disease here, but we've introduced it. We've presented these worthy negroes with smallpox, tuberculosis, syphilis, and alcohol. They aren't protected against these things as we are, and therefore they go off suddenly.

THE DOCTOR, *laughing*

There may be a lot of truth in that.

THE ASSISTANT

Of course there is. I went to a neighbouring town last year, and what happened, d'you think?

THE DOCTOR

What?

THE ASSISTANT

I infected them with smallpox, and all the same I hadn't got it myself.

THE DOCTOR

Odd, that. How do you explain it?

THE ASSISTANT

Very easily. Amongst ourselves, all the weak organisms unable to resist illness, heavy work, and alcohol, have died out. Lightning won't hurt those of us who remain. We carry the germs of disease in our bodies as easily as a watch in our pockets. Thus it is that while we white men do splendidly here, the negroes depart for the next world with an astounding unanimity.

THE DOCTOR

As long as they go alone, eh?

THE ASSISTANT

It's little loss.

THE DOCTOR

Besides, there's material enough while it lasts.

THE ASSISTANT

It won't last long. What happened to the Redskins when the Yankees came? We know how to follow the lead.

THE DOCTOR

Well, I'm going the rounds. Where's the other assistant?

THE ASSISTANT

I hope you'll excuse him. I don't think he'll be here.

THE DOCTOR

What's happened to him?

THE ASSISTANT

I saw him last night in that cabaret they've just started, with a negress; he seemed pretty far gone.

THE DOCTOR

Boys will be boys. What's the cabaret like?

THE ASSISTANT

There's a taking programme. Yesterday was the debut of the ex-Princess Mahu, who does the danse de ventre, naked, in the style of the Moulin Rouge of Paris.

THE DOCTOR

A sensational item.

THE ASSISTANT

Rather! by a Princess.

THE DOCTOR

Genuine?

THE ASSISTANT

Absolutely.

THE DOCTOR

We're getting on in Bu-Tata.

THE ASSISTANT

I should say so. There's a little of everything. Sodom, Gomorrah, Babylon, Lesbos, all in one.

THE DOCTOR

Do you mean to say so?

THE ASSISTANT

Certainly. You don't go out at night. If you did, you would know. At every street corner you will find maidens of various hue ready to make you the most amazing proposals. And drunken niggers all over the place.

THE DOCTOR

Really?

THE ASSISTANT

Yes; our consumption of absinthe is something extraordinary.

THE DOCTOR

I had no idea.

THE ASSISTANT

Yes, Sir. Moreover the whites ill-treat the blacks, and the blacks, when they have the chance, get their own back by murdering the whites.

THE DOCTOR

Very nice.

THE ASSISTANT

They're the benefits of civilisation.

THE DOCTOR

Well, I'm going the rounds.

XII

A Press-Cutting

From the Bu-Tata "Echo":

At the end of the service the Abbé Viret preached a moving sermon. In it he praised the Army as the school of all manly virtues, and the bulwark of Justice. His concluding words were: "My brothers, let us thank God that true civilisation, the civilisation of peace and brotherly love in Christ, has at last entered the Kingdom of Uganda, never to depart again."

THE END

Translated by Nevill Barbour

The Restlessness of Shanti Andia

CHAPTER 7

HATE EXPLODES

I informed Allen and Ugarte that we must leave at once.

"Why is that?" asked Ugarte, pretending to be surprised.

"For no reason at all. Only some well-intentioned person has told Sandow what kind of people we are and where we came from."

"Who could it have been?" he asked brazenly.

"That's something you know better than anyone else," I answered him in Castilian Spanish.

Allen was listening to our exchange, well aware of Ugarte's falseness.

"I don't know what you mean by that," muttered Ugarte now. And then, seeing that I did not deign an answer, he added cynically: "The truth is that the little note has gotten under your skin."

"I should think so!"

"And what did the captain say to you?"

"He told me that informers make him sick with loathing, and for that reason alone we should go."

Ugarte turned pale. Allen, who now understood everything, exclaimed: "Ah! Is he the one that denounced us?"

"You stay out of what doesn't concern you, animal!"

The Irishman burst out in invective, and I had to struggle with him to keep him from hurling himself on Ugarte.

On the last night we spent in Sandow's house, I wrote a long letter to Ana. The three of us were in the library; Ugarte and Allen had stretched out on their bed, but they were awake.

When I had finished writing, I left the library, stuck the letter into a book, called the maid, and told her to see that the captain's daughter received the book. I was afraid that if I stayed away from my companions too long, I would return to find them in a deadly struggle.

None of us was able to fall asleep. Allen was burning with indignation against Ugarte. Before dawn, we quit the house without taking leave of anyone. It was a cold day outside. We followed the highway and walked along the coast, plagued by a thin rain.

Allen and Ugarte refused to address each other. To avoid all communication between them, Ugarte spoke to me in Castilian and Allen addressed me in English.

"That we should have to slog through the rain because of a dog like him!" Allen muttered between his teeth.

That night, soaked to the bone, we found an inn, half tavern and half cottage, called the "Hunter's Rest." It was a simple cabin, with walls and roof completely covered with ivy, and two windows with red curtains, illuminated by an interior light. From outside, it looked like the shaggy, bristly head of a monster with two red eyes.

Though we were now quite near the city for which we were bound, we decided to spend the night where we were. We sat down at the table and ordered supper. Ugarte began to mimic and mock Captain Sandow and his daughter. At first, his ridicule made me indignant; but I soon felt pity and a kind of shame for Ugarte, aware that he was falling into another of his fits of mad spite and aggression. But he kept on talking so much and hurling such insults that at last I asked him in some surprise: "What have I done to you that you should hate me in this fashion?"

"You're in my way," he screamed. "One of us is more than enough in this world."

And in a paroxysm of rage he began to insult me furiously, screaming that he wished me dead, because I was his downfall and his bird of ill omen.

Allen, pale with anger and hatred of Ugarte, cried out: "I wouldn't stand for it."

"You dare butt in? Stay out of it, you dog, you cur!" yelled Ugarte.

And, in his fury, he pulled out one of the files that we had brought with us from the prison ship, which he still carried, and jabbed at the Irishman, striking him in the cheek.

Allen jumped up, grabbed the bench he had been sitting on, raised it high in the air, and brought it down on Ugarte's head with such force that he left him dead on the floor.

The Irishman continued pounding the corpse and even the table like a madman, with the insane and mechanical force of a wounded elephant, until at length the bench broke and he was left with a fragment of wood in his hand, gazing at it like a sleep-walker just awakened. Then he threw the broken bench to the floor and broke out in tears. Everyone in the tavern had witnessed the affair, and sided with Allen.

"Come on," I finally urged him. "We've got to get out of here."

"No, no. What for?"

I was forced to remain at his side. Luckily, the wound on his face was a slight one.

"You go on. I'll stay here."

"No. I can't abandon you."

"There are witnesses here to what happened. It's best if you escape. You can help me more if you're free than if you're in jail. Take the money I've got left, and if you get to France, write the maid at Sandow's house about what happened."

I did as he said, and left the tavern; as soon as I was on the street, I began to run. There was a wind in my face that held me back somewhat; it was a humid wind, filled with the odors of the sea. I could hear the sound of voices in the distance, of people who also seemed to be running. Perhaps it was the police, who might have been alerted. I hid beside the highway for a while. Then I began running slowly again, and continued until I reached the city, where I made my way along a small narrow street. The wind wailed at intersections, the dogs howled, and the rain began to come down in buckets. I decided to stop at the first inn or eating house that I chanced upon. The first one that I encountered had a sign with a horse on it, and was called the White Horse. It was one of those quiet, unfrequented places that are to be found in the British Isles, and which are characterized by cleanliness and respectability.

A very lively girl came to ask me if I had yet had supper; I told her I had, and she led me to a room; a little while later, she appeared once again, bearing a large warming pan to warm the bed.

Outside, a veritable deluge was falling.

"I'll pay you now," I told the girl, "because I want to leave very early tomorrow morning."

"Just as you wish."

"Will the door be open at dawn?"

"Yes, it's usually open from about that time."

I paid her what she asked, and went to bed. It was still raining heavily outside; the water lashed the windows, and the wind whistled furiously, with surprisingly high, piercing notes. I fell asleep very quickly. It was a little before dawn when I awoke with a start, and peered out the window; it was no longer raining, and I dressed rapidly. When I went downstairs I found the door was not open. It immediately occurred to me that someone had told the people in the inn to close the door. But then perhaps they had secured it because of the wind.

I went back up and looked out the window. The distance to the ground was not too great, and so I jumped down, without mishap.

Finding myself alone, without the company of Allen and Ugarte, I felt driven by a greater energy and a more pressing fear of being recaptured. I would have preferred anything to being returned to the prison ship. The memory of those black headlands, the gray sea, the muddy swamps horrified me.

I spent a night in the fields, and the next morning, as the sun was coming up, I walked into Wexford port. I soon found a schooner getting ready to sail for Saint-Malo. In speaking to the captain about taking me, I found I had to overcome strong resistance. I handed over what money I had, and promised to pay him more when we reached France.

The captain was the image of an ill-tempered bear.

We made a horrible crossing, in the foulest type of weather and in a stormy sea. The captain apparently did not make a practice of concerning himself with his ship and its navigation, for as soon as we were at sea, he disappeared into his cabin and proceeded to get drunk on whiskey. Within an hour he appeared on deck in a state of drunkenness, his nose inflamed and his speech slurred. In view of the raging storm, he began to talk of changing his course and putting into England. After a while he seemed to forget it; we told him it would be absurd to change course, and, since he was rather muddled in his head, he did what he heard was best. At length we reached Saint-Malo.

I wrote immediately to Ana Sandow telling her what had happened after we left her house and asked her to intercede for poor Allen.

After a while I received a letter from Ana and a clipping

from a newspaper, in which there was an account of the death of Ugarte in an inn near Wexford called the "Hunter's Rest."

Only, the dead man was given the name Juan de Aguirre, and I, whose whereabouts was listed as unknown, appeared as Tristán de Ugarte.

From what Ana wrote, Allen's situation was favorable, considering the circumstances; all the witnesses had declared in his behalf; the fact that the dead man was a foreign adventurer and he a native of the country worked in his favor.

As for me, I had a difficult time finding employment. Inasmuch as all that part of France, that is, Normandy and Brittany, carried on its principal commerce with England, and since I felt no attraction for the air of perfidious Albion, there was no ship's berth that suited me. Finally, I found work in a warehouse in Le Havre.

My life was animated by one enthusiasm: the woman who thought of me. I wrote her constantly, and I wrote Allen, to whom I regularly sent part of my wages.

Allen was imprisoned for a very short time. As soon as he was released he went to visit Ana. Captain Sandow was increasingly brutal and despotic in his relations with his daughter. Allen and she decided to act; and so one day, to my great astonishment, I looked up to see them both walk into my house.

Ana and I were soon married. Eventually, we had a daughter, and we called her Mary.

With my daughter's future in mind, I determined to find out what was going on in Lúzaro; I wrote my mother, and she wrote back to tell me that they had thought me dead and had even held funeral services for me.

My life with Ana might have been a happy one; but my wife's health was very delicate. That sweet and fragile creature, so simple, so ingenuous and so innocent, died in my arms at the end of a slow and tortuous battle with life.

I always recall her in the somber house of her father, and to the memory of her I join always the memory of Walter Scott and his most feminine heroines. I read the novels of the Scottish author in the days that I first knew her, and I can not ever separate my beloved from the literary personages of that great author.

When she died, I decided to leave France and return to Lúzaro with my daughter and Allen, who had made up his mind to link his fate to mine.

This, then, has been my life. Errors, faults, I have committed in plenty. And who has not?

So read the manuscript of my uncle, Juan de Aguirre.

CHAPTER 8

PATRICK ALLEN AND ZALDUMBIDE'S TREASURE

One autumn day, towards nightfall, two suspicious-looking foreigners appeared in Chiquierdi's inn at Lúzaro.

They descended from the diligence, entered the kitchen of the inn, and, while they ate, made pointed inquiries about Don Santiago Andía. The woman who ran the inn told them that I had not lived in Lúzaro for some time, but was now at Izarte; when they learned this fact, they asked the distance from the town to our settlement.

The next morning, the mailman, who brought me the newspaper, furnished me with the facts of the visit and told me that the foreigners would certainly call on me. I waited for them, somewhat intrigued, and just before noon I saw them approach the house.

One of the pair was tall, red, heavy; the other was small, black-haired, and boasted a pair of lively eyes. I watched them from between the curtains of my room. At first glance, they did not seem to me at all suspicious-looking.

They rang at the door, and the maid showed them into my room.

The tall, heavy man seemed rather confused; the other man, smiling an insinuating smile, spoke up at once, with an Andalusian accent.

"Could you grant us a half hour of your time to listen to what we have to say?"

"Gladly, sir. Please be seated."

"Thank you," answered the short man. Then he added in English, addressing his companion, "Sit down, Smiles."

The two of them sat down.

"Aren't you Spanish?" I asked the dark-haired man.

"No, I'm English. I was born in Gibraltar. I'm a rock scorpion, as the English call people from the Rock. My name is Small,

Richard Small. My father was English, my mother from Cádiz; that's the reason that I speak Spanish fairly well."

"Not fairly well, but very well; better than I speak it."

"Thank you very much! I will tell you, in the fewest possible words, the reason for our visit. Until a few months ago, I lived in Liverpool in humble circumstances; I worked in a shop and was on the point of getting married, when I met an Irishman of advanced years, the brother of my girl's mother, an Irishman by the name of Patrick Allen."

"Patrick Allen!" I exclaimed. "The man who lived here for so many years!"

"The same man. Allen came back to his sister's house and told us all the story of Captain Zaldumbide's treasure; he told us how you had given him the exact location of the burial site, which had been written in Basque in a prayer book. From that day, the day Allen told us the story of the treasure, my girl's house was turned upside down; my girl, her brothers, the entire family saw nothing but millions in every direction. They urged me to find a rich man who would contribute the necessary funds to underwrite a search for the treasure, and I found Mr. Smiles."

"Present!" unexpectedly called out the tall, red-faced man, as he saluted in military fashion.

"That'll do, Smiles," interjected the dark young man. "As I was saying I found Mr. Smiles, who owned a saloon in Liverpool. Mr. Smiles leased out his saloon, I gave up my job, and, in the company of Allen, the three of us, fully equipped, went to Las Palmas in the Canary Islands. There we rented a schooner, with crew and all, and headed for the Nun River. The skipper of the schooner had orders to stand by for a week to wait for us at the mouth of the river; if we did not appear, he was to return at full moon for a period of six months. We disembarked from the schooner and ascended the river in a small boat until we were off the ruins of a hilltop fortress. We tied the boat to a tree on the river bank, and carefully made our way, watching and hiding every so often among the rocks, until we reached the ruins. We had met or seen no one en route. From what Allen said, we had to find a wall with an elephant drawn or incised on it. The first to see it was myself: 'There it is!' I cried out.

"Allen ran up to the wall, stood with his back to it, and took out a small spyglass from his pocket. Smiles and I were anxiously watching him when we suddenly saw two white men creeping around a wall to get a better view of what Allen was doing.

They quickly realized that we had seen them, and the pair rushed us, followed by a dozen or so Moors who had been in hiding. We had no opportunity to make use of our weapons, and were made prisoners on the spot.

"Allen knew the two men: They were Ryp Timmermans, cook on the 'Dragon,' and a Dutch sailor named Van Stein. The two of them had been searching for the treasure for more than a year, but had been unable to find any trace of it. Some other former members of the 'Dragon''s crew, released from prison, had also appeared on the scene to make excavations in all the rises of the ground along the river bank, but Zaldumbide's coffers still lay buried, as far as we could tell.

"Ryp and Van Stein, more persistent than the others, had remained on the spot; they had renounced their religion and, becoming converts to Islam, had married Moorish women; they were the chiefs of a little settlement established in a small oasis which contained some brackish wells and a few palm, honey-locust, and argan trees.

"The two renegades and their Moors led Smiles, Allen, and myself to the oasis. The settlement itself consisted of a few wretched cottages, constructed of tree trunks, stones, and clay, covered over with a fabric made of camel or goat hair. They shut us up in a hut, and Ryp and Van Stein began to question us. Smiles and I told them the truth, which was that we had heard that a treasure was buried thereabouts and we had come to look for it.

"Ryp assumed that we had some special information on the matter, and he asserted that we would not be released until we had told all we knew. Allen was determined to tell them nothing. Smiles and I could not tell them anything, because we did not know anything of importance.

"We were kept in that hovel for a month; as food, we were given a little bread, salted fish, milk, and honey.

"Most of the Moors in the settlement were real savages, of mixed Negro blood. The women were the only ones who worked. The men, licentious dogs, spent their lives with a rifle on their shoulder, idly prattling. The women meanwhile cultivated the ground and stored the harvests, smoked and dried the meat and fish, and made fishhooks and arrows.

"Though the men would not work, they did occasionally hunt, pastured the goats, and would buy and sell tanned skins, capes, brimstone, camels, and oxen.

"Every year, at a certain season, the entire band would make a trek inland for a couple of months, on a Negro-stealing expedition. On reaching a Negro village, they would surround it during the night, and then, at a signal, would commence firing shots in the air and screaming wildly. The unfortunate Negroes would panic and begin to run out of the village, where the marauders would catch them like rabbits. Grouped into caravans, the prisoners would be sold to slave dealers, who would send them to Fez, Marrakech, and Tafilelt.

"It was difficult to see how Ryp and Van Stein could have gained mastery over that band of bloodthirsty Moorish bandits; nevertheless, the truth was that they held the Moors in the palm of their hands. Those jackals would have been happy to tear us to pieces, but Ryp protected us. The cook was sure that Allen possessed the exact instructions for finding the treasure; he had him searched, of course, but nothing was found. He next tried to reach an agreement with Allen, whereby they would share equally in the treasure, if Allen could find it.

"Allen was terribly changeable in this arrangement; he made the agreement, then changed his mind, then agreed again to a division, and then announced he would have no part of it. He had reached a point where he placed greater importance on the treasure than on his life. 'You want me to tell you where the treasure is, so you can get it and then get rid of me?' he would say to Ryp as an argument. 'No, my boy, nothing doing.'

"Smiles and I urged him to come to agreement with Ryp; for my part, I was increasingly anxious to get out of there on any terms, even with empty hands. Allen, however, could not be pushed.

"One day he announced again that he was willing to work with Ryp. He called the ex-cook of the 'Dragon,' and we made an agreement to go to the river bank in a body, the five of us white men escorted by a party of ten armed Moors. We reached the ruined fortress, and Allen insisted that he be left alone. He spent a quarter of an hour by himself, and then he marched toward the river; he walked up to a certain stone, reached out and touched it, and said: 'Here it is.'

"The words were scarcely out of his mouth when Van Stein drew his pistol and fired point blank, killing Allen on the spot.

"Smiles and I started to run furiously, sure that our lives were at stake. Luck was with us, for the rest of the party did not trust each other long enough to pursue us, and they all began to dig in a frenzy, thus giving us a chance to get away. We arrived at the edge of the sea in a state of exhaustion; we were in the middle of an immense beach, formed of sand dunes that the wind had made and unmade. The two of us hid, for hours and hours, with every sense on the alert, in a crevice formed in one of the dunes.

"Of a sudden, in the calm of the night, we heard voices around us. It was Ryp and Van Stein.

" 'Can you see anybody down there?' asked Ryp.

" 'Nobody.'

" 'Maybe they crossed the river.'

" 'What do we care what they've done?' said Van Stein.

" 'What do we care? Why I wouldn't be surprised if the dark one knew where the treasure is,' yelled Ryp.

"Smiles and I listened to the conversation; when the two voices could no longer be heard, Smiles said:

" 'They didn't find anything.'

" 'No doubt about it.'

"I did not know whether to be glad or sad; since they had not found the treasure, they would make some attempt to find us. As soon as night had fallen, we left our hiding place, and started down the wide beach. Where were we bound? We did not know; we had no objective. Smiles suddenly exclaimed:

" 'Damnation: There's a full moon tonight. If it clears a little, we'll be visible for miles.'

"Sure enough, a little later a full moon shone down on us, lighting up the beach so that every rise and crest was plainly outlined.

"A moment later, I recalled the fact that the skipper of the schooner hired in the Canaries had agreed to appear off the mouth of the river at the full of the moon for a period of six months. We were still in the fifth month. If he had kept his word and had brought the schooner to the river mouth we were saved. Inspired by the thought, Smiles and I began running and leaping over the shifting sand dunes, and ran towards the river mouth.

"There was the schooner. But she seemed on the point of putting out to sea!

" 'Help! Help!' yelled Smiles and I.

"At first they must not have heard us, but then we saw the ship sailing straight for us, its sails unfurled and gleaming white in the moonlight.

"Ryp's people, too, had apparently heard our shouts, for we began to be fired upon from further down the shore. Smiles and I dived into the water and began desperately to swim for the schooner.

"A few moments later, when I found myself on the ship's deck, I swore never to set foot in Africa again. We were soon back in the Canaries, and from there we went on to Liverpool. I was sure that the family of my future wife, once they learned of Allen's death and heard from us about our adventures, would find themselves cured of their passion for finding a treasure, but such was not to be the case. Quite the contrary.

" 'You've got to go,' my future mother-in-law urged me, 'to see that Spaniard, the one that can tell you where Zaldumbide's treasure really is.' And that's why we're here. We beg you to make known your conditions."

"I don't have any conditions," I said. "I'm well off; I don't need a thing. I'll be glad to give you the necessary information. Fortunately I have kept the piece of paper upon which I first jotted down the secret, word by word. I only hope you have better luck than everyone else connected with the treasure."

"But still . . ."

"No, no, no. I want nothing."

I gave them the directions translated from the Basque of Allen's prayer book, and the two Englishmen went away, after thanking me effusively.

A year later, I received a letter from the young man, Small, together with a package. The letter read:

The treasure has given us bad luck. We went back to the Nun with an escort of fifteen well-armed men. We found the treasure at once. But when Ryp's men, from their hiding place, saw us actually bringing up the coffers and getting ready to take them away, they attacked us with desperation. In the battle that followed, Smiles and Ryp were killed. Van Stein was badly wounded and two of our men fell prisoner. I caught a fever, of which I'm still not cured.

The accompanying package contained two large pearls sent me by Small. The thought of having them in the house was repugnant to me. I did not even want to show them to my wife, and, climbing Mount Izarra, I threw them into the sea.

They will make a nice ornament, I thought, for one of those undines Yurrumendi knew.

EPILOGUE

Many years have passed, years of normal, easy, everyday life. Juan Machín has never appeared among us again. Perhaps he is wandering the seas, lost in some far corner. As if upholding a family tradition, he has become the restless Aguirre who is lost somewhere on the face of the world. Is he alive? Is he dead? Will he return to us? I do not know. I must confess that at first I would not have wanted him to come back; now, I would; I would be happy to see him and to shake his hand.

As regards me, I am a little ashamed to say that I am happy, very happy. It is true that I have not deserved happiness, but nevertheless such is the case.

When I think of my wife, I, too, recall the heroines of Scott, especially Diana Vernon in *Rob Roy*. But I do not, like my Uncle Juan de Aguirre or Scott's hero, have to think of my heroine as dead, but rather can look around and find her alive at my side. Today, with her fifty years and her gray hair, she seems to me more enchanting than ever.

My mother lives with us in our house in Izarte. She likes to spend her time in the kitchen, gossiping with the maids and with my daughter, putting wood on the stove, and murmuring against my wife.

Basically the two of them understand each other perfectly. But my mother must quarrel a bit; and so she accuses my wife of being bossy and of always wanting her own way.

All my children have been rocked in their grandmother's arms, and it will not be long before my mother can rock her first great-grandchild.

Every day I am becoming more indolent and more distracted. Often, in the early morning, when the weather is good, I get up very early and follow the open road, listening to the rumor of the fields. The birds sing in the groves, a brilliant sun pours over the earth.

On my return, I stand outside my house and contemplate it, standing as it does atop the garden which serves it by way of pedestal. The red geraniums shimmer along the wooden balcony; in the midst of the vegetable garden the sunflowers stand about on their giant stalks. I climb the staircase and come out on the balcony. The cows are at pasture in our meadow; my children follow them, protected from the sun by large straw hats. In front of me I can see the scattered houses of Izarte, which seem like play houses, spouting smoke from their chimneys; farther off lie the mountains.

My wife knows that sometimes I must wander a bit, and she leaves me to my devices. She used to accompany me on my walks, and sometimes, when we would watch the evening star, she would recite that poem of Ossian, which the two of us had read in a book belonging to Ana Sandow, and which begins in the following manner:

> Star of twilight, shining sovereign in the East,
> Radiant face appearing from behind the clouds
> As you stroll majestically atop the peaks:
> What do you see through the foliage?

I would listen to the verse with tears in my eyes. Ossian's songs to me seemed wondrous. Nowadays my wife has too many cares to allow her to roam in the country. Our clan has increased, and she is the administrative authority. I believe she is a fine tyrant, an intelligent dictator, the representative of the ideal government for the idle and lazy.

I am the vagabond of the family.

As the seasons change I feel the nostalgia given off by the sea's profound peacefulness, its solitude and abandon. Then I go to stroll along the Beach of Souls, and there I gaze, as if it were for the first time, at the three-pronged spray of the waves as they break on the sand.

Spring arouses deep joy in me, and autumn a profound sadness; but the sadness is of so strange a nature that it seems to me that I would be most unfortunate not to feel it from time to time.

On those November days, when the mist and rain and the dominion of gray returns, when the vague and blurred lines everywhere appear, when the sharp winds whistle, when the arroyo of Sorguiñ-Erreca turns into a torrent, then I like to walk along the beach and become saturated in the enormous melancholy of the sea and be soaked in the profundity of sadness.

Later, when I am saturated with the wind and sense of spray, and the waves, and the howl of the wind, I climb along the Crest of the Dogs up to the highest point and walk through the corn fields. There below lies the quiet village where I live, there live those that belong to me. I walk toward my house; my family, gathered around the fire in the kitchen on these winter days, is waiting for me.

Back in the kitchen, I recount my adventures to the younger children, embellishing the stories with details taken from my imagination. I have told all the stories so many times that my wife reproaches me in a mocking tone for telling them again.

Sometimes I have wondered if any of my sons will turn out to be a sailor or an adventurer. I have searched for signs in them of a sailor's devotion to the sea.

`But no, they have no inclination for the mariner's lot, and I am happy. . . . And yet. . . .

In Lúzaro now, no one cares to go to sea; the sons of well-to-do families become engineers or doctors. The Basques are retiring from the sea.

Oh, gallant riggings! White, white sails! Haughty frigates, with prows on high and a figurehead on the cutwater! Round hookers, swift-sailing brigantines! How sad it is to think you will all disappear, that you will soon no longer be seen!

Yes, I am happy that my sons will not be seamen. . . . And yet . . .

Translated by Anthony Kerrigan

Ramón Pérez de Ayala

(1880-1962)

Born in Oviedo, Asturias, he attended Jesuit schools, an experience he later used as the basis for a novel. He studied at the University of Oviedo, where one of his teachers was Clarín, worked as a foreign correspondent during the First World War, traveled extensively over Europe, and served as Ambassador to England under the Spanish Republic. Possessing a vast culture, Pérez de Ayala wrote some beautiful, if intellectual, poetry, penetrating essays on Spanish life, and about a dozen novels, through which he achieved his greatest reputation as a writer. After 1930 he wrote almost nothing except some short stories, published as a collection in 1962, and some scattered essays.

Pérez de Ayala's novels combine psychological penetration, ironic and at times almost grotesque humor, fantasy, and realism. His first important novel, *AMDG* (1910), takes its title from "Ad majorem Dei gloriam," the Jesuit motto. It is an autobiographical recollection of the author's unhappy experiences in a Jesuit school, and the protagonist, Alberto Díaz de Guzmán, is Pérez de Ayala. The author contends that one cannot maintain intellectual integrity in a bigoted and anti-intellectual atmosphere such as the Jesuits perpetuated. *Twilight on the Peaks* (1907), *The Vixen's Paw* (1912), and *Mummers and Dancers* (1913) continue the adventures of Guzmán, as they dissect the sensual and intellectual life of Spain. His three poematic novels, *Prometheus, Sunday's Light,* and *The Fall of the Limones* (1916), concern abnormal and degenerate victims of an unfair world. His two most important novels, undoubtedly, are *Belarmino and Apolonio* (1921) and *Tiger Juan* (1926). The former, a story of two shoemakers in Pilares, Pérez de Ayala's favorite setting for his fiction, discusses the dual aspect of human life as represented by Belarmino, the introvert philosopher, and Apolonio, the extrovert actor-dramatist. Belarmino, fascinated by the power of words, seeks the meaning of the world through control of his new language. At the end he is reconciled with Apolonio, as the author seems to plead for the need for communication between reason and faith, thought and action. *Tiger Juan* examines aspects of the Don Juan theme and parodies Calderonian fantasies about honor.

In his novels Pérez de Ayala sought to unify the real and subjective worlds. He wrote intellectual novels about the tragic sense of life, the problem of time, the relationship of art and life, and the interrelationships of fantasy and reality. In spite of his overintellectualized approach to life and a remarkably ironic humor, which occasionally verged on cruelty, he conveyed a sense of tolerance and understanding for human weakness.

The selection given is the complete first chapter of *Belarmino and Apolonio*.

Belarmino and Apolonio

DON GUILLEN AND LA PINTA

One Tuesday in Holy Week, at luncheon, there appeared at our table a new boarder: a prebendal cleric. Had I met him in the street, had I sat opposite him in the tram or beside him in a railway-station buffet, I should barely have given him an absent-minded glance. But here we were gathered about a *casa de huéspedes*[1] table. The worthy Don Amaranto was right. All the other boarders and myself at once began brazenly staring at this grand clergyman, as if it was a duty we had to perform. But he was quite indifferent to our curiosity. Bull-fighters, priests and comedians are not annoyed by being stared at, accustomed as they are to the limelight, in the ring, on the stage, or in the pulpit.

The "grand clergyman," I remarked above, and no adjective could have been better chosen. He looked like a brand-new, shiny cardboard saint. His glistening merino cassock might have been varnished, and his neckband was a splash of red, almost of crimson. His face, where his mustache and beard had been shaved away, was a pale-blue-to-purple color, and the rest of his countenance was extremely ruddy, while his eyes were dark and deep-set. He was forty at the most; and once one got over one's first impression of being in the presence of a little artificial saint, one discovered in the priest's physiognomy something or other that was distinctly personal and suggestive. The ruddiness of his cheeks was pathologic; he must suffer from heart-trouble. But he made a fine appearance; and after all, he was quite young for the ecclesiastical dignity that his costume proclaimed. A malicious person might have deduced that he had attained his rank with the omnipotent

---

1. *Casa de huéspedes:* a boarding house. (*Editor's note.*)

aid of petticoats; but on the other hand, there was nothing about him that suggested the "ladies' man,"—nothing, even, to indicate that he was especially popular with the sex. His was not the assurance of the conquering curate, nor the hypocritical humility and sweetness of the little skirt-clinging clergyman. If he owed his rise in the world to the women, it probably had been without solicitation on his part. Such, at least, were my meditations between the soup and the roast.

Doña Emerenciana, an eldering widow who, from lack of better-born gallants, spent the greater part of her life in running after Fidel, our waiter,—Doña Emerenciana was visibly on pins and needles, and she was the first to address the new boarder.

"Don't you find it fearfully warm in Madrid? And here it is, only April! I suppose you come from a cooler province, Don——May I inquire your name?"

"My name is Pedro, Lope, Francisco, Guillén, Euripides, take your choice," replied the clergyman, in a deep, musical voice and with a frank and winning smile.

We all smiled in turn, except the old lady, who had not yet made up her mind whether this reply was a serious or an ironical one.

"You are very funny!" she exclaimed at length, trusting that it was irony.

"No, Madam," the priest informed her, "I didn't say that to be funny."

"But Euripides, that's no Christian name, is it? If it is, it must come from the province of Palencia, for they do have the oddest names down there."

"No, Madam, it is not a Christian name, but it seems that didn't make any difference to the curate who christened me. And if they canonize me, there'll be a St. Euripides, the first of the name."

"How funny you are! But thank heaven, you have plenty of first names."

"It was a whim of my father's. He was a playwright and a shoemaker, or a shoemaker and a playwright, according to the order of precedence that you prefer. My baptismal names are those of the most famous dramatists of old: Pedro Calderón de la Barca; Lope de Vega; Francisco de Rojas Zorrilla——"

"I've heard of that Zorrilla; he was the author of *Tenorio;*[1] I

---

1. The point here lies in Doña Emerenciana's confusion of the two

heard of him when I was a girl," broke in Doña Emerenciana.

"Guillén de Castro," continued the priest with a smile, "Euripides——"

As he paused for a second, Doña Emerenciana gave a start: "Euripides who?"

"Euripides López y Rodriguez," replied the priest, as solemn as an owl.

"He must have been from the lower classes," was Doña Emerenciana's comment. "And now, what are we going to call you?"

"Some call me by one name and some by another. Pick the one you like."

"I prefer Guillén."

"The ladies always do," observed Don Guillén, with a satirical inflection.

"So far as I'm concerned, if you don't mind, I'm going to call you Mr. Euripides; it has more of a republican flavor," put in Don Celedonio de Obeso, an avowed atheist and an aggressive republican, a paltry chap at bottom, as plain as mud. For of course, we had to have one recognized republican at our boardinghouse-table. This Don Celedonio had become the leader of the republican party of Tarazona. He had the gift of gab and a nanny-goat beard.

"As you like," said Don Guillén, on the spur of the moment.

Before the meal was over, Don Guillén had won everyone's confidence and good will,—to such an extent that Don Celedonio had the nerve to ask him, point-blank:

"Do you believe in God?"

"Do you believe in the Republic?" countered Don Guillén, unperturbed.

"Yes, like the good republican that I am."

"And I as a priest, am a believer."

"No intelligent person believes in God."

"I have heard intelligent persons say: 'No intelligent person believes in the Republic.'"

"But the primitive Christians," and our Don Obeso hastily lowered his voice, "the primitive Christians were republicans."

"Worse than that, they were anarchists. But seeing that the Christians, starting with the idea of God, achieved that of the Re-

---

dramatists, Rojas-Zorrilla, born in 1607, and José Zorrilla, 1818-1893, the author of *Don Juan Tenorio,* an extremely popular piece in the Spanish romantic theatre. (*Translator's note.*)

public, so you, starting with the Republic, might very well attain
to the idea of God."

"I'm not putting down any money on it," said Don Celedonio;
and Don Guillén laughed in friendly fashion at this witticism.

It is a remarkable fact that, during the whole of this conversation, Don Guillén had not exhibited the least acrimoniousness; he
had not been the least bit belligerent or contemptuous. Our good-
will toward him grew. As we left the dining-room, Don Celedonio
whispered to me: "He's a good scout! Those curates are all right!"

After lunch, I learned that Don Guillén was connected with the
Cathedral of Castrofuerte, and that he was the Holy Week preacher
in the chapel of the Royal Palace. He must surely be a "spell-
binder."

Doña Trina's house harbored so many boarders and transient
guests that the huge apartment in the calle de Hortaleza, the
mother country so to speak, was not big enough to hold them, and
Doña Trina had had to send out colonies into the adjoining streets
and about the neighborhood. One of these colonies, the one where
I had set up my household gods, was in the calle de la Reina. I
mention this by way of emphasizing the fact that the colonials
enjoyed more freedom, especially at night, than did the residents
of the mother country. During the night hours, these streets and
side-streets were a rendezvous and a constant market-place for
frightful prostitutes and their unprepossessing male attendants. To
get to my room, I was forced to make my way through this endless
army of occupation; and as I did so, I was subject to a constant
fire from the courtezans, and was harassed by verbal and more
imperious invitations, for occasionally one of them would slip her
arm through my own. To get rid of them, and also for the sake
of a little rest, I would sometimes look in at the little café where
all the girls hung out. I would make myself agreeable to the
fiercest of the lot, and would leave them well fed, satisfied and
in a much better humor. They aroused my sympathy, and I was
always considerate with them. I admit that prostitution is a terrible
disgrace and one that stinks to heaven. But is one to blame the
ulcer if it finds lodging in a rotten body, where it quite naturally
has a chance to spread out? In a society in which everything is
prostituted, feminine prostitution is almost praiseworthy, for the
reason that it is a warning symptom. Often, after having put them
into a better frame of mind, I would stay in the little café for a
while to talk to these unfortunate creatures. I drew a great deal
of spiritual profit from their conversation, for pity such as they

inspired is a purge for the soul. I also observed the characters, amazing, most of them, which were to be met with here in this dive. From the very first, my curiosity was aroused by one particular woman. She was a nice, quiet blonde, and her face was not all plastered up and rouged like the others. She was always alone, and always sat without stirring, over in a corner, a glass of coffee in front of her, which she never touched. She looked like a Raphael virgin, a trifle faded. One evening, after I had stood looking at this girl for a long time, the *"Piernavieja"* or "Old Peg-Leg," so called because she dragged one leg a little,—"Old Peg-Leg," who was the most tattered and aggressive unit in the army of occupation, said to me:

"What are you looking at? That shrimp over there? That's Angustias, la Pinta. She lives with the 'Gallowsbird.' He's a good-for-nothing bum; he makes her stay here till he comes past to pick her up in the morning."

"Ask her to come over and have something," I said to the *Piernavieja*.

"Hey, there!" cried my limping friend. "Come over here, la Pinta. This gentleman's asking you to have something."

La Pinta blushed and excused herself. It was in vain that the *Piernavieja* insisted.

"La Pinta," I said, "is that a nickname?"

"Not at all; it's her right name. Her name is Angustias Pinto. What an idea, to keep your family name in a trade like ours! She's just a stick, no good for anything."

Little by little after a number of evenings, I became friends with la Pinta. She was a meek little thing, sad and not at all talkative, or, as the *Piernavieja* had put it, a stick, no good for anything. One night, she told me that she was a little over thirty; she didn't look it. Another night, she told me where she was born: in the town of Pilares. But that evening—I remember very well—that Tuesday evening of Holy Week, the evening of the day that the ruddy and jovial canon had made his appearance among our "paying-guests," la Pinta had been astonishingly communicative.

"My father was a shoemaker, but he was something more—a bilateral philosopher, as he called himself. I heard those big words so often when I was young that I have never forgotten them. The professors from the university used to come to the shop were we lived. To hear my mother tell it,—she had a very bad temper—my father was the drone of the hive, and those who came to listen to him were simply making a fool of him. But my father was a saint."

Involuntarily, I thought of Don Pedro-Guillén-Euripides, son of a shoemaker and a dramatist. La Pinta went on:

"It was a curate who was my undoing."

"The villain!" I muttered, instinctively.

"No, he was not a villain," la Pinta corrected me, and she turned to me her long-suffering face. "He was not a curate then; he was only a seminary student. He wanted to marry me. We went away together. His father came and got him. My mother refused to take me back. And after that, well, you can see—— But I am sure my sweetheart loves me yet. His father, you know, couldn't stand my family. I wonder what's become of him, Perico——?"

"Was that his name, Perico?"

"Yes, Perico Caramanzana. And how his name suited him. His face was as ripe and rosy and as merry as an apple."

"Is that why they called him Caramanzana (apple-face)?"

"It's his real name. His father's name is Apolonio Caramanzana. You must have heard of him. Ah! he was the best shoemaker in Spain. Even the gentlemen from Bilbao and Barcelona used to come to have their shoes made by him. He also wrote plays."

I had a good deal on my mind as I left the café that evening. I went to bed, but it was a long time before I could sleep. In the room next to mine, I could hear a loud clearing of the throat, followed by a deep sigh. It was Don Guillén. A diabolic idea came to me: "What if, tomorrow, I were to bring la Pinta to Don Guillén's room?" I fell asleep turning this idea over in my mind.

The next day, a fast day, Don Guillén did not appear at table.

"Where is Señor Caramanzana?" inquired the widow, who had already succeeded in learning the canon's family name.

"He's not eating today," replied Fidel; "his stomach's a little squeamish. Haven't you noticed how flushed he is?"

"It's undoubtedly pyrosis," said Don Celedonio. "All the monks and clergy have pyrosis, from eating too much rich food and from too much alcohol."

"That will be enough from you, you old heretic," scolded Doña Emerenciana, threatening him with her fan.

"By the way, Fidel, I hope you haven't forgotten what I told you. I hope you've told our landlady that all this farce about fast days and other days doesn't mean a thing to me, and that, even on the holy days of Holy Week, I want fish and meat. I mix them or jumble them or whatever you choose to call it."

This from Don Celedonio.

"Jesus, Mary and Joseph! What a Judas Iscariot! It's a good

thing that Don Guillén isn't here; he'd blush to listen to such blasphemy."

But Fidel, the waiter, wore a sly smile.

When I had done eating, I left the mother country and set out for the colonies. Some twenty paces in front of me was Fidel, carrying a large tray covered with a napkin.

"Pst!" And he motioned with his head for me to come up. "Lift up the napkin."

I lifted a corner of it and discovered a plentiful supply of food, including a good healthy slice of roast beef.

"It's Don Guillén's dinner," said the waiter. "He may not mix 'em or jumble 'em or whatever you call it; but one thing's certain, he's not doing without his meat."

At this moment, Don Guillén's door opened, and the dark figure of the priest himself was outlined against a rectangle of grizzled light; he had caught me in the act,—a domestic spy, shameful and ashamed. His tousled hair lighted up like a halo about his head. He wore red morocco slippers. Those two details struck me like a pair of off-key notes, during that brief moment of surprise and silent suspense: that beaming aureole and the bleeding feet.

"Come in," he said; then he added, for my benefit: "Come in, Sir!"

I accepted. I had not yet recovered from the humiliation I felt.

"Sit down," he insisted.

I wanted to make my apologies and go; but I was conscious of a note of entreaty in the canon's voice, as he said to me:

"Won't you give me the honor of your company for a moment, please?"

This request and the tone of voice in which it was uttered made me my normal self once more. I sat down beside a table littered with books, papers, pipes, spectacles and, enthroned amid these intellectual tools and accessories, the photograph of a woman in a silver frame, like a reliquary. I ventured to glance at it, discreetly. It was like one of Raphael's child virgins, those of his Umbrian period.

"Put the tray here, Fidel. You brought some wine? Take it back; I have some that's better."

He turned to me.

"What are you looking at, that frame? It's a sixteenth-century reliquary, a gem."

"No, I was looking at the portrait."

"One of my sisters; she's no more."

"No more?"

"Lost; dropped out of sight."

"Ah, so she's dead," I observed doubtfully, to give him the opening for an explanation.

"It was some years ago." Then, after a pause: "Do have a little glass of cognac."

He brought out a bottle of old cognac and another of mellow wine, taking them from a pig's-skin bag the elegance of which was more befitting a man of the world than a clergyman. He sat down at the table; and the longer I looked at him, the less he seemed to me a priest, and the more he seemed a man of the world.

"By the merest accident," he remarked, as he ate leisurely, "you have invaded my personal life. If, a moment ago, when I found you——"

"In the act of spying upon you," I broke in; "but it was at the waiter's suggestion, and without knowing what it was all about."

"What difference does it make? What I was going to say was that if, at that moment, I had retired, you would have taken me for an unscrupulous and insincere priest. I couldn't let you go away without a few explanations."

"It is I who should——"

"You? Why? Putting the worst possible construction upon matters, your curiosity got the better of you slightly; while I, in the opinion of the timorous, have been guilty of a grave sin."

"But I am not one of the timorous."

"Nevertheless, I owe you an explanation. Just as, in the State, there are certain artificial crimes, so in the Church there are artificial sins. Artificial crimes and sins are those which, without offending or abating either justice or dogma, the respective pivots of Church and State, are, yet, a contravention of or a disobedience to certain disciplinary regulations which are purely accidental and temporal by nature. Among these temporal regulations is the obligation to fast four days during Holy Week. The idea might very well occur to the present pope or his successor to diminish or even to abolish that obligation. The State is a material community sustained by mutual interests; the Church is a spiritual community sustained by mutual love. And the disciplinary spirit of the Church is quite different from that of the State. In the State, discipline is a matter of the interests involved; for without discipline, the common interest would not be protected. In the Church, discipline is a matter of generous impulses; it is the will to sacrifice. Just as lovers, to make sure of their mutual love, put that love to the test by all sorts of whimsical demands,—for to love is to obey—so the Church imposes upon the faithful certain disciplinary obligations, by way of spurring on the slothful and compelling them to evince their love by putting it into practice. But for those persons, priests or laymen, whose faith is well-grounded and whose minds are wholesome, such disciplinary obligations are of no avail. The essential thing is dogma. The State readily grants the right of free thought,—the mind is never guilty—but do not try to carry that freedom over into action, for discipline would thereby be impaired. The Church is tolerant in the matter of actions and intransigent in the matter of ideas: it is only in thought that we sin. All sins, however monstrous they may be, are given absolution in the confessional; but the slightest doubt or lack of faith on the part of the sinner, and we are forbidden to absolve him. All that I have just said to you is mere common sense, and so, must be kept a secret from all those, priests or laymen who are not endowed with common sense. Do you understand?"

"I understand, I understand," I said approvingly. The truth is, I had understood very well all that he had said; that was not so hard to do. But I did not understand him. What sort of man was this sitting in front of me, philosophizing as he ate, masticating and reasoning so nonchalantly, and with such an air of worldly serenity, dressed like a worldling and without any obvious sign of his ecclesiastical state, and who, even as he spoke, would occasionally glance at the portrait of a woman whom he himself had pushed down into the nameless abyss of prostitution? What manner of man was he? A hedonist? An unbeliever? A hypocrite and a sophist, deceiving himself and others? A disillusioned being? A tormented soul? The explanation he had just given me interested me far less than all this. What difference did it make to me whether he fasted or not?

What happened now was like one of those cases of immediate thought-transference which sometimes occurs between two persons who are extremely intimate.

"But that," he said, "is the least of your concerns, whether I fast or not. The important thing is that, by the merest accident, you have been led to invade my private life, my life as a man. For all of us, monks, curates and ecclesiastical big-wigs, we all of us, under our merino and our furbelows, are men in disguise. I can say with the pagan poet: *Homo sum*.[1]

---

1. *Homo sum*: "I am a man." The complete quotation is: "Homo sum: humani nil a me alienum puto." It is from Terence's *Heautontimorumenos*, known in English as *The Self Tormentor*. The passage has been quoted by Cicero, Sir Richard Steele, and many others. (*Editor's note.*)

I saw him again, in imagination, with the beaming aureole and the flaming-red feet.

"You have surprised me without my ministerial trappings. When you came upon me, I was no longer God's minister, but one of God's creatures, wretched and imperfect, like all His creatures. In a few hours, I shall be speaking before the King, or rather, over the King; and it will be something more than a few pulpit steps that lift me above the crowned head of the Lord's anointed; the distance will be an infinite one, for the reason that I shall stand for that incorruptible and eternal consciousness which soars over thrones, over sceptres and over empires, at an inaccessible height. But here, in this mean little room, seated opposite you, I am no longer the voice of conscience; I am but a miserable concave object filled with darkness, where the voice of conscience echoes vainly."

This was becoming serious. Not knowing what to say, I sat there with my head dropped, and fixed my gaze upon a certain point, which chanced to be the portrait in the reliquary.

"You like that frame?" inquired Don Guillén.

"I like the portrait. I know that woman," I asserted bluntly. Don Guillén was not taken aback.

"You have made a mistake," he said. "It is undoubtedly another very similar face that you have in mind. You could not know that woman. I have already told you that she is my sister, and that she is no more."

He stressed the words *sister* and *no more*.

Following his dinner, Don Guillén took a small glass of cognac, and speeded up the conversation, which took a humorous and a lively turn. He was a man as witty as he was intelligent.

At the moment of leaving, he said to me:

"I shan't be eating at the table these days. What do you say if we dine together, here in my room? How Doña Emerenciana would envy you!"

In the course of these surreptitious dinners, and during the leisurely moments after dinner, my friend, Don Guillén, told me his story by snatches, the story of Angustias Pinto and that of their fathers, Belarmino and Apolonio. And then, later, I made certain discoveries of my own which were so important as to cause the tale of Caramanzana and la Pinta to take a secondary place in my mind.

Translated by Samuel Putnam

Ramón Sender

(1902-   )

Born in Aragon, Sender moved with his family to Zaragoza. At the age of fourteen, having quarreled with his father, he left home and thereafter supported himself through a variety of professions, but he managed to take his degree at the University of Madrid. The experiences, hopes, and dreams of the young Sender were beautifully portrayed in the author's novels published under the general title of *The Journey* over a period of years and published in definitive form in 1967. Sender writes and rewrites his novels, often under different titles, until he achieves what he feels is a definitive version. *Chronicle of the Dawn, The Violent Hippogryph, The Villa Julieta, The Youth and the Heroes, The Ounce of Gold,* and *The Levels of Existence,* through the protagonist, Pepe Garcés, trace his education, his growing understanding of man, the business world, revolutionary activities, the struggles between right and left, his withdrawal to live in a village with his grandfather, and his final realization that one owes a duty to one's fellow man and to society. The novels end as the hero, in jail and awaiting death, spends his time arranging his memoirs. Sender fought in the African campaign during 1922-24. His terrible experiences there formed the raw material for his first important novel, *Magnet* (1929), in which the hero took refuge in the dead carcass of a horse to escape capture, viewed a pig running through the fields with a human arm in its mouth, and experienced other nightmarish events. On his return to Spain, Sender interested himself in several left-wing groups. *Seven Red Sundays* (1932) describes these activities.

During the Spanish Civil War he fought on the Republican side. He lost several members of his family as a result of that conflict. Sender wrote an account of that war, *Counter Attack* (1937), biographical and literary studies, poetry, and several dramas, but he achieved his principal fame as a novelist. For Pío Baroja he was the greatest twentieth-century novelist, a judgment many share today. Since 1942 he has lived in the United States as a professor of Spanish literature.

Among his many other novels are *Public Order* (1931), which relates his jail experiences under Primo de Rivera; *Mister Witt Among the Rebels* (1935), which, against the background of the revolt of the Cantons against the First Spanish Republic in 1873, studies the jealousy of a man who feels the loss of his virility and approaching old age; *A Man's Place* (1939), filled with macabre humor, which seeks the value

114

of man in a society in conflict; *Proverb of Death* (1939), rewritten several times as *The Sphere*, of which the latest version was published in 1949, a symbolical and philosophical novel about good and evil; *Dark Wedding* (1942), a novel about a Caribbean penal colony, which studies beasts who try to become men; and *The Affable Hangman* (1952), which insists that all men share complicity in man's evil nature. Since few men can face this truth, it is the hangman who takes upon himself the moral blame of the crimes of all people and is thus a kind of martyr. *Requiem for a Spanish Peasant* (1961), originally entitled *Mosén Millán*, a study of man's inhumanity to man, reveals the betrayal of a priest who recalls that event in a series of flashbacks while waiting to perform a requiem mass, a kind of symbolical atonement, paid for by those who had been responsible for the victim's death.

In all his novels Sender stresses the need for regeneration, existentialist despair, and faith in humanity. It is love for the latter that motivates him, as he searches for meaning in this life. As the author says: "I live, and I do not know who I am; I travel along the road of life, but I know not whither, but I am content to be and to travel."

The selections consist of the entire twelfth chapter of *A Man's Place* and the concluding pages of *Requiem for a Spanish Peasant*.

A Man's Place

CHAPTER 12

When the Civil Guard left them again in the Castelnovo jail, they told the sergeant that they wanted to make a statement to the magistrate.

"All you've got to say is where the body is," the sergeant answered, "and you're going to say that today, no later."

In the afternoon Vicente's wife asked permission to go in and see her husband, but the guards drove her away with threats and insults. Before she left she shouted so that the prisoners heard her in their cell, that a lawyer was coming from the city to see them that evening.

The news filled the prisoners with hope, but the sergeant wanted to solve the problem of the corpse before the lawyer could get there, and in the midafternoon he went into the cell with other guards to start the questioning. They had ropes, and lashes reinforced with bits of lead. High up in the cell was a wooden bar with the ends fire-hardened and cut out, so that a cord thrown over it would not slip off. The bar hung from a small pulley and could be raised or lowered by hauling in or slacking off a rope tied to the cell door. This was used for hanging up pigs intended for the home for the aged. When the animals' throats had been cut and their hides scraped and washed, they were hung up here by their hind legs to be butchered. The sergeant thought he could use this to make the prisoners confess.

First he said almost with friendliness, "You ought to come clean. Where is the body?"

His manner heartened Juan and Vicente. "Look here, sergeant— This is all some kind of a nightmare. We're honest men but we can't get anyone to believe us, we can't even get anyone to listen to us. But the truth is that if we knew where the body was we'd tell you. We can't tell you because we don't know anything about it."

The sergeant turned white with anger. "You rats!" he said. "Do you think I'm not as tough as the sergeant who handled you before?"

Vicente thought that the tortures were coming again and there was no help for it. They were trapped in the nightmare and they could not get out. It was better to die and be done with it. For, how could they tell where Sabino's body was?

Where were they going to find it? They would have given half the little time for living they thought remained to them to find out, tell, and be let alone. They would go to the gallows when the time came, but even that was impossible now because "the *corpus* was missing."

"Where's the body?"

Vicente looked at Juan. He was conscious only of his animal fear of the whips and ropes. The sergeant started to tie them up. When Juan drew back in terror, the sergeant told them that they were to go to Ontiñena again to see the magistrate. Then they let him tie them, and when they were defenceless and unable to move the guards began knocking them about. The wounds in Vicente's eyelids had reopened and he bled freely. The two being prostrate, they lowered the bar, tied one of Juan's feet to each end, as he seemed the least damaged, and hoisted it until he was hanging free. Then they laughed, saying that the pig did not weigh much, gave him a kick in the teeth, and left without wasting time on further questions.

Outside the door, the sergeant shouted through the barred wicket, "When you've got something to say, call me."

A drop of blood fell at long intervals from Juan's swollen lips, thickening the blackened splotches that at other times had dripped from the pigs' snouts. This, too, was a dark, thick blood. Vicente groaned dully from a corner where he had dragged himself on all fours. Juan kept on bleeding and tried in vain to speak. His arms hung below his head and at times the drop of blood did not reach the floor but fell on a hand or on his shirt-sleeve.

They both wondered where Sabino's body could be. It would have been the greatest happiness to have been able to tell. They had never dreamed that legal procedure was so complicated, and it was a shame that confessing the crime did not suffice. They distrusted each other again. Vicente asked Juan if he really did know where the corpse was. Juan wanted to answer but his head was full of blood and his teeth and his rapidly inflaming lips hurt. Juan had a hope rather than a suspicion that Vicente might know something about Sabino's corpse.

Juan shouted and the guards came. One of them threw a handful of dirt on the blood clotting on the floor and asked:

"Are you going to tell where the body is?"

Juan said yes. Once again Vicente thought Juan probably had murdered Sabino. They let Juan down, promising him that if he did not tell everything as he should they would hang him up again. Vicente looked at the guards in terror through the curtain of blood which fell from his lids and which he could not get at to wipe with his sleeve.

Juan said, looking at the floor, "You can't find the body because we cut it up, and fed it to the hogs."

The cross-bar, the ropes, the dry blood on the floor, had suggested the thought of pigs to him. The guards looked at each other, shocked.

"There's a crime for you."

The others said nothing.

"How were they going to admit that?" the corporal remarked. "That's an extra touch that'll cost them their lives."

Now they understood his trickery in the fields.

They brought them bread and water, and a hot gruel of maize and crushed millet, also a basin so that they could wash off the blood. Vicente washed meticulously, not on account of the blood, but because since he had fallen on the corpse in the cemetery he

had felt as if his skin were on fire. They were both so weak that
the effort of washing, and drying themselves with their jackets
left them exhausted.

They ate a little and sat in silence, hoping for the lawyer to
come—if he really was going to, for they didn't have much faith
in that. It seemed to them irregular for anyone to concern himself
with them.

The lawyer arrived at dusk. Before he went to the cell he
asked the guards which was better, the inn in the town or the
Sign of the Monk. Then he was left alone with the prisoners. He
was hasty, wanting to get away because the place smelled very
badly. There was an inner window, covered with spider webs,
which once gave on a corral, and now, as a wall had been put
up converting that corner of the corral into a drain for the Town
Hall toilets, received the stench of the sewer directly. Juan was
upset by the idea that the lawyer might think that the smell came
from nastinesses committed by themselves. The lawyer asked if
they accepted him as defender, and put in their hands a paper
and his fountain pen. They both signed. Before going into the
matter he asked them if don Manuel were really a rich man and if
the Liberals had influence in Ontiñena. The prisoners thought that
perhaps the lawyer had been hired by don Manuel. They told
him he was very rich, which seemed to please the lawyer', and as
to what influence the Liberals might have in Ontiñena, they knew
nothing.

He thanked them for signing the agreement, and as the smell
grew worse, called the sergeant and asked him to take the prisoners
to the room that served as the guards' station.

The sergeant consented. "They've spilled it all, Señor, but the
law's the law."

He meant that for creatures like these the laws should not
allow a defence, but swifter, summary procedures. The lawyer
had a big briefcase and in it a condensation of the docket, which
he looked over casually.

In the room he asked to have the prisoners untied, but the
sergeant said that that was solely under the Civil Guard's juris-
diction as they were responsible for criminals and would be called
to account if they ran away. The lawyer waved his hand without
answering and asked to be left alone with his clients. The guards
went out and stayed watching the doors.

Vicente hastened to tell the lawyer that in the town, in his

parents' and his friends' houses, they would tell him they were
innocent. The lawyer nodded his head without having heard, and
taking a paper from his briefcase, read the beginning of it.

"It seems you have confessed," he remarked.

Vicente protested; it was enough to look at his face to understand that that statement had been torn from them by torture.
Juan, who could hardly speak, uncovered parts of his body and
showed him wounds and bloody bruises. The lawyer did not seem
impressed. The plea of torture was of no use because it laid an
accusation against so respected an institution as the Civil Guard,
the heads of which always belonged to families of great political
power. Such an argument could not be used without undermining
the foundations of the State. The lawyer's manner was bored and
displeased, and rather than listening to the defendants it could be
seen that he was preoccupied with the inconveniences of visiting
this town.

But he did go on questioning them. "It seems that they have
not found the body."

"No, sir."

"In what stage are the proceedings?"

They did not know what that meant. He explained that he
wanted to know what had happened that morning, to learn their
last statements, the statements that the sergeant meant when he
said that "they'd spilled it all."

They gave him details. When he learned that the corpse had
been cut up and given to the pigs to eat, he seemed overwhelmed.

Vicente explained, "You will understand that this is all a story."

They thought their innocence so obvious that anyone not a
Civil Guard or a magistrate would have to see it for himself. But
the lawyer seemed deeply disgusted.

"There's been a serious mistake."

"What?" asked Vicente.

"Getting rid of the corpse like that."

Vicente started. "But it's a lie, Mr. Attorney. He," he pointed
to Juan, "said it because they had hung him up by the feet."

He insisted that he could not use this business of torture as an
argument without damaging institutions of the State. Even if he
used it, it would not be admitted, for the same reason.

One could see that the sergeant had more power and authority
than all the lawyers in the world, and that frightened Vicente.

"It was a serious mistake," the lawyer repeated.

All three were silent. The lawyer added, "The defence is easier if the body does not appear, because one can always keep the possibility of innocence in the air, and at least you do not receive a capital sentence. This statement will make trouble for us."

The lawyer believed them both guilty. In an almost desperate manner, in the fear that everyone, even their defender, should think thus, Vicente went up to him and took his arm with his bound hands.

"We are innocent, Mr. Attorney. We didn't kill no one. I'm an honest man and I can go in the streets before all men with my head up."

The lawyer looked at him with some misgiving, and told him to calm himself and sit down.

Then he said with conviction, "The situation is not hopeless. It's not lost nor anything like it. I've seen other cases as difficult as this, and we've come out ahead."

Then he told them that don Jacinto had interested himself in their families and that on learning of it, don Manuel intervened and gave a job to Vicente's wife and money to Juan's, at which don Jacinto had to withdraw. But his good intentions had made a good impression in Castelnovo, where it seemed they had not liked him much before the crime.

This was more interesting to the lawyer than the specific question of torture and false confessions. He added that don Jacinto had invited the magistrate of Ontiñena to shoot with him and had sent his car for the morning's proceedings. Don Jacinto was a powerful enemy. Vicente and Juan saw that all the lawyer's machinations started from the assumption of the murder, including the disappearance of the corpse in the jaws of the pigs. The lawyer did not want to discuss that because it was all beyond discussion.

The very marks of the agonies they had undergone gave them a suspicious look to him, who saw in the fact that they had been beaten an element of culpability. "Punishment" being obvious, guilt must also be clear. This was not reasonable, but man's vital problems are never solved by reason.

The lawyer looked at Juan. "What do you say?" he asked.

Juan pointed to his injured mouth and hesitated, then he tried to talk.

"I didn't do nothing, either. This morning they beat me in the cemetery, too."

He spoke with a guttural and nasal accent, making m, which

he could not pronounce, into b. This, taken with the inflammation of the lower part of his face and the sombre look in his eyes (his teeth pained him dreadfully), gave him a savage, stupid appearance, and the lawyer saw the business as even more difficult, now that he had heard the sound of that voice.

"We shall see. Don't give up hope. We've got out of things just as bad as this."

He recited ritual words that he had spoken thousands of times.

In the same unconcerned manner he set about instructing them what to say in their new statements before the magistrate, in order to prepare their defence. The two listened, now fatalistically accepting their conviction and seeking the lesser evil.

He told Juan that since by his own confession he was the more deeply involved, he must take advantage of the fact that the victim's wife, Adela, was a woman of loose habits, and the crime must be made to seem one of passion. He had not killed Sabino to rob him, but because Juan was having intimate relations with Adela (as had so many others) and Sabino knew it, they met on the road at night, quarrelled, and Juan killed Sabino in self-defence.

Juan protested. "What will my wife say? I never was untrue to her."

The lawyer said flatly, "It is the only way to keep the prosecutor from asking capital punishment."

As for Vicente, he helped carry the corpse to the side of a solitary house near the river, and perhaps he went through the pockets and kept the money from them. The pigs of the farm-house (if there was one where several ran loose) ate the body and Vicente threw the remains into the river. This would lessen his share in the murder. The lawyer divided the guilt between them so that each one's part became less serious.

He repeated these instructions minutely. "You," he told Vicente, "did not intervene in any way in the murder, and you"—to Juan—"did not touch a penny of Sabino's money, nor have anything to do with getting rid of the body. And above all, do not forget that you slept with Adela and that before you killed Sabino you had a fight with him."

He repeated the instruction yet once more, dwelling on the points from which neither of the two must depart in the slightest. Then he called the sergeant and asked him to soften as much as possible the conditions under which the prisoners were confined.

The sergeant interrupted him. "They know well enough that if they behave decently and confess their crimes nothing will happen to them."

He added that they would probably be taken to Ontiñena the next day.

The lawyer departed and the prisoners went back to their cell. Neither of them any longer had the slightest suspicion of the other's guilt after having seen the means of defence prepared by the lawyer, and that it was nothing but a string of deliberate lies. If a series of deceptions could save them from death, so could they be brought to it by the same means.

Vicente felt great indifference and great fatigue. Nonetheless they were both a little calmer.

Translated by Oliver La Farge

Requiem for a Spanish Peasant

A few days later in the *carasol*,[1] the woman resumed her banter, mingling it with oaths and threats.

Nobody knew when people were killed. Or perhaps they knew but had not seen the killings. They were performed at night and during the day the village seemed to be peaceful.

Between the village and the *carasol*, four more corpses had been found: the bodies of four of the councilmen.

Many of the inhabitants were outside the village, harvesting. The womenfolk still went to the *carasol* and repeated the names of those who were falling. Sometimes they prayed, but afterwards, in apprehensive voices, they set themselves to reviling the wives of the wealthy, especially La Gumersinda and La Valeriana. According to La Jerónima, Señor Cástulo's wife was the worst of the lot and it was for her that the cobbler had been killed.

"It's not true," said someone. "It was because he was a Red agent, they say."

Nobody knew what "Red agent" meant and they all thought of Red, the bakery shop mare. But this made no sense. Neither

---

1. *Carasol*: A sunny place in the village outskirts where the village women gathered to gossip. (*Editor's note.*)

did anything else that was happening in the town. Not daring to
raise their voices, they began their *dijendas:*[1]

"The Cástulo woman is a hairy wart."

"A lazy good-for-nothing."

"A big, fat scorpion," put in La Jerónima, not to be outdone.

"A greasy louse's egg."

"Her house smells of piss in the fireplace," added La Jerónima.

They had heard that the *señoritos* from the city were going
to kill everyone who had voted against the King. La Jerónima, in
the midst of the catastrophe, sensed something magical and supernatural in the air, and she smelled blood everywhere. However,
when from the *carasol* she heard the bells ringing and at times the
blacksmith's anvil sounding in counterpoint, she was unable to
forbear swishing and swaying her skirts. Then she started cursing
again and called La Gumersinda "smelly feet." She tried to find
out what had become of Paco del Molino, but all anyone could
tell her was that he was being hunted. La Jerónima pretended to
be in the know and observed: "They won't catch that fine fellow
easily."

Again she referred to what she had seen when he was an infant
and she had changed his diapers.

From the sacristy, Mosén Millán's mind went back to the
dreadful confusion of those days and he felt grieved and perplexed.
Shots in the night, blood, evil passions, gossip, the foul behavior of
those strangers who, nevertheless, appeared to be educated. And
Don Valeriano complaining about what was happening while
simultaneously urging the *señoritos* from the city to kill more
people. The priest thought of Paco. His father stayed close to
home during those days. Cástulo Pérez had vouched for him,
saying that he was "clean wheat." The other wealthy men dared
not do anything against him, hoping to lay hold on his son.

No one but Paco's father knew where Paco was. Mosén Millán
went to his house.

Somewhat pale, Paco's father listened in silence. The parish
priest went on talking. He saw the young wife moving about like
a shadow, neither laughing nor crying. Nobody laughed or cried
in the village. Mosén Millán reflected that without laughter or
tears life could be as frightful as a nightmare.

By one of those gestures which friendship sometimes needs

---

1. *Dijendas:* Jerónima's pet name for gossip or impertinent speech.
(*Editor's note.*)

in order to prove itself worthy, Mosén Millán gave the impression that he knew where Paco was hidden. By letting it be understood that he knew, he made Paco's wife and father grateful to him for his silence. The priest did not say definitely that he knew, but he let it be understood. By one of life's ironies, Paco's father fell into the trap. He looked at the priest, thinking precisely what Mosén Millán wanted him to think: "If he knows and hasn't squealed, he's an honorable man, a man of integrity." This reflection made him feel better.

In the course of conversation, Paco's father revealed his son's hiding place, believing he was telling the priest nothing new. Upon hearing it, Mosén Millán was tremendously moved. "Ah," he said to himself, "it would have been better if he hadn't told me. Why must I be the one to know that Paco is hiding out in the Pardinas property?" Mosén Millán was afraid, and of what, he did not know exactly. He left soon afterward and was eager to confront the pistol-carrying strangers to prove to himself his strength of character and loyalty to Paco. And so it was. In vain the centurion and his friends spent the entire afternoon talking with him. That night Mosén Millán said his prayers and slept with a tranquillity he had not known for a long while.

Next day there was a meeting in the town hall and the strangers made speeches and shouted. Then they burned the tricolor flag and saw to it that all the townspeople came and saluted, raising their arms when the centurion so commanded. This fellow had a kindly face and wore dark glasses. It was hard to imagine him killing anyone. The countryfolk thought that those men who made unnecessary gestures and clicked their heels and shouted were weak in the head; but seeing Mosén Millán and Don Valeriano seated in places of honor they were nonplussed. Aside from the assassinations, the only thing these men had done in the village was to return the pasture lands to the Duke.

Two days later, Don Valeriano was in the abbey confronting the priest. Thumbs in the armholes of his vest—which made the charms on his watch-chain more conspicuous—he looked Mosén Millán straight in the eye and said, "I'm not after anybody's undoing, so to speak, but isn't Paco one of the most notorious? What I mean is, Señor Priest, others have fallen for less."

"Leave him alone," said Mosén Millán. "Why shed more blood?"

Yet it gave him pleasure to hint that he knew where Paco was hiding. By so doing he showed the mayor his capacity for loyalty. As a matter of fact, they were searching frantically for Paco.

Hunting dogs had been brought to his house to pick up the scent from his shoes and old clothes.

Just then, the centurion with the kindly face and dark glasses arrived with two others and, having heard the priest's words, declared, "We don't want people with softening of the brain. We're mopping up the town and the ones who aren't for us are against us."

"Do you people think I have softening of the brain?" asked Mosén Millán.

Then everybody became reasonable.

"The last executions were carried out without depriving the condemned of anything," the centurion stated. "They were even given extreme unction. What are you complaining about?"

Mosén Millán mentioned some honorable men who had fallen, and he insisted that all this madness should come to an end.

"Tell the truth," said the centurion, taking out his pistol and putting it on the table. "You know where Paco del Molino is hiding."

Mosén Millán wondered whether the centurion had taken out the pistol to threaten him or only to lighten his belt of its load. It was a movement he had seen him make before. And the priest was thinking of Paco whom he had baptized, and whom he had married. At that moment he was recalling trifling details such as the night owls and the pungent odor of marinated partridge. Paco's life might depend on his answer. He loved Paco. He loved him a great deal, but his love was in the name of God, not for the man himself. An affection over and above life and death. And he could not lie.

"Do you know where he's hiding?" all four men asked at once.

Mosén Millán responded by lowering his head. It was an affirmation. It could be an affirmation. When he realized this, it was too late. Then he begged them to promise not to kill Paco. They could try him and if he were guilty of something, lock him up, but they must not commit another crime. The kind-faced centurion promised. Then Mosén Millán disclosed Paco's hiding place. Afterward he tried to point out other qualities in the young man's favor, but they were not listening. They hurried away and the priest remained alone.

A half hour later, Señor Cástulo arrived, saying that the *carasol* was done with because the *señoritos* from the city had sprayed it twice with a machine gun, that some of the women had fallen and others had hurried off screaming, leaving trails of blood, like a flock of birds after a blast of grape-shot. Among those who managed to get away was La Jerónima and when Cástulo mentioned her name, he added: "Everybody knows. A bad penny . . ."

Seeing Cástulo laugh, the priest raised his hands to his head, ashy-pale. And yet, all the same, that man had possibly not revealed anyone's hiding place. "Why am I so shocked?" Mosén Millán asked himself in horror, and again he prayed.

Cástulo continued talking and said that there were ten or twelve women wounded in addition to those who had died in the *carasol* itself.

Next day, the centurion returned without Paco. He was indignant. He said that as he and his men were about to enter the Pardinas, the fugitive had met them with gunfire. He had one of the rural guards' rifles, and to approach the Pardinas was to risk one's life.

He asked the priest to go intercede with Paco. Two of the *señoritos* were wounded and he did not want to expose any more to danger.

Now, a year later, Mosén Millán recalled these episodes as if he had experienced them the previous day. When he saw Señor Cástulo—the one who had laughed at the *carasol* crimes a year before—come into the sacristy, he half closed his eyes again and said to himself: "I gave away Paco's hideout. I went to reason with him. And now . . ." He opened his eyes and saw the three men sitting there, facing him. Don Gumersindo, in the center, was slightly taller than the other two. Their three faces were looking impassively at Mosén Millán. In the tower, the bells ceased tolling, resounding three last times, solemnly, slowly, at long intervals, the reverberations remaining in the air for a while.

"With all due respect, I should like to pay for the Mass, Mosén Millán," said Señor Cástulo, thrusting his hand into his pocket.

The priest refused, and once more asked the acolyte to go see if there were any people. The boy went out, as always the ballad in his mind:

> Paco's kerchief drops and catches
> In the brambles on the way.
> The birds fly quickly overhead,
> The drifting clouds are slow and gray

Once more Mosén Millán shut his eyes, resting his right elbow on the chair arm and his forehead in his hand. Although he had come to the end of his prayers, he pretended to go on with them, in order to be left in peace. Don Valeriano and Don Gumersindo were explaining to Cástulo—both talking at once and each trying to drown out the other's voice—they, too, had wanted to pay for the Mass.

The acolyte came back very much excited and unable to say all he had to say at once. At last he said: "There's a mule in the church."

"What?"

"A mule. No one's in there, but a mule has got in somehow and is walking between the benches."

The three men left and returned to say that it was not a mule but Paco's colt, accustomed to running loose through the town. Everyone knew that Paco's father was a sick man and the women of the house half crazy. The animals and what small amount of property they had left were uncared for and neglected.

"Did you leave the church door open when you went out?" the priest asked the acolyte.

The three men assured him the doors were shut. Smiling sourly, Don Valeriano added, "It's a trick. A malicious act."

They began to wonder who could have put the colt in the church. Cástulo mentioned La Jerónima. Mosén Millán made a gesture of weariness and asked them to get the animal out of the church. The three men left with the acolyte. They strung out in a line and went after the colt with arms outspread. Don Valeriano claimed that it was a sacrilege and that perhaps the church would have to be reconsecrated. The others thought not.

They continued bearing down upon the creature. On a metal grille of the chapel of Christ, a wrought-iron devil seemed to wink. St. John in his niche raised a finger and showed his naked, feminine knee. Don Valeriano and Cástulo shouted in their excitement as if they were in a stable:

"Gee-haw! Haw there!"

The colt ran all over the church at will. The women of the *carasol*, if it had still existed, would have had something interesting to talk about. When the mayor and Don Gumersindo corraled the colt, it leaped between them and ran to the other side, with a gay whinny.

Señor Cástulo had a happy inspiration. "Open both wings of the door," he cried, "like they do for processions! Then the brute will see it has a clear way out."

The sacristan ran off to do so, against the better judgment of Don Valeriano, who could not bear to have Señor Cástulo show any initiative in his presence. When the great doors were opened wide, the colt was dazzled by the flood of light. Beyond the atrium the village square could be seen, deserted, with one house painted yellow, another whitewashed and trimmed in blue. The sacristan called the animal towards the exit. Finally convinced that this was not its place, it went out.

Under his breath, the acolyte was still reciting:

> *. . . the flocks of swallows come to rest*
> *Atop the cemetery cross.*

They closed the doors and the church was again in darkness. St. Michael, with his naked girlish arm, raised his sword over the dragon. In a corner, a lamp sputtered above the baptistry.

Don Valeriano, Don Gumersindo, and Señor Cástulo sat down on the front bench.

The acolyte went to the chancel, genuflected as he crossed in front of the altar, and disappeared into the sacristy.

"He's gone now, Mosén Millán," he said.

The priest was still reviewing his memories of the year before. The pistol-carrying strangers had compelled Mosén Millán to go with them to the Pardinas and once there, allowed him to approach alone.

"Paco," he cried, somewhat fearfully, "It's I. Don't you see it's I?"

No one answered. The barrel of a rifle showed in a window.

"Paco, don't be a fool," Mosén Millán shouted again. "It's better to surrender."

From the shadows of the window came the sound of a voice:

"I'll die before I surrender! Stand aside and let the others come forward, if they dare."

Mosén Millán adopted a tone of great sincerity. "Paco, in the name of all you love most—in the name of your wife, of your mother—surrender!"

There was no answer. At last Paco's voice was heard again.

"Where are my parents? And my wife?"

"Where do you want them to be? At home."

"Has nothing happened to them?"

"No, but if you keep on like this, who knows what may happen?"

After these words of the priest there was another long silence. Mosén Millán called Paco by name but nobody replied. At last Paco peered out. He still held the rifle and looked pale and tired.

"Answer my questions, Mosén Millán."

"Yes, son."

"Did I kill any of the men who came looking for me yesterday?"

"No. . . ."

"Not a one? Are you sure?"

"May God punish me if I'm lying. Not a one."

This seemed to improve matters. Realizing it, the priest added: "I've come here on condition that they won't do anything to you. I mean, you'll be tried before a court and if found guilty, you'll go to jail. But nothing more."

"Are you sure?"

The priest took some time in answering. Finally he said: "Those were my terms. In any case, son, think of your family. They don't deserve to pay because of you."

Paco looked about him, in silence. Then he said, "All right, I have fifty rounds left and could sell my life for a high price. Tell the others to come and not be afraid, for I'll give myself up."

From behind a fence the centurion gave a command.

"Throw the rifle out the window."

Paco obeyed.

Moments later, they had taken him from the Pardinas and were shoving and kicking him towards the village. They had tied Paco's hands behind his back. He was limping a great deal and this limp plus the two weeks' growth of beard darkening his face, had altered his appearance. To Mosén Millán's eyes, he had a guilty look. They locked him up in the village jail.

That same afternoon the *señoritos* from the city herded the people into the square and made speeches which nobody understood, speaking of Empire and Immortal Destiny, of Law and Order and the Holy Faith. Then they sang a hymn with arms raised and hands outstretched, whereupon everyone was ordered to go home and forbidden, under serious penalty, to go out again until the following day.

When the square was empty, Paco and two other peasants were taken out of jail and marched to the cemetery. It was almost night when they arrived. A dread silence was left behind in the village.

The centurion, as he stood them against the wall, remembered that they had not received confession, and sent for Mosén Millán. The priest was surprised to be taken in Señor Cástulo's car, which had been presented to the new authorities.

The car went right up to the place of the execution.

Mosén Millán had not dared to ask any questions, and when he saw Paco he felt no surprise at all, only a profound dejection. The three made their confessions. One of them was a man who had worked in Paco's house. Horrorstruck and not knowing what he was doing, the poor fellow repeated under his breath again and again: "I confess, Father . . . I confess, Father . . ." Señor Cástulo's car was used as a confessional, one door being left open, the priest sitting inside, the condemned man kneeling on the running board. When Mosén Millán said *Ego te absolvo,* two men snatched the penitent away and took him back to the wall.

Paco was the last to be confessed.

"In an evil hour I see you," he said to Mosén Millán in a voice the priest had never heard before. "But you know me, Mosén Millán. You know who I am."

"Yes, son."

"You promised me I'd be taken before a court and tried."

"I was deceived, too. What can I do? Think of your soul, my son, and forget all the rest if you can."

"Why are they killing me? What have I done? We haven't killed anyone. Say I haven't done anything. You know I'm innocent —that the three of us are innocent."

"Yes, son, you're all innocent. But what can I do?"

"If they kill me because I defended myself in the Pardinas, all right. But the other two haven't done anything."

Paco clung to Mosén Millán's cassock and repeated, "They haven't done anything and they're going to be killed. They haven't done anything."

"Sometimes, my son," said the priest, moved to the verge of tears, "God allows an innocent man to die. He even permitted the death of His own Son, who was more innocent than the three of you."

These words left Paco mute and paralyzed. The priest was silent too. Far off in the village, dogs barked and a bell tolled. Nothing had been heard but that bell, day and night, for two weeks. At last, with desperate firmness, Paco spoke.

"Then if it's true we have no hope, Mosén Millán, I have a wife, and she's expecting a child. What will become of her? And of my parents?"

He spoke breathlessly, and Mosén Millán answered in a whisper, with the same frenzied haste. Sometimes they could not hear the words they pronounced, but between Paco and the priest, words were unnecessary. Confused and stammering, Mosén Millán talked about the designs of God and after a long lamentation, asked the final question.

"Do you repent of your sins?"

Paco did not understand him. It was the first of the priest's

expressions he did not understand. When the question was me-
chanically repeated for the fourth time, Paco nodded. At that
moment Mosén Millán raised his hand and said: *Ego te absolvo
in* . . . , whereupon two men grabbed Paco by the arms and led
him to the wall where the others were standing.

"Why do they kill these others?" Paco shouted. "They've done
nothing."

One of them lived in a cave, like the man to whom they had
once taken extreme unction.

The headlights of the car in which Mosén Millán was sitting
flashed on, and almost simultaneously a volley of shots rang out,
with orders from no one and not a single voice heard. The other
two peasants fell but Paco, covered with blood, ran toward the car.

"Mosén Millán, you know me!" he cried, demented.

He tried to climb in but could not. Everything was splattered
with his blood. Mosén Millán was silent, his eyes shut, praying.
The centurion thrust his revolver behind Paco's ear and somebody
said, alarmed, "No! Not there!"

They dragged Paco away. He kept repeating hoarsely. "Ask
Mosén Millán—he knows me."

Two or three more shots were heard. Then followed a silence
in which Paco kept on whispering: "He denounced me . . . , Mosén
Millán. Mosén Millán. . . ."

The priest was still in the car, wide-eyed, hearing his name
and unable to pray. Someone had turned the headlights on again.

"Now?" asked the centurion.

Mosén Millán climbed out and, helped by the acolyte, anointed
the three with holy oil. Then a man gave him Paco's watch—a
wedding present from his wife—and a pocket handkerchief.

They returned to the village. Through the car window, Mosén
Millán looked at the sky and, remembering the night when he had
gone with Paco to give extreme unction in the cave, he wrapped the
watch in the handkerchief and held it carefully in his joined hands.
Still he could not pray. They passed by the deserted *carasol*. The
great, naked rocks seemed to be leaning towards each other and
talking. Mosén Millán thought of those dead peasants, of the poor
women of the *carasol,* and he felt a kind of involuntary scorn which,
at the same time, made him feel guilty and ashamed.

Once back in the abbey, Mosén Millán remained for two weeks
without leaving it except for Mass. The entire village was silent
and gloomy, like an immense tomb. La Jerónima had come out of
her house again and had gone to the *carasol,* all alone, talking to

herself. When she thought nobody could hear her there, she shouted. But sometimes she stood there in silence, counting the bullet holes in the rocks.

A year had passed since all this had happened, but it seemed like a century. Yet Paco's death was so recent and fresh that Mosén Millán still thought he had bloodstains on his clothes.

He opened his eyes and spoke to the acolyte.

"You say the colt has gone away?"

"Yes, Señor."

And leaning first on one foot and then on the other, the boy recited under his breath:

> . . . . and yielded up his final sigh
> To God, the Lord of all creation.—Amen.

In a drawer of the sacristy chest was Paco's watch and handkerchief. Mosén Millán had not yet dared take them to the dead man's parents and widow.

He went out into the chancel and began the Mass. The only people in the church were Don Valeriano, Don Gumersindo, and Señor Cástulo. While Mosén Millán intoned *introibo ad altare Dei*, he thought of Paco and said to himself, "It's true. I baptized him, I gave him extreme unction. At least—may God forgive him— he was born, lived, and died in the bosom of Holy Mother Church." He thought he heard his name on the lips of the dying man, fallen to the ground: ". . . . Mosén Millán."

And both terrified and moved to pity, he reflected: "Now in suffrage of his soul, I say this Requiem Mass, for which his enemies wish to pay."

Translated by Elinor Randall

Camilo José Cela

(1916-)

Cela, who was born in Galicia, is the most important Spanish novelist to emerge after the Civil War. His *The Family of Pascual Duarte* set the pattern for a whole series of new novels by young Spanish novelists about the Spanish Civil War and its aftermath. Although he was at one time a member of the Falangist Party, his novels serve as a sharp condemnation of the Spanish situation and the somber, gray, and hopeless lives that modern Spaniards live. Some of his novels, consequently, have been published outside of Spain. Cela uses a "slice of life" technique in his neo-naturalistic or *tremendista* novels. These works have obviously been influenced by the picaresque tradition and, in some measure, by the novels of Dos Passos, Hemingway, Pío Baroja, and Valle-Inclán.

The Family of Pascual Duarte (1941) concerns the son of an alcoholic father and an unloving mother who is pushed by circumstances into a series of terrible acts. He kills several animals, his faithless wife, her lover, and finally his mother. Blood predominates throughout, as Cela combines humor and horror and tries to show there are no absolute or arbitrary values possible. *Pavilion of Repose* (1943) involves the lives of a series of tubercular patients in a sanitarium. Although it lacks *Pascual Duarte's* violence, the novel implies that they, too, find a life force in their escaping blood which unites them. Perhaps, says Cela, Spain itself is the sanitarium. *New Wanderings and Misadventures of Lazarillo de Tormes* (1944) reveals the sad economic realities to which modern Spain has been reduced, as cruelty and hunger rule the day. In *The Hive* (1951) Cela uses the same technique used by Huxley in *Point Counter Point*. His characters are deformed caricatures of men who lead brutal and dismal lives, which revolve around hunger and sex. One meets these victims of society in a shoddy cafe and follows them out into the hopelessness of the beehive of Madrid. *Mrs. Caldwell Speaks With Her Son* (1953) is a series of soliloquies in letter form of a woman who died insane in an institution. *The Blond* (1954) speaks of life in Venezuela, where horror and compassion also intermingle.

Cela has also written a number of travel books dealing with various sections of Spain. Among these are *Trip to Alcarria* (1948) and *Jews, Moors, and Christians* (1955). In these works and in his short stories Cela stresses his identification with the humble folk of Spain. He sums up his artistic creed as: "To ration tenderness and not to become blind

133

nor to pretend not to see the inhumanity is the most noble function of the writer of these times in which we have been destined to live."

The first selection, from *Pascual Duarte's Family,* includes Chapters 4 and 5 and a fragment of Chapter 6. The second selection, from *The Hive,* covers the last third of Chapter 5.

The selection, from *The Hive,* covers the last third of Chapter 5.

Pascual Duarte's Family

CHAPTER 4

I am hoping, sir, that you will forgive the disjointed way in which this story unfolds, the reason being that in keeping track of the people concerned, rather than following the order of events, I'm obliged to jump from one thing to another and all over the shop, like a grasshopper you're trying to lay hands on, but I find there's no other way except this that I could tell it, for not only would it probably not come out right at all any other way, but I'd constantly be running the risk of starting to talk and talk and talk, only to end up short of breath and in such a fix that I should never manage to disentangle myself.

The years went by for us as they do for everyone else; our life at home ran the same course as it always had, and if I'm not to go making things up, there's precious little I could tell you about that period which you can't very well imagine for yourself.

However, fifteen years after the girl was born and when, to judge by my mother's gaunt appearance, the last thing in the world one would have expected was that she might bear another child, especially given the length of time that had passed, bless me if she didn't swell out again in front, and God knows whose doing it was this time, though I suspect it was just about then that she got mixed up with the Señor Rafael; so it was merely a question of waiting for her appointed day and the newcomer duly arrived. The birth of poor Mario—which was the name they gave my little brother —was more distressing and troublesome than anything you can think of, because as if the hullabaloo my mother raised wasn't enough, the whole business coincided with my father's death, which if it hadn't been so tragic in itself would certainly have made one laugh fit to bust, it was really so funny when you stopped to think

about it. It was after we'd had Father shut up for a couple of days
in the closet that Mario came into the world; a mad dog had bitten
him, and though at first we didn't think he was going to be any
the worse for it, later on he was taken with shivering fits which
put us all on our guard. Señora Engracia gave us plainly to understand that the look in his eye was liable to bring on a miscarriage,
so that since the poor devil was beyond hope anyhow, we set to,
with the help of the neighbours, and got him out of harm's way,
though it wasn't an easy job and we had to watch out and mind
ourselves very carefully, for he tried so desperately to bite us that
if he had managed to get his teeth into somebody's arm they'd
surely have lost it. I still remember with fear and agony that
dreadful tussle. . . . You've no idea how we had to fight to get the
better of him! He lashed out like a lion, swearing he'd murder us
all, every man-jack of us, and his eyes flashed so that I'm convinced
he'd have been as good as his word, had God allowed it. It was
two days, as I say, since we had got him locked up, and he raised
such Cain and let out such hefty kicks at the door, which we
shored up with staves, that it doesn't surprise me, in the midst
of all this din and with Mother screaming her head off at the
same time, that young Mario should have entered the world
quaking with terror and sort of half-witted. My father finally
subsided the next night—Twelfth Night it was—and when we went
to have a look we found him inside there, huddled on the ground
and with such an unholy expression of panic on his face that it
honestly seemed he must have gone down into Hell. It frightened
me a good deal that Mother, instead of bursting into tears as I
expected, began to laugh, but I had to blink back a couple of
tears that came into my eyes when I saw the body's bloodshot
stare and its purple tongue half out of the gaping mouth. When
we came to bury him, Don Manuel, the priest, preached a bit of
sermon at me as soon as he saw me. I don't remember much of
what he said, but I know he spoke of the life to come, of Heaven
and Hell, of the Blessed Virgin, and my father's memory, and when
it occurred to me to suggest that so far as the old man's memory
was concerned the best thing to do was to give the whole subject
a miss, Don Manuel laid his hand on my head and told me something about the Angel of Death taking mortals from one kingdom
to the next and not liking us to hate those whom he had led into
the sight of God for judgement. Mind you, that wasn't how he
said it, but in very wise and solemn words; yet what he was trying
to impress on me wasn't far different from the way I've expressed

it here. After that, whenever I met Don Manuel I greeted him
and kissed his hand, but on getting married my wife would have
it that I looked like a nancy-boy doing things like that, so of course
I had to give up the habit, and later I learned how Don Manuel
had remarked that I was for all the world the same as a rose blooming on a dungheap, and Christ knows that I wanted to throttle
him when I heard it, but as my temper is more hasty than violent,
little by little I minded the thing less and I ended up by forgetting
it altogether, especially as after a time and on thinking it over I
was never again very sure of having understood the remark aright.
Maybe Don Manuel hadn't said anything of the sort—one should
not believe all the things people tell one—and even supposing he
did, who knows what he was getting at? Who knows whether he
really meant what I took him to mean?

If Mario had been in full possession of his senses when he
departed from this vale of tears it's pretty certain that, looking
back on it, he wouldn't have been sorry to leave. He wasn't with
us long; it was as if he'd got wind beforehand of the sort of family
he was about to join and preferred the company of the innocents
in limbo. God is my witness that he chose the right road when he
said good-bye to the miserable years of the life that lay in store
for him. He went from us when he hadn't yet reached the age
of ten, which may not have been a long enough time for all the
suffering that came his way, but should, one would have thought,
have been ample for him to learn to walk and talk, which he never
did. The poor wretch never got beyond crawling along the ground
like an adder, and making noises in his throat and nose that sounded
no better than the squeaking of a rat: that's all he ever accomplished. He hadn't been alive very long before we realized that
a half-wit he'd been born, poor creature, and a half-wit he'd
remain to his dying day. It took him eighteen months to grow
his first tooth, and even then he made such a sorry job of it that
Señora Engracia, who was always there when we needed her,
had to yank it out of his head on a string in case it should get
embedded in his tongue. About that time, I couldn't say whether
or not it was on account of all the blood he swallowed from the
tooth he had lost, but he came out in a measly rash, if you'll excuse
me mentioning it, on his behind, and what with the matter that
oozed from these sores and wetting himself on top of that, his
little arse looked quite flayed and raw, so that when we got down
to curing the affected parts with salt and vinegar the brat screeched

so pitifully that it would have melted the hardest heart to listen to him. From time to time he did have a few peaceful moments toying with a wine bottle, which was what seemed to appeal to him most, or lying out in the sun to recuperate a little in the doorway or in the corral; and that's how he got along, poor kid, neither very much better nor much worse but easier in his condition on the whole, until a day came—he was four at the time—when fate took such a skunner to him that, without his having hurt a soul or done anything wrong or offended God in any way, a hog (if you'll pardon me) chewed off his ears. Don Raimundo the chemist applied a little of some yellowish powder called seroform to the wounds, and it was such a pathetic sight to see him daubed that colour and missing both ears that all the neighbours wanted to comfort him, so they most of them brought him a lollipop on Sundays, or some almonds, and gave him olives soused in oil or a hunk of garlic sausage. Poor Mario, what a grateful light shone in his beady little black eyes when he grabbed these friendly offerings! Yet, badly as things had turned out for him before, there was plenty worse to follow after the business of the hog; from morning till night he hollered and wailed like a lost soul, and as Mother's small store of patience gave out just when it was most needed, the wretched kid lay around on the floor for months on end, eating whatever food was thrown to it and so filthy that even though I myself—why tell a lie?—seldom washed, the dirtiness of the brat quite revolted me. Whenever a pig came into view, which was a thing that happened in those parts continually, my baby brother used to go so raving mad it was awful to watch him: he bellowed louder than ever and tumbled over himself trying frantically to hide behind something, with such an expression of horror in his eyes and on his puckered face that I am sure it would have stopped Satan dead in his tracks if he had appeared out of Hell at that moment.

I remember one day—a Sunday—when he flew into one of these fits and was so overcome with terror and rage that in his haste to escape he made a beeline (God knows why) for Señor Rafael, who was in the house at the time, because since my father's death he'd taken to coming in and out as if he owned the place; and what did the crazy creature go and do but bite the old boy in his leg, which was unlucky for him, as with the other foot the man promptly gave him such a hell of a kick on one of the scars that it knocked him clean out and almost finished him off, so that he lay on the ground with a trickle from his ear that made me think he was bleeding to death. Señor Rafael howled with laughter, as if he was proud of what he had done, and I hated him so from that instant that—as I hope to be saved—I swear, if God had not removed him out of my reach, I'd have settled his hash at the first convenient opportunity.

The child was there between them, stretched out at full length on the floor, and I promise you it made my blood run cold to see how vilely my mother could behave, for, instead of picking it up, she just laughed in chorus with Señor Rafael. As for me, the Lord knows I didn't lack the strength of will to lift the poor little brute, but I thought it better to leave it be. . . . If the old man at that moment had called me a coward, I know I should have beaten him to a pulp under my mother's very eyes.

I went away out of the house to try to forget, and on the way I met my sister, who was hanging around the village at the time, and when I told her what had taken place she took on such a look of fury that it struck me what a dangerous person she would be to have up against one, and I brought Stretch to mind, I don't know why, but I couldn't help grinning at the thought that some day she might fix him, too, with that cold and vicious glare. . . .

When we got back, a good two hours later, Señor Rafael was taking his leave; Mario lay where I had last seen him, moaning softly with his mouth against the ground and the scar flaming a vivid red like a summer sunset. I thought Sis was going to let all hell loose, but she simply picked him up off the floor and laid him down on his back in the kneading-trough. . . . I have never liked the looks of her so well as when I saw her do that: in her blue dress the colour of heaven and with her fiercely maternal air she was the very image of young motherhood, which was never in fact to be her lot. . . .

When the Señor Rafael had gone at last my mother lifted Mario up in her arms, laid him in her lap, and sat with him all night through, licking his wounds like a bitch tending her new-born puppies. The nipper let her fondle him, and smiled. He fell asleep after a while, and it showed on his lips where the smile had been. . . . That night I'm sure was the only time in his life that I saw him smile.

CHAPTER 5

Some time went by after that without his suffering any further mishap, but when Fate has it in for you there's no way out, whatever you do to escape and however you try to hide, so a day came when, not knowing where on earth he had got to, we discovered him at last, drowned in a vat of oil. It was my sister Rosario who found him. . . . He had toppled over, head downwards, like a thieving owl caught by a gust of wind, with his nose on the muddy bottom of the jar. . . . When we pulled him out, a driblet of oil hung from his mouth as if he were spinning a thread of gold in his stomach, and his hair, which in life had always been of a dull ashen colour, was so shiny and bright now that you would have said it had come alive when he himself died. This is the only odd thing I remember about Mario's death.

My mother didn't cry, either, at the death of her child. Her heart must have shrivelled up inside her for a woman not to have so much as a single tear left to shed over the loss of her offspring. . . . For my part I may say that I wept, and I'm not ashamed to confess it, and so did my sister; but I developed such a hatred against my mother, and in no time it grew so much stronger, that I was seized with fear of myself. A woman who doesn't weep is like a spring that doesn't flow and is therefore useless, or like a bird that doesn't sing in the sky and which God, if He chose, would deprive of its wings, because foxes and other vermin don't have wings or deserve them.

Often and often I've wondered and considered, and to this day, truth to tell, I still wonder how it was that I first came to lose all respect for my mother and later on, as time went by, every bit of affection or outward sign of it as well. I've thought about this deeply and long because I wanted to clear a space in my memory so that I could discern when it was that she ceased for me to be my mother and about what time afterwards she actually became an enemy. A deadly enemy, because there's no hatred like the hatred of blood for its own blood; an enemy who roused the very worst in me, because there is nobody one hates so intensely as someone who is like oneself, when one takes a loathing to that likeness. After much reflection and very little result the most I can

say is that, so far as the respect part of it goes, I lost all the respect
I ever had for her a long time back when I didn't notice a single
good quality in her that I could imitate, nor any gift from God
that I might covet, so that it must have dropped out of my heart
when she struck me as being so wicked that I couldn't fathom the
evil that was in her. As for hating her—really hating her—that came
later, quite some time later (Rome after all wasn't built in a day),
and if I were to plump for about when Mario died I doubt if I
should be far out in my dates.

We had to dry the small body with strips of flax so that he
should not appear all greasy before the Seat of Judgement, and
we rigged him up to look very nice in some muslin that there was
about the house and a pair of espadrilles which I went down into
the village to buy, and we tied a ribbon the colour of mallow about
his neck in a bow, so that it looked as if a butterfly, in its innocence,
had settled on the dead child's throat. Señor Rafael was stirred by
a feeling of charity towards the deceased whom in life he had
treated so cruelly; he helped us now to assemble a coffin, hurrying
to and fro with some nails or a piece of three-ply or a pot of white
lead, as beaming and busy as a bride, which I must say kept me
guessing, for, try as I might, I was unable to make out either at
the time or since whether in his heart of hearts he was as pleased
as Punch, like his behaviour gave me to believe, or not. When he
kept murmuring in an offhand way: "It is God's will! There's
another little cherub in Heaven," I was so thoroughly puzzled that
to this day I'm not sure what I felt about it all. While he ham-
mered planks or plied the paint-brush he'd repeat, like a refrain:
"Another little cherub, another little cherub, another little cherub
in Heaven," and his words throbbed inside my heart like the
ticking of a clock—a clock that sounded as if it was about to burst,
a clock that registered each measured syllable as it fell softly and
precisely from his lips, while his bright and moist little blue eyes,
like a viper's, gazed at me in the kindliest fashion when all that
I could feel for him in return was the uttermost loathing. . . . It
disgusts me still to remember it.

"A new little cherub in Heaven!" The son of a bitch, what a
show he put on! Let's not dwell on it any longer.

Frankly I had never known (nor did I give serious thought
to the matter) what angels were like. At one time I pictured them
as being fair and dressed in flowing skirts of pink or blue; at another
I imagined they might be the same colour as the clouds and
thinner even than stalks of wheat. However, what I can guarantee

is that my idea of them bore no likeness to my brother Mario, which is probably why it struck me that there was more than met the eye in Señor Rafael's remark and that it was something as cunning and unkind as you would expect from such a perfect swine.

The kid's funeral was as shabby and dismal an affair as my father's had been a few years before. Without exaggerating, there weren't above five or six mourners to follow the coffin—Don Manuel, Santiago the altar-boy, Lola, two or three old women, and me. Santiago went in front with the cross, whistling most of the time and kicking at pebbles; then the coffin and, behind that, Don Manuel with his white vestment over his cassock, like a night-shirt; and the old crones bringing up the rear with such a deal of sobbing and sniffling that honestly you'd have thought the whole pack of them together were the mothers of the body we were accompanying on its journey to the grave.

Lola was already by way of being my sweetheart at the time, and I'm not saying outright that she was my sweetheart because, although we had taken rather a fancy to each other, I hadn't yet screwed up the courage to court her openly. I was afraid maybe she'd turn me down, and although more often than not she pre-sented me with opportunities for making up my mind, I was always too timid and sheered off at once, so that time kept slipping by and nothing was done about it. I must have been around twenty-eight or thirty, and she, being younger than my sister Rosario, may have been twenty-one or twenty-two. She was tall, with a dark complexion and black hair, and her eyes were so large and deep that it was disturbing to look into them. Her body was firm and as you might say hardened by the very health there was in her, yet it was so fully developed that anyone would have taken her for a young mother in her prime. Nevertheless, before I proceed and risk forgetting to mention it, I want to tell you, for the sake of truth, that at this time I'm speaking of she was as pure as on the day of her birth and as untouched by man as any novice in a convent. It's a point I wish to stress, so that no wrong idea should be formed of her. As to what she may have done later, that's up to her and her own conscience—God alone knows the full story—but with regard to her conduct at the time, I am so certain no lecherous thought ever crossed her mind that I wouldn't hesitate for a moment to deliver up my soul to the Devil if he could produce proof to the contrary. She walked with such a lithe, sure step, she carried herself with so proud a grace and so confident a swing, that she might have been anything but a poor country girl, and her thick plait of hair at the nape of her bended head had such an appearance of vigour that months afterwards, when she was mine, my wedded wife, I used to love to beat it against my cheeks, it was so sweet-smelling and silky, redolent of sunshine and thyme and of the chill little beads of sweat that mingled, when she was stirred, with the down at her temples.

To revert to our subject, the burial was easy: the hole had been dug beforehand, so all we had to do was to pop my brother into it and finish shovelling the earth on to him. Don Manuel prayed in Latin and the women knelt beside the grave. When Lola went down on her knees you could see the smooth white flesh above the black edge of her stockings. . . . I am ashamed of what I am about to say, but may God not hold it against me in saving my soul alive, on account of how hard it has been to bring myself to confess it: at that moment I was glad for the death of my brother. . . . Lola's thighs glistened like silver, the blood beat in my forehead, and I thought my heart would burst within me. . . .

I did not notice Don Manuel nor the women leave. I was sort of daft when I began to come round again from my trance, sitting on the heap of fresh earth that covered Mario's corpse; why I was there and how long I'd stayed in that position are two things I never found out. I remember the blood was still thumping in my brain, my heart still tugged this way and that as if in an effort to escape from my chest, where it was trapped. . . . The sun was sinking; its last rays gilded the sad cypress, my sole companion. . . . It was hot; my whole body shook; I couldn't move, it was as though I was transfixed by the stare of a wolf. . . .

Suddenly Lola appeared by my side, her bosom rising and sinking as she breathed. . . .

"So·that's where you were."

"Hullo."

"What are you up to?"

"Why, nothing . . . Just sitting here."

I got to my feet and held her by the arm.

"What are you doing here?"

"Nothing. Can't you see? I'm doing nothing. . . ."

Lola gazed at me in a frightening way. Her voice came out of the beyond, the solemn and hollow voice of a ghost. "You're exactly like your brother!"

"Who? Me?"

"Yes. Just the same as your poor brother. . . ."

It was a fierce struggle. Thrown to the ground, and pinned under my weight, she was handsomer than ever. . . . Her breasts heaved faster and faster, as she panted for breath. I seized her by the hair and held her down securely. She twisted and strained, trying to slip from my grasp. . . .

I bit her till she bled, till she was quiet and submissive as a young mare. . . .

"Is that what you wanted?"

"Yes. Oh, yes. . . ."

Lola smiled at me with the fine smile of her even teeth. . . . Then she stroked my hair.

"You're not like your brother after all. You're a man!"

The words were a deep echo in her throat. . . .

"You're a man! A man!"

The earth was soft—how well I remember its softness! And there, strewn over my brother's grave, were six blood-red poppies. . . . A blood-offering spilled on the freshly turned earth. . .

"You're not like your brother. You're a man!"

"Do you love me?"

"Yes! I love you!"

CHAPTER 6

A whole fortnight it's been, as things have turned out, since I last put pen to paper, because during that time, what with questioning and visits from Counsel for the Defence on the one hand, and being moved here to these new quarters on the other, I haven't had a free moment to write. Now after rereading this still not very bulky wad of papers, all sorts of different ideas besiege my brain in such a jumble and hurry that, try as I will, I don't know where to make a fresh start. An exceedingly gloomy tale it is that I have had to tell so far, as you will have observed, and I'm afraid of not finding the heart to go on with it when I come to tackle what remains to be told, which is sadder still. It scares the wits out of me when I realize how faithfully and well my memory is serving me now that everything that's happened in my life, which can no longer be undone, is going on record permanently in black and white. It's funny to think—though wretched too, God knows—that if only I had made the same effort some years back to see things as clear as I'm seeing them now, instead of having to write them down at all I'd be sitting quietly taking the sun in the stable-yard, or fishing for eels in the stream, or out after rabbits among the hills at home. . . . I'd be doing any of those things that most people do without so much as a passing thought. I should be free, as the majority of my fellow-men are free, without thinking twice about that, either, and there would stretch before me a span of God's good years such as most of mankind can look forward to without stopping to consider that they may spend them as unhurriedly as they like. . . .

Where they've brought me to now is a better place. You look out of the window into a little garden that's as neat and tidy as any parlour, and over the wall beyond, as far as the ridge of hills, broad and brown as the tan on a man's face, lies the open plain, across which pass from time to time a string of mules headed for Portugal, jogging donkeys on their way to outlying farmsteads, women and children who go no farther than the well. . . .

Translated by John Marks

The Hive

Lola and Don Roque have a talk sitting side by side on the couch. Don Roque is still in his overcoat and holds his hat on his knees. Lola is naked, with her legs crossed. An oilstove burns in the room; it is fairly warm. The wardrobe mirror throws back the image of their two figures, a truly strange pair: Don Roque muffled up and looking worried, Lola naked and in a bad temper. Don Roque has finished talking.

"That's all."

Lola scratches her navel, after which she smells her finger.

"D'you know what I think?"

"What?"

"That your daughter and I are birds of a feather and could shake hands."

Don Roque shouts at her: "Shut up, I tell you. Shut up!"

"All right, I can shut up."

Both are smoking. Lola, plump, naked, and puffing smoke, looks like a performing seal.

"Your girl's story about the photographer is the same as yours about your sick friend—"

"Will you shut up?"

"Now that's enough of your 'shut ups' and your silly rubbish. It's just as if you hadn't got any eyes in your head."

In another place we have already said the following: "With bristling mustache and a gentle look in his eyes, Don Obdulio protects, like a malevolent yet roguish cupid, the clandestine affairs which make it possible for his widow to have something to eat."

Don Obdulio is on the right-hand side of the wardrobe, behind a flower stand. On the left hangs a portrait of the mistress of the house in her youth, surrounded by lap dogs.

"Come on, get dressed. I'm no good for anything now."

"All right."

Lola thinks: "That girl is going to pay me for this, as sure as God's in Heaven. She's going to pay for it, and how!"

Don Roque asks her: "Will you go out first?"

"No, you go, I'll get dressed in the meantime."

Don Roque leaves, and Lola bolts the door.

"Nobody will miss him if he isn't here," she thinks.

She unhooks Don Obdulio and puts him in her bag. Then she damps down her hair at the basin and lights a cigarette.

Captain Tesifonte seems to respond at last. "Right . . . we'll try our luck. . . ."

"You don't really mean it?"

"Yes, certainly, you'll see. One day when you're going on a spree, call for me and we'll go together. Agreed?"

"Yes, sir, agreed. Next time I go on the prowl, I'll let you know."

The junk dealer's name is José Sanz Madrid. He has two pawnshops where he buys and sells secondhand clothes and *"objets d'art,"* and where he hires out dress suits to students and morning coats to penniless bridegrooms.

"Go in there and try some on, there's plenty to choose from."

Indeed there is plenty to choose from: hung on hundreds of clothes-hangers, hundreds of suits are waiting for the customer who will give them an airing.

One of the pawnshops is in the Calle de los Estudios and the other, the more important one, in the Calle de la Magdalena, about halfway up.

After his evening snack, Señor José takes Purita to the pictures; he likes to relax before going to bed. They go to the Ideal Cinema, opposite the Calderón, where they are showing *His Brother and He* with Antonio Vico and *A Family Affair* with Mercedes Vecino, both "passed by the censor." The Ideal has the advantage that the performance is continuous and that it is so large that there are always some seats.

The usher shows them the way with his torch.

"Which seats?"

"These will do. We'll be all right here."

Purita and Señor José sit down in the back row. Señor José puts his arm round the girl's neck.

"Well, what news?"

"Nothing at all."

Purita stares at the screen. Señor José takes both her hands.

"You're cold."

"Yes, it's very cold."

For a few moments they stay silent. Señor José is not comfortable in his seat, he shifts round continually.

"Listen."

"Yes?"

"What are you thinking about?"

"Psh . . ."

"Don't rack your brains, I'm going to settle that thing with Paquito for you. I've got a friend with a lot of influence in the Social Aid organization—he's first cousin of the Civil Governor of thingumajig."

Señor José lets his hand slide down to the open neck of the girl's blouse.

"Ooh, that's cold!"

"Never mind, it will get warm."

The man puts his hand into Purita's armpit, outside the blouse.

"How warm you're here under the arm!"

"Yes."

Purita's armpit is hot, as if she were not well.

"So you think they'll take on Paquito?"

"I should say so, my dear. Even if my friend hadn't so much influence, he'd get him in."

"And will your friend do it?"

Señor José has his other hand on one of Purita's suspenders. In the winter Purita wears a suspender belt: the round garters don't keep up her stocking properly because she is rather thin.

In the summer she goes without stockings. Though it may not
sound like it, it saves quite a lot of money.

"My friend does what I tell him to; he owes it to me for all the
favors I've done him."

"I hope you're right, God grant it."

"You'll see."

The girl is lost in thought, her eyes wistful and far away.
Señor José pushes her thighs a little apart and pinches them.

"With Paquito in the day nursery, things would be different."

Paquito is the girl's youngest brother. There are five brothers
and sisters, with Purita herself, six. Ramón, the eldest, is twenty-
two—he is doing his military service in Morocco; then comes
Mariana, who is eighteen and an invalid, poor thing, tied to her
bed; then Julio, an apprentice at a printer's, who is going on
fourteen; Rosita, who is eleven; and Paquito, who is nine. Purita
is the second eldest, she is twenty, although she may look a little
more than her age.

The six live on their own. Their father was shot against a wall
for one of those things, and the mother died of T.B. and under-
nourishment in 1941.

Julio gets four pesetas a day at the printer's. The rest of the
money Purita has to scratch together by walking the streets all
day and coming to port after supper at Doña Jesusa's house.

The children live in a garret in the Calle de la Ternera, Purita
in a lodging house, where she is freer and can get telephone
messages. About noon every morning Purita goes to see them.
Occasionally, when she has no date, she has lunch with them;
at the lodging house they keep her lunch for her so that she can
have it instead of supper if she likes.

Señor José has had his hand down the girl's low neck for some
time.

"Shall we go now?"

"If you want to."

Señor José helps the girl into her cotton overcoat.

"Only for a little while, eh? The wife's smelling a rat as it is."

"Just as you like."

        ✲   ✲   ✲   ✲

"Here, that's for you."

Señor José stows a twenty-five peseta note into Purita's hand-
bag, which has a blue dye that tends to stain the hands.

"May God reward you."

At the door of the room the pair say good-by.

"Tell me, what's your name?"

"José Sanz Madrid. And yours? Is your name really Purita?"

"Yes. Why should I tell you a lie? My name's Pura Bartolomé Alonso."

The two stay there for a brief moment, both staring at the umbrella stand.

"Well, I must go."

" 'Bye, Pepe. Won't you give me a kiss?"

"Yes, dear."

"And listen, do give me a ring as soon as you've news about Paquito."

"Of course, don't fret, I'll ring you up here."

Doña Matilde shouts out to her boarders: "Don Tesi! Don Ventura! Supper's ready!"

The moment she sees Don Tesifonte, she tells him: "I've ordered liver for tomorrow, let's see how you like that."

The captain does not even look at her, his mind is occupied with other things.

"Yes, that young fellow may be right. Hanging about here like a big booby isn't the way to have conquests, and that's a fact."

Doña Montserrat has had her bag stolen during the laying-by of the Holy Host. It's a disgrace, nowadays there are thieves even in church. There wasn't more in it than three pesetas and a few coppers, but the bag itself was still quite good, quite serviceable.

They had already started on the *Tantum Ergo*[1]—which Doña Montserrat's irreverent nephew José María used to sing to the tune of the German national anthem—and the only people left in the seats were a few women who stayed behind to perform their acts of private devotion.

Doña Montserrat was meditating the text she had just read: "This Thursday brings to the soul the fragrance of lilies, and with it the sweet taste of the tears of perfect contrition. In innocence an angel, in penitence rivaling the austerities of the Thebaid . . ."[2]

Doña Montserrat turned her head, and her bag had gone.

At first she hardly noticed it; her imagination was too full of transmutations, apparitions and disappearances.

---

1. *Tantum Ergo*: The last two stanzas of a hymn sung when the Eucharist is borne in procession.

2. *Thebaid*: A Latin epic poem by Statius, which treats of the Seven against Thebes.

At home, Julita puts her notebook away again and, like Doña Matilde's boarders, goes to supper.

Her mother tenderly pinches her cheek. "Have you been crying? Your eyes look a bit red."

Julita answers, with a pout: "No, Mamma, I've been thinking."

Doña Visi smiles with a roguish air. "Of him?"

"Yes."

The two women link arms.

"Won't you tell me his name?"

"Ventura."

"Oh, you sly puss, that's why you picked the name Ventura for the Chinese baby!"

The girl averts her eyes.

"Yes."

"Then you must have known him quite some time?"

"Oh, yes, we've seen each other off and on for the last six or eight weeks."

Her mother turns almost grave.

"And how is it you never told me about it?"

"I didn't want to say anything to you as long as he hadn't declared himself."

"That's quite true. I am silly. You were absolutely right, darling, it's best not to say anything till the moment things are quite clear and settled. Women have to be so careful."

Julita feels a cramp in her legs and a slight sensation of heat in her chest.

"Yes, Mamma, very careful indeed."

Again, Doña Visi smiles and asks: "Tell me, what does he do?"

"He's preparing for an exam as a notary."

"It would be grand if he got an assignment."

"Well, we shall see if he's lucky, Mamma. I've made a vow that I'll light two candles if he gets placed in the first category, and one candle if he only gets into the second."

"Quite right of you, darling. Pray to God and wield the sword. I'll make the same vow myself. But now tell me, what's his surname?"

"Aguado."

"That's rather nice: Ventura Aguado."

Doña Visi laughs excitedly. "Oh, my dear, what a prospect! Julita Moisés de Aguado—have you thought of that?"

The girl has a faraway look. "Oh, yes."

Rapidly, afraid that it may all be a dream and shatter any

moment into as many pieces as a smashed electric bulb, her mother starts to count her chicks before they are hatched.

"And if your first-born is a boy, Julita, then we'll call him Roque after his grandfather. Roque Aguado Moisés. What a joy that would be! Oh, when your father hears of this, how pleased he'll be!"

Now Julita has reached the other side, has crossed her river, she speaks of herself as of another person; nothing else matters to her but her mother's simple candor.

"If it's a girl, I'll call her after you, Mamma. Visitación Aguado Moisés doesn't sound so bad either."

"Thank you, darling, oh, thank you. I'm so touched! But let's pray for a boy; there's always a great need for men."

Again the girl feels her legs trembling. "Yes, Mamma, there's a great need."

With her hands clasped over her stomach, her mother says: "Just think—perhaps God will grant him a vocation."

"Who knows?"

Doña Visi lifts her eyes to the heights above. The ceiling, the room's smooth sky, shows several damp patches.

"All my life I have longed to have a son who's a priest."

At this moment, Doña Visi is the happiest woman in Madrid. She takes her daughter by the waist—very much like Ventura does when they are at Doña Celia's—and sways her to and fro like a small child.

"Maybe it will be my grandson, pet. Perhaps it will."

Both women laugh, locked in a tender embrace.

"Oh, I do so want to live to see it!"

Julita means to improve on her handiwork.

"Yes, Mamma, life's full of delightful things."

She drops her voice, giving it a muted, solemn fall.

"I do believe my meeting with Ventura"—there is a faint buzzing in the girl's ears—"has been my good fortune."

Her mother chooses to sound the note of common sense.

"We shall see, darling, we shall see. Pray God you're right. We must have faith in Him. Yes—why shouldn't it be so? A little grandson who shall be a priest and edify us all by his example! A great orator in the pulpit. It sounds like a joke now, but one day we may well read an announcement of spiritual exercises conducted by the Reverend Father Roque Aguado Moisés. I would be an old woman by then, but my heart would be bursting with pride!"

"And mine too, Mamma."

Martin quickly recovers and walks on, proud of himself.

"A good lesson for her. Ha, ha!"

Martin quickens his step. He is almost running, sometimes he is giving a little hop.

"I wonder what that wild sow has got to say after this."

The wild sow is Doña Rosa.

On reaching the Glorieta de San Bernardo, Martin remembers the present for Nati.

Perhaps Rómulo is still in his shop. Rómulo is a secondhand bookseller who sometimes has an interesting print in his cubbyhole.

Martin makes for Rómulo's lair, turning down to the right after the university.

On the door hangs a notice that says: "Closed. Messages to be handed in at the back door." The light is on in the shop. Rómulo must be tidying up his papers or sorting out an order.

Martin knocks at the small back door that leads into the courtyard.

"Hullo there, Rómulo."

"Oh, hullo, Martin. How nice to see you."

Martin produces his cigarettes and the two men smoke, sitting close to the brazier which Rómulo has brought out from under the table.

"I was just writing to my sister, the one in Jaén. Nowadays I'm living in this place and don't go out except for meals. Sometimes I don't feel like eating and then I don't stir from here all day long. They bring me coffee from across the street, and that's all."

Martin looks at some books lying on a rush-bottomed chair with its back all to pieces, which is only good to put things on.

"Not much here."

"No, there isn't. This thing by Romanones, *A Lifetime's Jottings,* is quite interesting. It's very rare."

"Oh, yes."

Martin puts the books on the floor.

"Listen, I'd like an engraving, but a nice one."

"How much d'you want to spend on it?"

"Twenty to twenty-five."

"For twenty-five I can let you have one that's quite charming. It isn't very large, I admit, but it's genuine. What's more, it's framed and all that, just as I bought it. If you want it for a present, it's the very thing."

"Yes, it's meant to be a present for a girl."

"For a girl? Well, if she isn't a cloistered nun it's absolutely right, I'll show it to you. But first let's smoke our cigarettes in peace, there's no hurry about it."

"What's it like?"

"You'll see it in a minute. It's a Venus with several small figures underneath, and some verses in Tuscan or Provençal, I don't know which."

Rómulo leaves his cigarette on the table and switches on the light in the passage. He comes back immediately with a frame which he wipes with the sleeve of his overall.

"Look."

The print is attractive and it is tinted.

"The coloring was done at the same period as the print."

"It looks like it."

"Oh, yes, there's no doubt about that."

The engraving shows a fair-haired Venus, completely naked and with a wreath on her head. She is standing, surrounded by a gilded ornamental border. Her tresses flow down her back to her knees. On her belly there is a drawing of the four points of the compass; it is all highly symbolic. Her right hand holds a flower, her left hand a book. Her body is outlined against a blue, starry sky. Still within the ornamental border, but lower down, are two small circles, the one underneath the book containing the sign of Taurus, the one underneath the flower, the sign of Libra. The bottom part of the engraving shows a meadow surrounded by trees; two musicians are playing, one the lute and the other the harp, while three couples, two seated and the third sauntering, are deep in conversation. In the upper corners two angels are blowing with puffed cheeks. Right at the bottom are four lines of unintelligible verse.

"What does it say here?"

"It's written on the back. I got Rodríguez Entrena to translate it for me, you know, the professor at the Cardinal Cisneros Institute."

The pencil note on the back reads:

> Venus, passion's grenade, sets afire
> Gentle hearts that music doth inspire,
> Through the joys of dance and lazy play
> Leading them to love the sweetest way.

"Do you like it?"

"I love that sort of thing. The great charm of all such verse is its vagueness, don't you think?"

"I entirely agree."

Martin takes out his packet of cigarettes again.

"You're well off for tobacco."

"Today, yes. Some days I haven't got a shred and have to pick up the stubs my brother-in-law leaves about, as you well know."

Rómulo gives no answer, it seems the wiser course to him. He knows that Marco loses his head when he touches the subject of his brother-in-law.

"For how much will you let me have it?"

"Well, let's say twenty. I told you it was twenty-five, but if you give me twenty, it's yours. I paid fifteen for it and it's been sitting on the shelf there nearly a year. Is twenty all right for you?"

"Good, give me five pesetas change."

Martin puts his hand in his pocket. For an instant he stays still, frowning as though in thought. He pulls out his handkerchief and spreads it on his knees.

"I'd swear I had it in here."

He gets up.

"I can't understand . . ."

He searches in his trouser pockets and turns out their linings.

"Well, that's torn it. It's the last straw."

"What's the matter with you?"

"Nothing. I'd rather not think about it."

Martin looks through the pockets of his jacket, takes out his old, dilapidated wallet stuffed with his friends' visiting cards and newspaper cuttings.

"That's finished me."

"Have you lost something?"

"The twenty-five pesetas . . ."

Julita has a queer sensation. At times she feels something like a depression, and at times she has to make an effort not to smile.

"The human brain," she thinks, "is by no means a perfect instrument. If one could read the thoughts in people's minds like a book. . . . No, it's better as it is, it's better we can't read anything and don't understand one another except for the things we choose to say, even if they're all damn lies!"

Occasionally Julita likes to use strong words when she is alone.

They walk along the street hand in hand, looking like an uncle with his niece whom he takes out for a walk.

As she goes past the porter's lodge, the girl turns her head away. She is so absorbed in her thoughts that she fails to see the first step of the staircase.

"Take care, don't hurt yourself."

"No."

Doña Celia comes to open the door.

"Good evening, Don Francisco."

"Hullo, my dear. Let the girl go in, I want a word with you first."

"Certainly. Go in there, my child, and sit down where you like."

The girl sits down on the edge of an easy chair with green upholstery. She is thirteen years old and her breasts are small and pointed, like tiny roses about to burst the bud. Her name is Merceditas Olivar Vallejo; her girl friends call her Merche. She lost her whole family in the war. Some are dead, others in exile. Merche lives with her grandmother's sister-in-law, an old lady swathed in lace and painted like a monkey; she wears a wig and her name is Doña Carmen. Among her neighbors Doña Carmen is known by the unpleasant nickname of "Old Corpse hair." The children in her street prefer to call her the "Grasshopper."

Doña Carmen has sold Merceditas for five hundred pesetas, and Don Francisco, the one with the popular clinic, has bought her. She told the man: "First fruits, Don Francisco, first fruits. A carnation in bud."

And to the girl she said: "Look, child, all that Don Francisco wants is just to play. Anyway, it's got to happen one day, don't you see?"

The Moisés family has a gay time at supper tonight. Doña Visi is radiant, Julita all smiles, almost blushing. Inside her head, her thoughts go marching on.

Don Roque and his other two daughters have caught the infection of gaiety, without knowing the cause. Only at certain moments does Don Roque recall the words Julita said to him on the stairs: "From . . . from the photographer's." And then the fork trembles between his fingers; until this is over, he dare not look at his daughter.

*　*　*　*

After she has gone to bed, Doña Visi takes a long time to go to sleep. Her head seems to be spinning round the one subject.

"Do you know our girl has got herself a young man?"

"Julita, you mean?"

"Yes, and he's going to be a notary."

Don Roque turns over between the sheets.

"Now, don't you set the bells ringing yet. I know you're fond of giving out every piece of news straight away through the town crier. Let's first wait and see what comes of it."

"Oh, but you always pour cold water on everything!"

Doña Visi's sleep is full of sweet dreams. After several hours she is wakened by the sound of a small bell that calls a convent of poor nuns to the first prayer at daybreak.

Doña Visi is in a mood to see in everything good omens, happy auguries, and reliable signs of joy and future blessings.

Translated by J. M. Cohen

José María Gironella

(1917-   )

Born in Gerona, the setting for his most famous novel, Gironella attended a seminary but soon decided he had no calling for the priesthood. He held a variety of positions from bank messenger to bookseller. During the Civil War he fought on the Nationalist side. Nevertheless, he lived among the Spanish refugees in France for a time. He wrote some poetry, but his fame came with the publication of his first novel in 1946, *A Man*, which won the Nadal Prize. In 1948 *The Tide*, an anti-German work about man's inhumanity to man, caused him some unpopularity. He published his best-known novel, *The Cypresses Believe in God*, the first part of a long trilogy about the events leading up to the Spanish Civil War, the War, and its aftermath, in France in 1952. This novel deals with the period before the War, and it was published without difficulty. The second and third volumes were banned for several years.

Gironella seeks in the first volume the causes of the outbreak of fighting and introduces us to Ignacio Alvear of Gerona and to his family and friends. We meet aristocrats, conservatives, liberals, communists, and anarchists, as Gironella objectively (he claims) tries to analyze the psychology of the Spanish people. The second volume, *A Million Dead* (1961), continues the saga of the middle-class Alvear family. Ignacio's parents are Franco supporters. Ignacio faces a difficult decision in trying to choose between tradition and his sweetheart on the one hand and his need for a kind of regeneration on the other. He finally decides to fight at the front, first with the Loyalists and then with the Nationalists. The third volume, *Peace Has Broken Out*, published in 1966, covers the events of the Post Civil War period.

Gironella holds out the hope for moderation and spiritual solace in his work. It remains to be seen whether or not he achieves his stated aims of making this trilogy a definitive reply to all foreign works written about the Spanish Civil War as well as a "chronicle for the Spaniards themselves, so poorly endowed to encompass without passion the totality of the events." He has, however, amply succeeded in another endeavor. that of attempting to "capture the everyday traits, the mentality, the inner ambience of my compatriots in all their pettiness and all their grandeur."

The selection used is Chapter 24 of Part II of *The Cypresses Believe in God* and covers the historical period between November 22, 1933 and October 6, 1934.

The Cypresses Believe in God

CHAPTER 24

When Carmen Elgazu saw the can of anchovies Ignacio had brought her, she let out a squeal of admiration. "What a present, son!" She weighed it up and down in her hand. "Over two pounds! And they know how to prepare them so well in San Felíu!"

"We've got enough for all winter."

"What do you say, shall we open it?"

Matías blew out a puff of smoke. "I'm in favor."

"Me, too."

"Me, too."

"The ayes have it."

"Wait a minute," said Ignacio. "There are other things."

He opened his suitcase. Fishhooks of all sizes and shapes, a roll of line specially recommended by the owner of the boat *Ana María*.

Matías half-closed his eyes, which was his way of making them laugh, and looked into the suitcase. "Let's see, let's see! Gosh all fishhooks, son, these are real presents!"

Pilar was watching everything. Shirts, soap, handkerchiefs, more fishhooks . . . "Where's my present?"

Ignacio bit his lips. He looked at her roguishly, to gain time, as though implying that he had a surprise. Finally he said: "Don't think I forgot," closing the suitcase, "but I thought: it will be better if she tells me what she wants."

Pilar was frankly disappointed. She shrugged her shoulders disconsolately. "Never mind, it doesn't matter."

Carmen Elgazu spoke up: "She would have liked something from San Felíu, you know."

Matías, still examining the line, poured oil on the troubled waters. "No lamentations, now. Let Pilar say what she wants and Ignacio will go right out and buy it."

"Nothing, it doesn't make any difference."

"Don't be stubborn."

The girl finally gave in. Biting her finger, she asked: "You'll really buy it for me?"

"Of course I will."

"Well then—" She paused a moment. "How much do you want to spend?"

"That's a good question." Ignacio smiled and took out his wallet, which was flat.

"Have you got enough for a pair of green sandals?"

"How much do they cost?"

"The ones I like are twelve fifty."

"Good enough."

César looked at Ignacio and said: "Before you go out, look in your room. What's on the bed is from all the family. What's on the night table is from Pilar and me."

Ignacio scratched his nose. He did not know whether César was in earnest or not. Carmen Elgazu winked at him, and in a couple of strides he was at his door, the whole family behind him. On the bed lay all his first-term law textbooks.

The boy stood looking at them, not knowing what to say. Then he went over to the night table: there was a little image, about ten inches high, of St. Ignatius Loyola.

He ran his fingers through his hair and turned toward his family. "Study and pray, isn't that it?" There was a silence. "Come on, Pilar. Let's go get those sandals."

Besides his family, several other people were eagerly awaiting Ignacio's return.

First, Don Emilio Santos, to tell him that it was a fact that his son Mateo would be coming to Gerona in October, to help him in the *Tabacalera* and to study law.

Second, the teller of the Arús Bank. The news of the children of the strikers of Zaragoza who had been distributed among families in Barcelona had given him and his wife, who lived alone, an idea: they would adopt a child from the orphanage. They had talked it over with their brother-in-law, the Izquierda Republicana deputy, Joaquín Santaló, and he had approved of the plan and had helped with all the legal details. They had gone to the orphanage and chosen a boy about eleven, by the name of Paco, whom they had liked because everyone had told them that he was highly gifted at drawing. They were going to send him to the School of Fine Arts. Ignacio would have to meet him. It was touching to see how hard Paco tried to adjust himself to his new home, without quite managing it yet. When he did he would be completely happy, as the teller and his wife already were.

Then—Doña Amparo Campo was waiting for him. She had been practically alone the whole summer, with Julio running hither and yon, a briefcase under his arm. And the Police Commissioner had not been dismissed, so the excuse Julio had given her for not taking a vacation was probably just an invention. "I'll never forgive him for that, Ignacio. Thank God I've got friends like you who come to see me once in a while."

"Friends—?"

"Yes. Dr. Rosselló from the hospital often comes, and the architect Ribas. Very refined people."

Besides all these, they were waiting for Ignacio at the bank. He got in from San Felíu Sunday night and he had to be at work at the bank on Monday. Heavens, what a change of scene! It all seemed so strange to him—the faces, the face of the assistant manager, Tower of Babel, Cosme Vila, the electric fans, the messengers squaring their shoulders for the sacks of money.

He hardly recognized his creaking chair, his desk covered with papers. All those ink spots on his desk! He had never noticed them before.

Ignacio missed swimming so much that he decided to go to the swimming pool in the afternoons, taking advantage of the fact that they would have a short work day until September 15, thanks to the UGT. There he saw El Responsable's daughters, who gave him an ironic look. And El Cojo and El Grandullón. Blasco was in San Felíu. El Rubio, whom they now called "Goat," did not go around with them any longer. El Responsable never went to the pool. Ignacio paid no attention to their looks. And as his mother had forbidden him to go to the pool, he told them at home that he went swimming in the Ter.

With what ease Ignacio lied now! He had come back from San Felíu completely changed. Time was silting over in his memory all the good examples he might have brought back with him. All he remembered were those which upset his spirit: Olga's neckline, the boys smoking in bed, the summer visitors pushing their way through the Esperantists.

He could not say why, but his resentment at having to leave San Felíu when so many *señoritos* were staying on as long as they liked seared him deeper and deeper. He had not even deigned to give the spires of San Felíx and the Cathedral a friendly look. He was irritable at the table. Without knowing why, he made Pilar his whipping boy. He teased her until she was in a rage. But the girl gave him as good as she got. She revenged herself by pinching him and telling him that hair worn in coils over the ears was ridiculous and completely out of date.

Ignacio managed to calm his nerves at such moments by concentrating his thoughts on his family: his father fishing in the Ter with the new tackle he had brought; Carmen Elgazu, so pleased with the can of anchovies; Pilar with her green sandals; and César, who was away from home all day. But the bank and its monotonous routine burned him up. For that reason he liked going to the swimming pool, where he could swim and see exciting necklines. There were times when he thought he must avoid being alone with Doña Amparo Campo at all costs.

He noticed that a kind of slackness had come over him. In bed he lay sprawled full-length, his legs wide apart, claiming that the nights were stifling. His laughter was noisy, his gestures were exaggerated. His textbooks lay piled up in the corner.

At the barbershop, when he walked in, the barber from Málaga slapped him on the back. He wondered at this familiarity. "How little respect I must inspire!" he thought. He went to the Cataluña Bar, and nothing said by the new patrons who had invaded the café—football-players and taxi-drivers—hurt his ears.

At times he tried to efface the memory of Ana María from his mind completely. Again, he would sit on a bench in the Dehesa and with equal tenacity evoke her image and, in all their details, the days they had spent together. He had not written to her. He had not yet written to her. He liked something about the situation that his silence created.

The heat had people overpowered, unable to think. Everybody moved languidly. The city was practically defenseless. The Oñar smelled bad. Its principal water-supply was the sewers.

Little by little several silhouettes possessed his mind. There were the cars of the summer visitors to San Felíu. He saw them rolling majestically along, the tops down, and in them men dressed in white, wearing odd eyeshades, and dark beauties with sun glasses. They were rich, they were the rich who in one day at the Casino spent more than all his books cost. They went into the stores laughing, poking fun at the owner or the clerks, paying and looking disdainfully at what they had bought, giving the impression that they had bought it because, at the moment, they felt like it, and that very possibly they were going to throw it away at once. Sometimes, to amuse themselves, they bargained over the price. They haggled about a penny and insisted that around the corner they could get the thing cheaper. The earnest efforts of the clerks to assure them that they were mistaken seemed to feed their vanity. In the end the women would pat the clerks on the arm as though tired out. "Now, don't be silly. It doesn't matter that much."

They lived completely apart from the people of the town. There were families who had spent the summer in San Felíu year after year and knew nobody in the town. Ignacio asked himself if that was why there were Esperantists there, and whether that cork-cutter would have committed suicide if he had found understanding and human warmth in one or two of the factory-owners.

David and Olga, who were back, assured him that complaining was futile, and that only Socialism could solve the situation, for it would give the downtrodden means of defense. And yet what did the word "socialism" mean? There were so many kinds of socialism. Did it mean doing away with the restricted zone? In that case Ana María would not bathe there, nor Major Martínez de Soria. They would go to one of those small, hidden beaches which could be seen from the hermitage of Sant Elm. All right, then they would drive them away from there. Well and good, they would build their own private pools, and if one day the stream began to empty workingmen into the pool, they would withdraw to their kitchen and bathe in a washbasin, as he had when he was three years old. In any case, fusion would never be achieved—there would be no mixing, to the delight of Don Jorge and his theories.

Why was he thinking all this when Ana María had so effortlessly consented to mingle with him, a bank clerk? . . . True, but that did not alter things. Ana María was completely at ease wherever she found herself, barelegged, running, diving, coming out of the water, while he had to be constantly on guard to keep from seeming common.

The rich, the rich! This was now his obsession. It gave him great satisfaction at the bank to ask the bookkeepers how much the wealthy families had in their accounts. Cosme Vila had the information jotted down in a notebook. The bookkeepers had told him, in spite of the fact that they were forbidden to divulge this information. Cosme Vila even claimed to know the value of the jewels the rich families kept in their safe-deposit boxes. Though that seemed impossible, for how could he open them?

All at once it made Ignacio feel good to be working in the company of people of his own social class. It gave him pleasure to think that all these people and their relatives shared his concerns, and that the excitement over a can of anchovies would have been the same in any of their homes. A sense of solidarity awoke in him. Among people of the same class, words have the same meaning. All of them knew what they were talking about. But at San Felíu, when one of those *señoritos* remarked: "That's the rind"—what did he mean?

Each of the bank employees had the account of his summer to relate. Several of them, like Tower of Babel, came back with new skin. The skin working at the bank was different, though the people were the same. In a word, skin was not important.

But the prize story was Cosme Vila's. Cosme Vila had gone off on a honeymoon with the daughter of the railroad-crossing watchman. He called her his "companion." His words were reminiscent of those used by David and Olga, but more despotic. David and Olga had recorded their union at the City Hall; Cosme Vila had not even done that. The girl's parents had been willing, so he and his companion had taken the train to Barcelona. There, according to Cosme Vila, they had seen various shows and had drunk lots of orgeat, which his companion loved. She had slept a lot. He had talked a lot with Comrade Vasiliev, an intelligent member of the Communist Party, and they had come home. Now they lived together and were expecting a child. No wedding presents or buying a dining-room set or a bedroom suite or lamps. Nothing bourgeois about their home. Austerity. He had forbidden his companion the use of cosmetics; but if she wanted to get her hair done, she could go to the barbershop he went to, the one with the pictures of Marx, Lenin, and Stalin, where the separation of the sexes had been done away with.

"Come and visit us some time and you'll see," Cosme Vila said to Ignacio. "But no," he added. "No matter what you do, you'll always be a bourgeois. You don't realize that some day this is all going to end. If they tell you that three hundred million people in China are starving, or in India, or Africa, or South America, it doesn't make a dent on you. You think that all you have to do is go to confession every so often and everything will be fixed up."

The orbit described during the day by Ignacio's mind, submitted to tests of this sort, and his own state, was obsessive. The result was that he did not write to Ana María, that he went on not writing. And that César looked at him somewhat fearfully.

The one counterweight that exercised any influence on him was the image of St. Ignatius that César had given him, which from its place on the night table presided over his room. It was impossible to enter the room without instantly encountering the eyes of the saint. The statue became a positive nightmare for Ignacio because the eyes not only looked at him when he came into the room, but followed him implacably wherever he went. They even watched him in the dark. It was a well-known optical phenomenon, but if it had only happened somewhere else! It was awkward to be thinking about El Responsable's daughters in their blue and yellow bathing suits with St. Ignatius's eyes looking into his.

He would gladly have turned the image to the wall. Because, in addition to the eyes, there was something else. The history of the saint, which César had rapturously told him, made him even more nervous: "a nobleman, an officer, founder of the Jesuits." *Company* of Jesus, *General* of the Order; he had left a military touch on everything. Allowing for differences, it reminded Ignacio of Major Martínez de Soria's fencing classes. Not to mention the fact that, in the opinion of all, it was the Jesuits who at the moment directed the policies of Spain, and that that was why there was talk of revolution.

But—he couldn't touch the image. For César adored it and was in love with the saint.

"Think of it, Ignacio," he said, "he wrote the *Spiritual Exercises.* And everything he accomplished was based on two virtues: obedience and action. And as though that weren't enough, he was from the province of Guipúzcoa!"

This last argument impressed Ignacio. For he knew that Carmen Elgazu had named him in fulfillment of a vow: "If my first child is a son I'll call him Ignacio in honor of the saint of Loyola," the Basque saint par excellence.

Matías Alvear had spent his vacation in Gerona fishing in the Ter. He had had the same time off as Ignacio. Twice he had taken his wife, César, and Pilar along, and they had eaten supper seated on the ground beside the river. Carmen Elgazu had made many admiring remarks about the scenery, the green of the trees and the grass, the water that flowed rushing by, the incredible colors of the sky toward Rocacorba and over the Cathedral. She had complained only a little about the mosquitoes, the absence of Ignacio, and the presence of the athletes who were strolling about, half-naked, and with handkerchiefs knotted at the four corners on their heads. It horrified Carmen that Pilar should be seeing all that, and besides she could not bear those knotted handkerchiefs. She said it made them look like devils or those wicked creatures that lived in the woods.

"Satyrs?" Matías suggested with a smile.

"That's it. That's what they are."

The handkerchiefs had very little effect on Pilar. She loved those country excursions, though she would have liked to ask several of her new friends at the dressmaking establishment to come with them. For she now had new friends, older than Nuri, María, and Asunción, whom she had not seen since the close of school, for they too had said good-by to the nuns; and besides they had left on their vacations at once. But she hardly missed them. With the older girls she had met at the sewing-room she had discovered new worlds. The things she heard from them interested her much more. There were times when her mother was wrong. Several of the girls at the shop liked men who wore handkerchiefs knotted at the corners on their head.

Pilar had been well received at the dressmaking establishment, which was run by two devout old maids—the Campistols—who always said they had never married because they were afraid of men. Their workroom was located over a herbalist's shop, on the way to San Félix. Because of this the girls frequently employed medicinal terms. "Come now, what you need is a cup of camomile tea." This remedy had been suggested many times to Pilar, whose education at a convent school at times made her the butt of their jokes.

But she was well received, because she was "cute." They found her very cute and very likable. And she did everything she could to make herself agreeable. Besides, there was Ignacio. On her second day there she took along some pictures of Ignacio, and that caused a flutter in the workroom, shocking the modest Campistol sisters. Two or three of the girls knew Ignacio by sight. "Pilar, see if you can fix me up with your brother."

"I'll do what I can, but I don't know. As he's going to study law—"

The conversations in the workroom influenced Pilar as those in the bank had affected Ignacio. The things she learned! When the two old maids were around, they all sewed quietly, and at the end of the afternoon they said the rosary. But when the two of them stepped out—the talk was of movies and dances. Pilar was so glad she had had her adventures, thanks to her operations on the stock-market. For if she hadn't, she would never have seen a movie and would have felt like a fool. Those who had sweethearts were cross-questioned about every detail of their relationship. They said to Pilar: "What did you do at the Sisters'? You're not going to tell us you didn't go walking with the boys at the Institute!"

The season, the oppressive heat, the smells that came up from the herbalist's shop, and the quiet of the workshop in the after-noon induced a special state of lassitude which was a fertile field for such ideas. Pilar's attention had been attracted by two sisters who were dark, wore long earrings, always brought their lunch wrapped in sheets of *El Demócrata,* and talked about the custom-ers the way Cosme Vila talked about the clients of the Arús Bank, and announced that there would soon be a revolution. It seemed that their father and brother were "revolutionaries." Pilar did know what party they belonged to, but she could see them: blue cover-alls, blackened hands, caps or berets jammed down to their eye-brows. They often criticized the officers, too, calling them *chulos,* especially a certain Lieutenant Martín. There were other girls who said: "I'm going to tell you something. A lieutenant wouldn't have to crook his finger twice at me." As Pilar bit off her thread, she thought to herself that there was something very attractive about a man in uniform.

Two of the girls sang in the choral society. The others belonged to the group of *sardana*-dancers known as "La Tramontana," which had won first prize in the last contest. Pilar was very careful to avoid treading on anyone's toes about regional matters. The first day she went to work, her father had warned her solemnly: "No arguments, you understand. So Catalonia is the best place? All right, it's the best."

César, who had improved greatly in health under Carmen Elgazu's care, divided his time among the Calle de la Barca, the Museum, and the Bernat factory.

He was kept busy at the Museum, for Mosén Alberto was sick. The priest was bothered a lot by his stomach, and that month of August he felt really sick and had to stay in bed. And it was when he was sick that the man really showed the stuff he was made of: he kept right on working in bed. He wrote all day long. Catechisms, articles, and the study of old manuscripts. And he tried not to be a burden. He had given orders to his maids that they were not to hover over him all the time. He was also preparing illustrations with the idea of teaching sacred history by means of slides. With a projector that he would buy on installments, he would visit all the schools of the city. "We have to use modern methods," he said.

It impressed César very much to see Mosén Alberto in bed enveloped in a white nightshirt. Priest and cassock were synonymous in his mind. There was something effeminate about Mosén Alberto in a nightshirt, with his sloping shoulders and his neck bare, showing the blue veins. Fortunately, plenty of hair showed over the top button.

Mosén Alberto said to César that it was necessary to be on the alert, for great events were in the making. "As soon as everybody is back from vacation . . ." The thing that distressed him most was not being able to say Mass. "You can't think what it means to a priest not to be able to officiate at Mass." He could shave himself, but he could not say Mass. Noguer the notary, who was back in town, came to see him, as did other priests, and people from his village of Torroella. On Saturdays some of the peasants came bringing him messages from his mother. César met a young priest at Mosén Alberto's, Mosén Francisco, who had taken the place in San Félix parish of the one who had gone to Fontilles to look after the lepers. Mosén Francisco resembled his predecessor. He wore a big broad-brimmed hat, which seemed to rest on the eaves of his ears. He was short and square, walked with long strides, and exuded vitality. He put his soul into every word. He knew César from seeing him in the Calle de la Barca. "Wonderful," he said to him. "I know the good work you are doing."

But César was worried about Ignacio. He had noticed the change the minute his brother got back from San Felíu. He watched Ignacio sprawl on the bed or gulp his milk at one swallow. And then go through those thousand and one daily acts about the house which César felt so important—pulling his chair up to the table, walking past his mother, opening the window, tearing a sheet off the calendar—absent-mindedly and as though routine. What was Ignacio thinking about? What could be more important than the immediate thing, than the contact with the people and objects with which one lives?

César was discreet and managed to avoid intruding himself. He did not talk to Ignacio about the Catholic Epistle of St. James the Apostle, nor even of what he was reading at the moment, selections from St. Teresa of Ávila, St. John of the Cross, and Fray Luis of Granada. Ignacio had cut him short from the start, saying that it took a special frame of mind to read the Spanish mystics. "Go to San Felíu for two weeks or to the swimming pool for an afternoon and you'll understand what I mean."

César had talked about Ignacio with Mosén Francisco, the new priest of San Félix; he knew it was no good mentioning the matter to Mosén Alberto. And Mosén Francisco had said to him: "Son, summer is a terrible time. I don't know how to control people's imagination in the summer. When you have charge of the confessional, you'll realize what it is."

"Good God," thought César, "why doesn't it snow, why don't we get a cold wave from the Pyrenees or the Alps?"

The seminarian took communion every day for Ignacio's sake. "Father, cleanse from my brother's mind every thought that is not pleasing to You, restore to him that joy of Christmas time, of the New Year. Remember that he has his degree now, that his will be a great responsibility."

"Get out, don't be foolish," Ignacio said to him at times. "I'm not so bad as you think." But at other times he could not control himself and made some cutting remark.

One day one of these remarks was so vicious that César cried as never before in his life. Ignacio was stretched out in bed reading and smoking. Suddenly he leaped up. "Take a look at this, César, just read it." And he handed him an article on the relations said to have existed between St. Francis of Assisi and St. Clara. It was a monstrous accusation, a satire that chilled the blood.

The seminarian looked up at Ignacio. "But, do you—?"

Ignacio lay down on the bed again. "I don't know, kid. After all, the saints were men, weren't they?"

César was aghast. An unfamiliar rage possessed him. St. Francis of Assisi! Without knowing what he was doing he rushed at Ignacio, snatched the magazine out of his hands, tore it to pieces, and then gave the mattress on which his brother was lying a kick.

Ignacio was up like a spring, reaching out to grab César by the lapel of his pajamas. There were tears in the seminarian's eyes. At that moment Ignacio caught a glimpse of himself in the wardrobe mirror and let César go. He ran his fingers through his hair, then quickly put on his clothes and left the house, banging the door behind him.

If only the Rambla were the sea! If he could have gone for a midnight swim!

Translated by Harriet de Onís

Juan Goytisolo

(1931-   )

Juan Goytisolo, of mixed Spanish, Basque, and French ancestry, comes from Barcelona. His mother died in a Civil War bombardment by the Franco forces; and Goytisolo, himself, lived in a refugee children's colony, a setting he later employed in one of his novels. He studied law, but he could not adapt himself to the conformity he found in Spanish universities. While still in his twenties he realized that he was unable to accept the empty values of Spanish society, and he went into voluntary exile in Paris, where he currently works for a publishing firm.

Goytisolo, in describing his fiction, said: "Many of those who are now writing novels were only children during the Civil War. With the eyes of children they saw, calmly, atrocious things. They forgot them. But there was a moment in their lives, as they grew up, in which they suddenly remembered them again. And they remembered them more and more, as their bones grew harder and their blood richer." Goytisolo's novels, whether of that past or of current reality, are almost all photographic documentaries. Nevertheless, he rejects the "objectivist" novel as defined by Robbe Grillet and others, for he is involved in the necessity for social reform and social justice and cannot remain aloof. Pío Baroja, Valle-Inclán, Carson McCullers, and Truman Capote have influenced his novels, which examine unhappy children in a land devoured by hunger and hate. As he shows, most of his juvenile delinquents and his abnormal degenerates are a product of the Spanish Civil War and the government that assumed control. Thus, an implicit condemnation of the Franco regime can be read into all of his novels.

His first important novel, *Juegos de manos* (1954), or *The Young Assassins,* treats of a group of unhappy adolescent intellectuals who plan the death of a political official. The young dreamer, David, chosen for the task, is unable to carry it out and pays with his life for his disloyalty to the group. *Duelo en el Paraíso* (1955), or *Children of Chaos,* concerns the death of a youngster whose torturers are other refugee children who have learned about death from their elders. In *The Circus* (1957), a young tough robs and kills one of the town's wealthy citizens. A half-mad character, typical of the personages in Goytisolo's novels, who seeks escape from the unpleasant real world, assumes the blame. *The Undertow* (1958) attacks the lack of social justice, the indifference of the

168

Catholic Church, and the decadence and degradation of a land where words such as "bread," "justice," and "liberty" have lost their significance. *Fiestas* (1958) continues the sordid examination of poverty-stricken people, frustrated idealists, and what it means to a boy to grow up in Spain. *The Island* (1961) leaves the world of children for a corrupt adult world and pictures Spain as an island where husbands and wives deceive one another, where lesbians and homosexuals flourish, and where "virginity has disappeared from the map." *The Feast's End* (1962), in four long stories, examines marital relationships. *Signs of Identity* (1966) is his most outspoken attack on the Franco regime.

Goytisolo has also written a critical study on the novel, a work on Fidel Castro's Cuba, and a series of travel books, done in a personal kind of reporter style, such as *Fields of Níjar* (1960) and *The Chanca* (1962), which examine aspects of the sad reality which Goytisolo views as inevitable in a nation without a soul.

The selection is part of Chapter 3, about halfway through the novel.

The Young Assassins

The light hung from the center of the ceiling, enveloped in a fluted paper shade, rough to the touch. At a sign from Agustín, David turned it off again. The gesture of turning it on had been purely mechanical. The reflex, perhaps, of an impish child.

"Be still," he said.

David obeyed him, looking at him curiously. They had been friends for a long time, and Agustín had never spoken to him like that. He felt filled with uneasiness and tenderness at the same time.

"You have known me a long time," Agustín continued. "I have told you how spoiled I was as a child. It wasn't my fault. My parents loved me too much, and they never dared refuse me anything. I was the only object in life for them; a kind of gift, or surprise, or grace. Three years before I was born my mother had given birth to a little brother, stillborn. My mother had to be sent to a sanatorium. The doctor had said that probably they would never have another child, and when I was, nevertheless, born, everybody received me with cries of joy and much applause.

"They probably still have hundreds of photographs of me at home: the day of my christening, my first steps, in a little sailor suit, by the sea, on the beach, and in the country. My mere existence gave them a kind of wild happiness. They were always taking me to the garden to take my picture. In time my face came to adapt itself to this comedy: all day long, it seemed to wait, patiently, with studied poses, for the click of the camera.

"Long before you knew me I considered myself a privileged character. Any praise, no matter how extravagant, seemed to me the result of careful and accurate thinking. Surrounded by people who smiled at me and flattered me, I floated about like a drunken insect, with the suggestive wings of a butterfly, and although I was coquettish enough to, I pretended not to notice the admiration that I aroused. In reality I lived as in a dream, filled with satisfaction, adorned with medals of a pretended humility, and smiling at everybody as though I were a bashful, timid child.

"Even as a child (it almost makes me blush to admit it), my tastes were already very special, but instead of what usually happens in such cases, my parents took great pains to encourage them. Because of their own artistic bent, they refused to consider it a tragedy that I should devote myself to drawing and to taking piano lessons from an old, half-crazy teacher.

"My father used to paint during the hours he had free from his work; and it was his ambition that I should be a painter. He continually regaled me with boxes of paints, canvases, and palettes. Many an afternoon he allowed me to go with him to his studio, where, seated on a stool, I followed the progress of his brush. He liked to consult me about colors, and when he finished, he would ask me quite seriously for my opinion. On other occasions he would encourage me to draw. He would ask me to make him a still life, a portrait, a water color. For hours I remained absorbed in my work, entirely satisfied. Sometimes, if he liked the picture, he would take it home and show it to my mother. All this may seem absurd, especially if you take into account that I was barely fourteen years old, but it all formed a part of the educational theory by which he was bringing me up.

"As for my mother, she had gotten the idea into her head that I was a great actor: on my sixteenth birthday she gave me a chest filled with costumes, beards, wigs, and masks. In the rear of the house there was a kind of stage where amateur artists would play in benefit performances organized by my mother. There I learned to recite Rimbaud's 'Le Bateau Ivre,' all dressed up in one of my costumes. One day she decided to bring my father, who did not suspect a thing. I recited the poem in its entirety, with all the emotion I was capable of, and when I finished, I discovered

that my parents were both weeping. From then on, it was decided
that I was to be an actor.

"I immediately began my studies in the school of dramatic
art, where I had to undergo a very rigid discipline: forced to
learn by heart abominable texts. But I took advantage of that
experience to recite at home the works that I loved: the doubts of
Macbeth, poems of Blake. I was burning with all sorts of ambitious
projects that I knew would cause astonishment and admiration.
And in my imagination I thought I could hear a chorus of fantastic
applause, distant and diffuse, like a confused humming.

"The continuous tribute that I received from my parents made
me swell with pride. As I said, my mere presence was enough to
give them happiness. In me they saw the unexpected, the mirac-
ulous. As a consequence, I was exempt from any law. Everything
contributed to making me feel that I was different. I listened to
people talk with obvious awe about my talent. Many times when
they thought I was asleep, they talked about the plans that they
were hatching for me, plans that I followed with closed eyes,
while my heart beat rapidly within my breast. Without realizing
it, I was storing up vanity, pretended humility, false love, com-
placency: all that which is generally called good sentiments. My
soul was an absurd mixture of contradictory virtues poorly matched.
And secretly I felt an asphyxiating sensation of ill-being.

"My mother said later that she already knew at that time that
I was condemned, and that my beauty, alas, was the beauty of
the devil. I can't say the same for myself: I didn't know anything.
I did not harbor against my parents any resentment, and their fawn-
ing, pawing devotion rather flattered me. My aim was to please:
I wanted to respond to the hopes pinned on me. It was later, years
later that I realized my narrowness and my oppression. I was
wearing one of the costumes which they had just given me; under
its great folds I felt a completely different being, and just a bit
insolent. Dressed as a Negro, I recited 'Une Saison en l'Enfer'[1]
before the wardrobe mirror in my room. When I reached the invo-
cation of the ancestors, I made the poet's anger my own; I felt
detached from myself and I forgot where I was.

"I admit without humility that I recited the lines quite well,
and I identified myself easily with the subject. Some of the phrases
seemed to spring spontaneously from within me. I was surprised,

---

1. One of the major works of Jean Arthur Rimbaud (1854-91).
(*Editor's note.*)

almost, to see them written down, such was the identity that bound us. The words of the poet had put me in touch with hatred, and its call awakened an ancient echo in my blood.

"As I was saying, my parents dazzled me with the spectacle of their devotion. They courted me, they praised me, they smiled upon me. And suddenly their subservience began to seem distasteful to me. I had never encountered any resistance in our relationship: only acquiescence. I always got what I wanted. Any decision reached by me acquired in their eyes an extraordinary value. They outdid themselves for me alone, and granted me a freedom of choice that no other boy of my age enjoyed. But by giving me the liberty to do what I wished, they were sacrificing themselves for my sake; on the other hand, through their very sacrifice they were actually making me beholden to them. The skein was extremely subtle, and it was not easy to disentangle. Behind the noble words I saw the bribe of love and the cowardice of sacrifice rear their heads. All right, I said to myself, I shall not be the one to surrender.

"My mother, especially, loved me with a tenderness that was truly tyrannical. The dream of her life had been to have a son like me, rebellious, impulsive, and proud; and in my first steps toward liberty I counted on her willing support. I did not bother informing my father, who was less intelligent than she, of the change: he lived locked up in his world, which my mother guarded and which was sufficient to make him happy, but not her. She realized that a personality like my father's was not enough to fulfill her. Tranquillity did not satisfy her. She had a need of company which nothing would satisfy, and she had to have the nearness of a being on which to rest the immense emptiness of her soul.

"I made her the confidante of my first escapades, and my father did not suspect anything, shut in as he was in his little world of glass. We formed between us a kind of society, from which my father was excluded and whose purpose was the revelation of our most intimate secrets. I kept her informed of my first amorous adventures, told her about my nights out, never omitting a single detail. At times my frankness went to inconceivable extremes. But my mother never said anything. She just gave me the money I needed, carefully keeping everything hidden from my father. The fact that I trusted her so much seemed to make her happy. In a way, it was for her a rather elegant manner of being unfaithful to my father.

"Those confidences, at first limited to the realm of my sexual experiences, grew later into my desire for freedom. Little by little I felt a hatred develop in me of everything around me. I was beginning to realize that another's love creates in us a multitude of ties that limit and coerce us. 'Love is soft, sticky, and pawing,' I told her. 'It weakens us and ends up by dominating us.' My mother listened to me without blinking an eyelash, as if nothing I said affected her. Perhaps she imagined that it did not apply to her: that I was talking in the abstract. When I had finished, she urged me to keep my silence: 'That is all very well; but don't ever tell that to anyone. A thought, once repeated, loses its value, evaporates. This must remain between the two of us.'

"Her obstinate love knew no limits: it wrapped itself around me like clothes that are too tight. My confessions, no matter how shameless, gave her one reason more for loving me. She never tried to stop them. She simply accepted them, as she accepted everything mine, without realizing that it was precisely her acceptance which was separating us most. In time I came to encompass her in my hatred, and my words had no other object than to torture her.

"I told her again and again to the point of satiety that my love had disintegrated, that I was looking for the opportune moment to leave her side. I even reproached her for the education I had received, the fruits of which she was feeling: 'There you are, that is what you have brought on yourself. Perhaps if you had been hard, everything would have been different. But now it is too late.' My mother listened to me, her face contracted with pain. All she could do was to bow her head submissively, and to my insults she responded obstinately: 'You are good, but you insist upon hiding it.'

"These conversations, always the same, ended up by tiring me. I found them useless and degrading. 'I don't know what pleasure you can get out of them,' I said to her. 'One would think you enjoy torturing yourself.'

"And my mother, refusing to answer, looked at me with relentless, pursuing eyes. 'Please,' she murmured, 'please; I beg of you.'

"My father, on the other hand, lived deceived to the very end. When he began to understand, it was too late: my mother's zealous vigilance had done its work. It took him suddenly, without giving him time to recover; hence, his defeat was the more deadly. He found himself faced with a consummate fact: the tumbling down of all his castles. And in his stupor he did not even have the strength to say a single word to me.

"I remember that around that time I decided to play a filthy trick on my mother. My father often had models around who posed for him. Most of them were pretty and attractive. There was one in particular, small and insinuating, who fascinated me a good deal. Her body, as harmonious as a statue's, seemed molded out of rubber. I called my father's attention to her, knowing his occasional weakness for women, and I encouraged him to take her on as his mistress. One afternoon at my instigation he made love to her in his studio, and that same evening I hastened to tell my mother all about it. 'Don't be angry with him,' I said to her. 'The whole thing was my doing.' I saw her turn pale, white with anger, but she didn't say a word. Only later when I was going to bed she came to my room, her eyes swollen from crying.

"'You're a beast, Agustín. I would not do a thing like that even to the person I hated most in the world.'

"Her answer made me understand that nothing would ever change her, and on the following day I told them of my intention to leave for Paris. I did it with the utmost brevity, without asking them for their consent. Naturally, they hastened to make it possible. They went immediately to buy my tickets. They overwhelmed me with their preparations. They understood absolutely nothing about my motives, and they hoped to soften me with their affection.

"They knew perfectly well that all their hopes for my future had just come to an end. It was enough to look at them to understand that they felt themselves frustrated and miserable. They asked me if I would write to them, and I answered no. Then they asked my permission to write to me. I replied that they could do so if they got any pleasure out of it, and that as far as I was concerned I saw no reason why they should not. They drove me to the station and during the ride they did not find a word to say. It seems to me now that they already knew that I would not ever go back to them.

"However, they tried not to give up hope. They imagined that Paris, Lisbon, Madrid would mean only stages, and that in the end reality would call me back again to Barcelona. They offered me sufficient money to establish a dramatic-arts school there. Nowhere, they said, could I find such opportunities to get ahead. They promised to let me live the type of life that I wanted to. Oh, they proved themselves absurdly magnanimous. They sacrificed themselves for me up to the very end.

"When I arrived in Paris, about five years ago, I rented a studio, where I began immediately to daub lots of canvases. I knew well

enough that I was no painter of genius, but I did hope to make
myself a place in the theater. However, I ran up against the in-
surmountable obstacle of my accent. Nothing ever came of the
tryouts I had. My voice did not interest anyone. Then I began to
work in a series of incredible places, the kind of jobs with which
American millionaires always start off their careers: newspaper boy,
waiter, elevator boy, dishwasher. On the way back to the studio
I would go marketing. I had rented an electric plate, and every
night I cooked a few strips of bacon and a large pot of coffee.

"I had nothing else to eat, and during the day I felt the walls
of my stomach contract as if they were made of rubber. Also, at
night in bed I suffered from the cold, and to try to get warm I
used to put a pan of water on to boil, and from time to time I'd
dip my hands in it. One day during that time I received a letter
from my mother with a blank check in it. I was stretched out on
the divan (a horrible one with scarlet flowers which I shall never
forget), alone with my hunger and the cold. That blank check filled
me with fury. Almost instantly I wrote my answer, a single word
—which you can imagine—and I ran out and deposited it in the
nearest mailbox.

"A fine rain was falling, and I felt a few drops of it run down
my neck; I was wrapped up in hatred, hunger, and cold, encased
in an impermeable film. I knew that I had just liberated myself
forever, since my only gratuitous act, yes the only one, lay in the
refusal of the money. The hatred that was choking in my throat
gave me back my identity. To have given in to my mother would
have been the equivalent of accepting her moral code. My ability
to refuse the money rescued me, and I believed myself freed at last.

"And in spite of it—how can I tell you, David—I feel dead.
Or what amounts to the same thing: I am bored. For hours at a
time I do nothing but cough and yawn and smoke innumerable
cigarettes. I have to invent alibis to prove to myself that I exist.
Alibis for what, against whom?" In the heavy atmosphere of the
room, his questions seemed to float, thin out, and hang in the air.
"Oh, I know they say I'm a fool. They tell me that I can still go
back. And yet—" his voice had become harsh, and David's heart was
beating violently, "and yet, I do not want to go back. I must burn
my bridges. Cut off the only way out. You understand?"

"Yes." David was breathless. "The coming of age."

"Kill! Kill!"

Translated by John Rust

PART II

Poetry

Rubén Darío

(1867-1916)

The author, a Nicaraguan mestizo whose real name was Félix Rubén García Sarmiento, took the name Darío from one of his great aunts who raised him. In spite of his origin, Darío always considered himself a cosmopolite, more at home in Paris than in his native land. As a leading modernist his sensuous, musical, rhythmic poetry became the most popular of its day and influenced, although briefly, that of Juan Ramón Jiménez, Antonio Machado, and other well-known Spanish poets. Darío served for a time as a teacher, library employee, and finally became a journalist in Chile and then in Argentina where he was a correspondent for *La Nación* of Buenos Aires. He married twice, unhappily, but he found happiness in Spain through his mistress, Francisca Sánchez, who became his spiritual and moral guide and support. His principal visits to Spain occurred in 1892 and again in 1898.

Rubén Darío was one of the great renovators of Spanish poetry. He stressed the evocative power of words, and in his verbal experimentation he employed a variety of metrical forms copied from medieval Spanish sources, from the Romantics, the French Symbolists and the Parnassians. In his early works he concentrated on exotic materials such as palaces or the swan, which became a symbol of the entire movement called Modernism. Although his poetry was emotional, sensual, and musical, it contained a fusion of many other disparate elements, a reflection, perhaps, of his background and inheritance, for he and his poetry were a strange combination of pagan, decadent, bohemian, aristocratic, and Catholic elements.

Probably Darío's three best-known collections of poetry are *Blue* (1888), a mixture of prose and poetry; *Profane Prose* (1896), the height of modernistic, ornamental style; and *Songs of Life and Hope* (1905), less elegant, if still chromatic, poetry, which more profoundly examines ideas and the meaning of life and which tries to express the poet's soul by examining and seeking to understand that of his fellow human beings.

The poems are given in their entirety. The selections "Sonatina" and "Symphony in Gray Major" are from *Profane Prose*. "Portico," "Nightfall in the Tropics" and "Canción of Autumn in Springtime" are from *Songs of Life and Hope*. Although "Nightfall in the Tropics" is from the last-named volume, it is one of his earliest poems, written in 1886, but Darío liked it so much he included it in his later volume.

SONATINA

The Princess mourns—Why is the Princess sighing?
Why from her lips are song and laughter dying?
   Why does she droop upon her chair of gold?
Hushed is the music of her royal bower;
Beside her in a vase; a single flower
   Swoons and forgets its petals to unfold.

The fool in scarlet pirouettes and flatters,
Within the hall the silly dueña chatters;
   Without, the peacok's regal plumage gleams.
The Princess heeds them not; her thoughts are veering
Out through the gates of Dawn, past sight and hearing,
   Where she pursues the phantoms of her dreams.

Is it a dream of China that allures her,
Or far Golconda's ruler who conjures her
   But to unveil the laughter of her eyes?—
He of the island realms of fragrant roses,
Whose treasure flashing diamond hoards discloses,
   And pearls of Ormuz, rich beyond surmise?

Alas! The Princess longs to be a swallow,
To be a butterfly, to soar, to follow
   The ray of light that climbs into the sun;
To greet the lilies, lost in Springtime wonder,
To ride upon the wind, to hear the thunder
   Of ocean waves where monstrous billows run.

Her silver distaff fallen in disfavor,
Her magic globe shorn of its magic savor,
   The swans that drift like snow across the lake,
The lotus in the garden pool—are mourning;
The dahlias and the jasmin flowers adorning
   The palace gardens, sorrow for her sake.

Poor little captive of the blue-eyed glances!
A hundred negroes with a hundred lances,

A hound, a sleepless dragon, guard her gates.
There in the marble of her palace prison
The little Princess of the roving vision,
    Caught in her gold and gauzes, dreams and waits.

"Oh" (sighs the Princess), "Oh, to leave behind me
My marble cage, the golden chains that bind me,
    The empty chrysalis the moth forsakes!
To fly to where a fairy Prince is dwelling—
O radiant vision past all mortal telling,
    Brighter, than April, or the day that breaks!"

"Hush little Princess," whispers the good fairy,
"With sword and goshawk; on his charger airy,
    The Prince draws near—the lover without blame.
Upon his wingéd steed the Prince is fleeting,
The conqueror of Death, to bring you greeting,
    And with his kiss to touch your lips to flame!"

Translated by John Pierrepont Rice

SYMPHONY IN GRAY MAJOR

The sea like a vast quicksilvered glass
Reflects the zinc of the graven sky;
The burnished background of pallid gray
Is flecked with distant birds flying by.

Round, opaque glass, the sun is climbing,
Slow as an invalid weak and worn;
The Triton sea wind rests in shade
Pillowed upon his curved black horn.

Leaden waves moan beneath the pier,
Shifting their swollen expanse of gray.
Upon a cable, smoking his pipe,
A sailor dreams of the misty shores
Of a hazy country far away.

An old sea dog. The fiery rays
Of Brazilian suns have tanned his skin,
The fierce typhoons of the China Sea
Have seen him swig his flask of gin.

Pungent with nitre and iodine,
The sea foam knows the sailor well
From his curls and biceps and ruddy nose
To his canvas cap and blouse of drill.

In the cloud of gray tobacco smoke
He visions a country far away
And a brigantine that spreads its sails
For that warm shore on a golden day.

Tropic siesta. The mariner sleeps.
All is wrapped in the gamut of gray.
Dim and more dim grows the curved horizon
As if it were softened and shaded away.

Tropic siesta. A harvest fly
Plucks his guitar in a senile drone;
On the single cord of his violin
A cricket preludes his monotone.

Translated by Alice Jane McVan

PORTICO

I am the singer who of late put by
    The verse azulean and the chant profane,
Across whose nights a rossignol would cry
    And prove himself a lark at morn again.

Lord was I of my garden-place of dreams,
    The heaping roses and swan-haunted brakes;
Lord of the doves; lord of the silver streams,
    Of gondolas and lyres upon the lakes.

And very eighteenth century; both old
    And very modern; bold, cosmopolite;
Like Hugo daring, like Verlaine half-told,
    And thirsting for illusions infinite.

From infancy, 'twas sorrow that I knew;
    My youth—was ever youth my own indeed?—
Its roses still their perfume round me strew,
    Their perfume of a melancholy seed—

A reinless colt, my instinct galloped free,
    My youth bestrode a colt without a rein;
Drunken I went, a belted blade with me;
    If I fell not—'twas God who did sustain—

Within my garden stood a statue fair,
    Of marble seeming yet of flesh and bone,
A gentle spirit was incarnate there
    Of sensitive and sentimental tone.

So timid of the world, it fain would hide
    And from its walls of silence issue not,
Save when the spring released upon its tide
    The hour of melody it had begot—

The hour of sunset and the hidden kiss;
    The hour of gloaming twilight and retreat;
The hour of madrigal, the hour of bliss,
    Of "I adore thee" and "Alas" too sweet.

And 'mid the gamut of the flute, perchance,
    Would come a ripple of crystal mysteries
Recalling Pan and his old Grecian dance
    With the intoning of old Latin keys.

With such a sweep and ardor so intense
    That on the statue suddenly were born
The muscled goat-thighs shaggy and immense
    And on the brows the satyr's pair of horn.

As Góngora's Galatea, so in fine
    The fair marquise of Verlaine captured me;[1]
And so unto the passion half divine
    Was joined a human sensuality;

1. The marquise represents sensual woman. Galatea, a character in
Góngora's famous poem, "Polifemo," represents the spiritual or divine
woman. (*Editor's note.*)

All longing, and all ardor, the mere sense
And natural vigor; and without a sign
Of stage effect or literature's pretence—
If there was ever soul sincere—'twas mine.

The ivory tower awakened my desire;
I longed to enclose myself in selfish bliss,
Yet hungered after space, my thirst on fire
For heaven, from out the shades of my abyss.

As with the sponge the salt sea saturates
Below the oozing wave, so was my heart
Tender and soft, bedrenched with bitter fates
The world and flesh and devil here impart.

But, through the grace of God, my conscience
Elected unto good its better part;
If there were hardness left in any sense,
It melted soft beneath the touch of Art.

My intellect was freed from baser thought,
My soul was bathed in the Castalian flood,
My heart a pilgrim went, and so I caught
The harmony from out the sacred wood.

O sacred wood! O rumor, that profound
Stirs from the sacred woodland's heart divine!
O plenteous fountain in whose power is wound
And overcome our destiny malign!

Grove of ideals, where the real halts,
Where flesh is flame alive, and Psyche floats;
The while the satyr makes his old assaults,
Let Philomel[1] loose her azure-drunken throats.

Fantastic pearl and music amorous
A-down the green and flowering laurel tops;
Hypsipyle[2] stealthily the rose doth buss
And the faun's mouth the tender stalking crops.

---

1. Philomel or Philomela was the daughter of the king of Athens who
was turned into a swallow. Ovid claimed she was turned into a nightingale. Rubén Darío follows Ovid here. (*Editor's note.*)
2. Hypsipyle: butterfly. (*Editor's note.*)

There, where the god pursues the flying maid,
    Where springs the reed of Pan from out the mire,
The Life Eternal hath its furrows laid
    And wakens the All-Father's mystic choir.

The soul that enters there, disrobed should go
    A-tremble with desire and longing pure,
Over the wounding spine and thorn below,—
    So should it dream, be stirred, and sing secure.

Life, Light, and Truth, as in a triple flame
    Produce the inner radiance infinite;
Art, pure as Christ, is heartened to exclaim:
    "I am indeed the Life, the Truth, the Light!"

The Life is mystery; the Light is blind;
    The Truth beyond our reach both daunts and fades;
The sheer perfection nowhere do we find;
    The ideal sleeps a secret in the shades.

Therefore to be sincere is to be strong.
    Bare as it is what glitter hath the star;
The water tells the fountain's soul in song
    And voice of crystal flowing out afar.

Such my intent was,—of my spirit pure
    To make a star, a fountain music-drawn,
With horror of the thing called literature—
    And mad with madness of the gloam and dawn.

From the blue twilight such as gives the word
    Which the celestial ecstasies inspire,
The haze and minor chord,—let flutes be heard!
    Aurora, daughter of the Sun,—sound, lyres!

Let pass the stone if any use the sling;
    Let pass, should hands of violence point the dart.
The stone from out the sling is for the waves a thing,
    Hate's arrow of the idle wind is part.

Virtue is with the tranquil and the brave;
    The fire interior burneth well and high;
The triumph is o'er rancor and the grave;
    Toward Bethlehem—the caravan goes by!

Translated by Thomas Walsh

NIGHTFALL IN THE TROPICS

There is twilight grey and gloomy
    Where the sea its velvet trails;
Out across the heavens roomy
    Draw the veils.

Bitter and sonorous rises
    The complaint from out the deeps,
And the wave the wind surprises
    Weeps.

Viols there amid the gloaming
    Hail the sun that dies,
And the white spray in its foaming
    "Miserere" sighs.

Harmony the heavens embraces,
    And the breeze is lifting free
To the chanting of the races
    Of the sea.

Clarions of horizons calling
    Strike a symphony most rare,
As if mountain voices calling
    Vibrate there.

As though dread, unseen, were waking,
    As though awesome echoes bore
On the distant breeze's quaking
    The lion's roar.

                                        T. W.

CANCIÓN OF AUTUMN IN SPRINGTIME

Days of youth, my sacred treasure,
Unreturning ye pass by!—

Would I weep?—no tears I measure;—
Then my tears—I know not why!—

My poor heart hath been divided
    In its days celestial here;
There was a gentle maid, unguided
    Through this world's affliction drear;

Like the white dawn was her vision;
    Like the flower her gentle smile;
And her dusky locks elysian
    Seemed of night and grief the style.

I was but a lad unknowing,—
    She, as natural, would play
Through my love's fond ermine, showing
    Herodias and Salomé.

Days of youth, my sacred treasure,
Unreturning ye pass by!—
Would I weep?—no tears I measure;—
Then my tears,—I know not why!—

There was another then, more tender,
    More sensitive, more subtly kind,
More soothing, more delight to render
    Than ever I had thought to find;

But 'neath her gentleness unceasing
    A violent passion was concealed
And through her filmy robe releasing,
    A wild Bacchante was revealed.

To breast she took my young ideal,
    And nursed it softly as a child;
Then slew it, left it sad, unreal,
    Of all its light and trust defiled.

Days of youth, my sacred treasure,
Unreturning ye pass by!—
Would I weep?—no tears I measure;—
Then my tears—I know not why!—

There was another took my kisses
  To be the casket of her flame;
She laughed amid our wildest blisses,—
  Her teeth against my heart-strings came!

Amid the maddest of her passion
  She looked across with wilful eyes,—
As though our fond embrace could fashion
  The essence of eternal skies;

As though our fragile flesh were tying
  The boughs of endless Edens here;
Unmindful that with Springtime dying
  The joys of body disappear.

Days of youth, my sacred treasure,
  Unreturning ye pass by!—
Would I weep?—no tears I measure;—
  Then my tears—I know not why!—

And all the others! In how many
  Lands and climes,—they ever were
Pretexts for a rhyme,—or any
  Notion in my heart astir!—

Vain my search for that high lady
  For whom I have awaited long.
But life is hard and grim and shady,—
  There was no princess, save in song!

In spite of Time's unyielding measure,
  My thirst for love has never died,—
My gray head bends to scent with pleasure
  The roses of the garden-side—

Days of youth, my sacred treasure,
  Unreturning ye pass by!—
Would I weep—no tears I measure;—
  Then my tears—I know not why!—

Mine is still the Dawn of golden treasure!—

                              T. W.

Miguel De Unamuno

(1864-1936)

We have already examined Unamuno's life and novels. His poetic creed, as given by himself, is fairly simple. A poet is one "who disrobes his soul with rhythmic language"; "The poet gives himself"; and "In poetry one never lies, even if he tries to do so." As with many modern Spanish writers genre distinctions are not too meaningful. Many critics find him more of a poet than a philosopher-essayist, the genre which brought him most fame. In essence, all his work is a kind of spiritual and emotional autobiography.

Unamuno's first collection of poetry was published in 1907 under the unoriginal title of *Poetry*. Many of these poems had been written years before their appearance in print. Among his other titles are *Rosary of Lyric Sonnets* (1911); *Rhymes from Within* (1923); *Teresa* (1924); *Cancionero* (1953), his most varied collection, published posthumously; and his generally acknowledged masterpiece, *The Christ of Velázquez* (1920) in blank verse. Supposedly inspired by his contemplation of the painting of Velázquez, this poem involves a complicated symbolic relationship among Christ as the moon, God as the sun, and the Virgin Mary as the earth. The constant quest for immortality and the interplay between life and death, as well as the profound Biblical inspiration, stand out in the author's greatest philosophical and religious poem.

In addition to the note of religious anguish, the desire for faith and immortality, apparent to greater or lesser degree in all his work, the Spanish countryside, its cities and mountains, patriotism, the hearth and the home also appear as themes. Along with Antonio Machado, Unamuno, in spite of his Basque ancestry, became the poet of the Castilian landscape. Unamuno rejected the refined verse of Darío to concentrate on complicated word plays and abstract ideas, but he also wrote warm and personal poetry. If his poetry appears uneven or even rough at times, it continues to impress by its virility, feeling, and spirit.

"Castile," "Salamanca," "Beauty," and "Sleep, My Soul, Sleep," are from *Poetry*. "Sow Your Self!" is from *Rosary of Lyric Sonnets*. These poems are complete. The first fragment of *The Christ of Velázquez* is from Part I; the second fragment, from Part II.

CASTILE

Oh, land of Castile, you do raise me up
to the sky in the rough palm of your hand;
to the sky that burns and refreshes you,
    the sky, your master.

Parched land, sinewy land and land of clear
horizons, mother of hearts and of arms,
the present takes in you the ancient coloring
    of long past glories.

At their outer edges, your bare brown fields
touch heaven with its concave meadow of sky,
the burning sun has its cradle in you,
    its tomb, its sanctuary.

The rounded dome of your space is all summit,
in you I feel myself raised up to heaven,
I breathe here on your desolate waste lands
    air from high mountains.

You are a vast altar, land of Castile,
into your air I shall set free my songs,
if worthy of you to the world they'll come
    down from the uplands.

Translated by Eleanor L. Turnbull

SALAMANCA

Tall grove of towers that as he goes down
back of the trees that embellish the cloudscape
the father Sun of Castile doth touch with
    his golden rays;

Great forest of stone that drew out the history
from the deep recesses of mother earth,
backwater of quietude, I bless thee,
    my Salamanca!

On one side, beyond the slow river Tormes,
thou dost see the dark foliage of the trees,
which like the foliage of thy stone is motionless,
    dense and perennial.

Thus under their eyes the emblem of love
redeems them from their dull studies, for when
the master is silent then do those benches
    tell them of love.

Oh Salamanca, midst thy golden stones
the students in their youth did learn of love
whilst the surrounding fields that hem thee in
    gave juicy fruit.

I keep thy vigorous soul in the depths
of my heart, oh my golden Salamanca,
keep thou then, when my last days shall have come,
    keep thou my memory.

And when the sun as it sinks to its rest
kindles the age old gold that adorns thee,
in thy tongue of eternal herald tell
    what I have been.

E. L. T.

BEAUTY

Sleeping waters,
dense verdure,
stones of gold,
silver sky!

From the water issues dense verdure,
from the verdure
like giant spears of wheat the towers
that etch their gold against the silver
of the sky.
There are four tiers:
the river, above that the trees,
the city tower
and the sky upon which it rests.
And all reposing on the water,
a fluid foundation,
water of centuries,
mirror of beauty.
The city painted on the sky
in motionless light;
all is motionless,
motionless water,
motionless poplars,
quiet towers on quiet sky.
And it is all the world;
beyond there is nothing.
I am alone before the city,
and God entire
breathes between it and me all of his glory.
Its towers rise to the glory of God,
to his glory the poplars,
to his glory the heavens,
and the waters rest in his glory.
Time retires;
the eternal unfolds its bowels;
cares and anxieties are washed
in the motionless waters,
in the motionless poplars,
in the towers painted against the sky,
sea of high worlds.
Repose reposes on the beauty
of the heart of God, which thus opens
to us the treasures of his glory.
I desire nothing,
my will reposes,
my will reclines
its head upon the lap of God

and sleeps and dreams . . .
Resting it dreams
of all this vision of deep beauty.
Beauty! Beauty!
The comfort of sorrowing souls,
sick for loving without hope.
Blessed beauty,
answer to the riddle!
You shall slay the Sphinx,
you rest on self without other foundation;
glory of God, thou art enough for self.
What do those towers desire?
What desires that sky,
what the verdure
and the waters?
Nothing, they have no desires;
their will has died;
they rest on the bosom
of eternal Beauty;
they are words of God free from all
human desire.
They are the prayer of God that cheers
singing to itself,
thus killing all pain.
. . . .

The night falls; awake,
my anguish returns,
and the splendid vision has melted;
once more I am man.
And now, Lord, tell me, whisper in my ear:
so much beauty,
will it kill our death?

E. L. T.

SLEEP, MY SOUL, SLEEP

Sleep, oh my soul, sleep,
    sleep thou and rest,
in the age-old cradle
    of hope; sleep thou,
        sleep!

See the sun of night,
    father of dawn,
'neath the sleeping world
    passes; sleep thou,
        sleep!

Sleep, be not afraid,
    sleep thou, my soul;
thou mayst trust in sleep,
    as in thy home;
        sleep!

On its serene breast,
    fountain of calm,
recline thy head
    if worn; sleep thou,
        sleep!

Thou that dost endure
    this anguished life,
lay thine anguish at
    its feet; sleep thou,
        sleep!

Sleep, for His hand that
    gives life and takes,
is rocking thy worn
    cradle; sleep thou,
        sleep!

"And if from my sleep
  I should not wake . . ."
That anguish alone
  passes in sleep;
    sleep!

"In the depths of sleep
  naught do I feel! . . ."
Sleep that those dreams in
  sleep may be healed;
    sleep!

"I dread the dark sleep
  that has no ending . . ."
Sleep and do not grieve,
  there is a morning;
    sleep!

Sleep, oh my soul, sleep,
  the day will dawn,
sleep, oh my soul,
    sleep!
the morn will come . . .
    sleep!

At last in the cradle
  of hope she slept . . .
she slept, my sad soul . . .
  morn, will it come,
    Sleep?

E. L. T.

SOW YOUR SELF!

Shake off your sadness and your will regain,
inert you may not look on fortune's wheel
that turns and as it passes rubs your heel,
for who would live, in him life now doth reign.

You only nourish thus that mortal pain
of dying slowly, net whose toils you feel;

to labor is to live, the only weal
is work; set hand to plow and sow the grain!

You, as you pass, your very self must sow,
not looking back, not looking on death's strife,
lest the past weigh upon the path to go.

In you no movement, in the furrows life
whose breathing passes not as clouds but rife
with works, whose reaping is the self you sow.

E. L .T.

THE CHRIST OF VELÁZQUEZ

My beloved is white . . .

(*Song of Songs*, v, 10)

Of what art Thou thinking, oh my dead Christ?
And why does that heavy curtain of night,
the abundant black hair of a Nazarite
fall over thy forehead? Thou look'st within,
there where is the kingdom of God, within
Thyself, there where dawns the eternal sun
of living souls. Thy body is as white
as the mirror of the father of light,
the sun, life-giver; thy body is white
as is the mocn, that dead revolves around
its mother, our tired wandering earth;
thy body is white as the host of heaven
of sovereign night, of that heaven as black
as the veil of thine abundant black hair
of a Nazarite.
                For Thou art the Christ,
the only Man who did willingly die,
the conqueror over death, that to life
through Thee was elevated. And since then
through Thee that death of thine gives to us life,
through Thee death has been made for us a mother,

through Thee death is the welcome, kindly aid
that sweetens the bitterness of our life,
through Thee, the Man dead, He that does not die,
white like the moon of night. Life is a sleep,
Christ, and death is a vigil. While the earth
is sleeping alone, the white moon keeps watch;
from his cross the Man keeps watch while men sleep;
the bloodless Man keeps vigil, the Man white
as is the moon of the black night; He watches,
the Man who gave all of his blood that men
might know that they are men. Thou didst save death,
thine arms open to the night which is black
and most beautiful, for the sun of life
has looked upon it with his eyes of fire:
for the dark night was made so by the sun,
made so beautiful. And the lonely moon,
the white moon, is beautiful in the star-lit
night that is black as the abundant black
hair of the Nazarite. The moon is white
as the body of the Man on the cross,
that is the mirror of the sun of life,
the sun of life that never, never dies.

Oh Master, the rays of thy quiet light
guide us in the dark night of this our world,
strengthening us with the enduring hope
of an eternal day! Fond night, oh night,
mother of tender dreams, mother of hope,
oh most gentle night, dark night of the soul,
thou art nurse of our hope in Christ the Saviour!

E. L. T.

"It is finished!" Thou didst cry like the roar
of a thousand cataracts, voice of thunder,
like the thunder of an army in combat
—Thou, fighting death to the death—; and thine outcry
overthrew the walls of the new proud Jericho
of the pagans, city of the palm trees
of Greek wisdom, the spiritual Alexandria,
and flung wide to Thee the portals of Rome.

There followed a silence, measureless, mystical,
as if the air with Thee had died, and then
new music surged forth of unearthly sound,
made stormy in the recesses of heaven
by the grief of thy passion. With the tendons
and muscles stretched taut, like strings on the harp
of the sad wood of thy cross, in their torture,
thy limbs emitted at the touch of love
—boundless love—, the triumphant song of life.
It is finished! At last, Death has died!

Thou wast alone with thy Father—and He
face to face with Thee—, glances intermingled
—the blue of heaven and the blue of thine eyes—,
at the sob of immensity, his breast,
the limitless sea of the spirit trembled,
and God, feeling Himself to be a man,
tasted death, solitude divine. Thy Father
desired to feel what it is to die,
He saw Himself for a moment alone
without his Creation, when bowing thy head,
Thou didst give thy human breath to the breathing
of God. To thy last groan responded only
in the far distance the pitying sea!

E. L. T.

Antonio Machado

(1875-1939)

The poet lived in Andalusia until 1883, when his family moved to Madrid, but he was to become the outstanding interpreter of the Castilian soul. He studied at the Institución Libre de Enseñanza and later finished his studies at the University of Madrid. In 1907 he became a teacher of French in Soria, where he became thoroughly enamored with the Castilian spirit. He fell in love and married Leonor Izquierdo, a young girl of sixteen, in 1909. The following year they went to Paris, a city Machado had lived in before, and here he studied under Henri Bergson. Leonor died in 1912, and Machado, unable to face the constant reminder of his loss in the area they both loved, returned to Andalusia where he remained until 1919. In that year he returned to Castile to teach at Segovia. In 1931 he went to Madrid and, unlike his brother Manuel, became an ardent supporter of the Second Republic and its principles. It was in these years that he dedicated his best love poetry to the second great love in his life, a lady known only as Guiomar. In late January 1939, sick in body, mind, and spirit over the defeat of the Republic, this simple, humble poet of the people escaped with his aged mother to Collioure, France, where he died on February 22.

Machado did not write a great deal. In addition to several editions of so-called *Complete Works* from 1917 on, his principal poetry appears in *Solitudes* (1903); *Solitudes, Galleries and Other Poems* (1907), a reworking of the earlier collection; *Fields of Castile* (1912), the spiritual and telluric masterpiece of the Generation of '98 in its evocation of the Castilian soul; and *New Songs* (1924). He produced some penetrating and ironically humorous prose memoirs about the apocryphal professor and critic Juan de Mairena and the equally unreal philosopher Abel Martín. In collaboration with his brother, Manuel, he wrote several dramas.

Machado's poetry appears simple, but the simplicity is deceptive. In spite of his varied meters, he largely rejected verbal pyrotechnics in his search for eternal philosophical, metaphysical, and spiritual values. Rubén Darío described him once as "luminous and profound." Machado's themes include a remembered childhood, the countryside, love, and patriotism. Constant notes, also, in his melancholy and anguished poetry, an anguish whose source he could never fully identify, are existential preoccupations about the passing of time, death, immortality, and his inability to achieve faith in a God he kept on seeking. In this preoccupation he greatly resembles Unamuno whom he admired.

In spite of its suppressed stylistic embellishments, his sober, stoic, simple, and moving poetry contains an eternal appeal. Although he was an enemy of "official" Spain and found identification with all mankind, he continues to be the most influential of all twentieth-century poets, and he may well be the greatest Spanish poetic voice since the seventeenth century.

"Childhood Memory" and "Gloss" are from *Solitudes, Galleries and Other Poems;* "Portrait" and "The Banks of the Duero" are from *Fields of Castile.* "The Crime Was in Granada" was first published in *Ayuda,* Madrid, October 17, 1936. All the selections are given in their entirety.

CHILDHOOD MEMORY

A drab and chilling afternoon
in winter. The class
is studying. Monotony
of rain outside the glass.

The classroom. A chart
shows a fugitive Cain
and Abel dead
beside a crimson stain.

In a sonorous, hollow tone
the master thunders, an old man,
shabby, lean and dry,
holding a book in his hand.

And a whole chorus of children
begins to chant the lesson:
a hundred squared, ten thousand,
a thousand squared, one million.

A drab and chilling afternoon
in winter. The class
is studying. Monotony
of rain outside the glass.

Translated by Willis Barnstone

GLOSS

Our lives are the rivers
that will open on the sea,
which is our dying. Great song!

Among all my poets
Manrique has an altar.

Sweet delight of living:
evil science of dying,
blind flight to the sea.

Beyond the fear of dying
is the joy of arriving.

Great joy!
But the horror of returning?
Great gloom!

W. B.

PORTRAIT

My childhood is memories of a patio in Seville
and a bright orchard where lemon trees ripen;
my youth, twenty years on the soil of Castile;
my life, a few events as well forgotten.

I've never played Lothario or Don Juan's part—
by now you know my plain, almost monkish dress—
yet I was struck by Cupid's intended dart
and I loved wherever I found welcomeness.

Coursing my veins are drops of Jacobinic blood,
but my poetry springs from a quiet fountain;
and in the good sense of the word, I am good,
better than the upright man who holds to doctrine.

I love beauty, and true to modern aesthetics
have cut old roses from the garden of Ronsard;
but I dislike the rouge of current cosmetics,
and am no chirping bird in the latest garb.

I disdain the romances of hollow tenors
and the choir of crickets singing to the moon.
I halt among the echoes of pretenders,
and hear—amid their voices—but one tune.

Am I classic or romantic? I don't know.
I would leave my verse as a warrior his blade:
known for the manly hand that made it glow,
not for the smithy's famous mark or trade.

I chat with the man who goes with me to the end—
who speaks alone hopes to speak to God one day—
my soliloquy is talk with this good friend
who showed me the secret of philanthropic ways.

In the end I owe you nothing. You owe me what I write.
By my work I pay for the house I rent,
the clothes that cover me, my bed at night,
the plain bread that gives me nourishment.

And when the day for my last trip arrives,
and the ship, never to return, is set to leave,
you will find me on board with scant supplies,
almost naked, like the children of the sea.

                                        W. B.

THE BANKS OF THE DUERO

It was near mid-July, a handsome day;
alone, through broken stones I made my way,
slowly searching out corners of shadow.
At intervals I stopped to dry my brow
and give some respite to my heaving chest,
or else, urging my step, forward my body pressed

until fatigued, when in my right hand I took
a leaning stick, a kind of shepherd's crook,
and scaling hills under soaring birds
of prey, I trod strong-smelling mountain herbs—
rosemary, sage, lavender, and thyme.
On the acrid fields fell a sun of flame.

A wide-winged vulture with majestic flight
was crossing alone the sky's blue light.
I discerned a sharp peak beyond distant fields,
and a round hill like an embroidered shield,
and livid crests on the brownish soil—
scattered rags of an ancient coat of mail—
the small bald mountains where the Duero swerves
to form an archer's crossbow curve
around Soria. Soria is a chain of power
linked to Aragon with Castilian towers.
I saw the horizon enclosed by dark knolls
and rimmed with northern and evergreen oaks;
denuded cliffsides and a humble green
where the merinos graze and the bull on its knees
broods in the grass; the borders of the river
where clear summer sun lights the green poplars;
and, silently, some distant travelers,
so minute!—carts, riders, and muleteers—
cross the long bridge, and below the arcades
of stone, waters of the Duero in dark shades
of silver.
          The Duero crosses the oaken heart
of Iberia and Castile.
          O land apart,
sad and noble: high plains, wastelands, and stone,
terrain without plow or streams, treeless zones,
decrepit cities, roads without inns, and throngs
of stupefied peasants, without dance or song,
who from dying hearths still break free,
like your long rivers, Castile, toward the sea!

Wretched Castile, triumphant yesterday,
clad in rags, despising unknown ways.
Does she hope, sleep, or dream? recall the blood
spilt when she had the fever of the sword?

All moves, flows, turns, or races by;
sea and mountain change as well as judging eye.
Has it passed? Over fields the phantom still soars
of a people who placed God above their wars.

A mother once rich in powerful captains,
stepmother now of humble ruffians.
Castile is no more that generous state
of My Cid, who rode with haughty gait,
proud of his opulence and new commands,
endowing Alfonso with Valencian lands;
or of him who gained fame in heroic sport
and begged the mother of soldiers, the royal court,
to conquer the mighty Indian streams;
leaders and warriors of great esteem
bringing gold to Spain in regal galleons—
for booty, ravens; for battle, lions.
Philosophers nurtured on convent salt
impassively ponder the starry vault,
and if as a far rumble in dreams they hear
the shouting traders on Levantine piers,
they will not even trouble to ask their fate.
The wars have already sundered their gate.

Wretched Castile, triumphant yesterday,
clad in rags, despising unknown ways.

The sun is setting. From the distant town
I hear the pulsing bells resound:
old women in mourning go to intone
their Rosary. Two weasels slip between big stones,
see me, run off, and gaping, reappear.
The fields are fading on the somber sphere.
Along the white road an inn, open, alone,
faces the dark fields and a desert of stone.

                                        W. B.

THE CRIME WAS IN GRANADA

I

THE CRIME

He was seen walking between rifles
down a long street,
coming upon the cold field
which still held stars of early dawn.
They killed Federico[1]
when daylight appeared.
The squad of executioners
dared not look upon his face.
All had shut their eyes.
They prayed: Not even God can save you!
Dead fell Federico—

blood on his forehead and lead in his entrails.
. . . Oh, that the crime took place in Granada.
Let all know it! Poor Granada! In his Granada!

II

THE POET AND DEATH

He was seen walking alone with her,
without fear of her scythe.
The sun was already on the towers; hammers
on the anvils, anvils and anvils of the forges.
Federico spoke,
flirting with death. She listened.
"Because the clapping of your dry palms
sounded yesterday in my verse, companion,
and you gave ice to my song and the edge
of your silver sickle to my tragedy,

---

1. Federico García Lorca (1898-1936). (*Editor's note.*)

I will sing you the flesh you do not have,
the eyes you lack,
the hair the wind was ruffling,
the red lips where they kissed you.
Today as yesterday, gypsy, my death,
how good it is alone with you
in these winds of Granada, my Granada!"

III

He was seen walking . . .
                  My friends, build
of stone and dream in the Alhambra,
a tomb for the poet,
over a fountain where water weeps
and says eternally:
The crime was in Granada, in his Granada!

W. B.

Juan Ramón Jiménez

(1881-1958)

Juan Ramón was born in Moguer, a small Andalusian town. He was a sickly, solitary child who went first to a Jesuit school and then studied law in Seville, although he was more interested in painting than in a legal career. In 1899 he went to Madrid, but the death of his father the following year caused him to have a nervous breakdown. He spent time in sanatoriums in France and Madrid between 1900 and 1905, returned to Moguer for almost seven years, and returned to Madrid in 1911. He lived in the Residencia de Estudiantes and became acquainted there with some of the great names in Spanish literature. In 1916 he went to the United States to marry Zenobia Camprubí whom he had met when she was studying at the International Institute for Girls, directed by Susan Huntington. His wife helped protect him from the annoyances of the outside world and also aided in his translation of the works of the Hindu poet Rabindranath Tagore. In Madrid Juan Ramón wrote several collections of poetry and contributed to countless literary reviews. When the Civil War broke out in 1936 the poet and his wife returned to the United States where he taught at several universities. They visited Cuba, Argentina, and Uruguay before returning to Puerto Rico to live. On October 26, 1956, two days before his wife's death, he received the Nobel Prize for Literature.

Juan Ramón's first collection was *Violet Souls* (1900), but it was not until *Sad Arias* (1903) that his work was recognized. *Distant Gardens* (1904); *Platero and I,* the marvelous prose poem about the little donkey of Moguer, written in 1914 and published in a complete edition in 1917; *The Complete Season* (1946); *Ballads of Coral Gables* (1948); and *Animal of the Depth* (1949) are others among his forty volumes. Jiménez started his writing with intangible, vague, sensual, musical, modernistic rhythms, which he soon purified and enriched. He eventually tired of impressionistic and embellished poetry and returned to a kind of pure poetry, which he termed "naked." His complete break with Modernist leanings took place in *Diary of a Recently Married Poet* (1917), after which his poetry became more serious in its preoccupations with life and death.

In addition to his quest for purity and perfection in language, the poet insists on beauty above all things. For this reason, even when his poetry seems to lack a message or even meaning, it conveys a sense of mystery and the transcendental. The themes of anguish and melancholy, which in Machado seem sincere expressions of a Spanish soul, in Jiménez often seem to be deliberately contrived poetic themes. His delicate and refined poetry of sensations, nevertheless, at times strikes sincere notes of human love, ill-defined sadness, death, religious striving, scorn of the everyday world, and a search for a God in whom the poet could never really believe. Juan Ramón's ego involvement stood in the way of Christian humility, and the poet and his production seemed to become the sole object of existence. He himself explained that his search for God involved an emotional encounter, then a reciprocal exchange, an intellectualized explanation, and finally an interiorization in which the poet identified himself with God and, in a sense, became God.

Jiménez saw God and Beauty in nature also, the central descriptive note in his poetic muse. Often it was a description in a subdued tone or, as one critic phrased it, "almost a Chopin nocturne played at twilight." The poet called himself a "mystic of nature," identified himself constantly with it, and animated it and personified it. His delight in nature helped overcome some of his earlier sadness and his eternal terror of death, and one can find, in his nature poems, purity, beauty, tenderness, and peace. His constant quest for beauty as well as his continual reworking of his poems cause some to consider him intellectual and cold, but one may view his poetry as the "controlled spontaneity" of an "esthetic mystic." He claimed that "a poem is never finished, only abandoned," and he remained true to that ideal of studied perfection to the very end.

All selections are complete. "There was no one" is from *Distant Gardens*; "Yellow Spring" is from *Magic and Sorrowful Poems* (1909); "The Last Journey" comes from *Heart in the Wind* (1910-11); "Fleeting Return" is from *Spiritual Sonnets* (1914-15); "Were I reborn," "You Light," and "Fortunate Creature" belong to *The Complete Season,* and "The Best That I Have" is from *Animal of the Depth.*

THERE WAS NO ONE . . .

—There was no one. Water.—No one?
And is the water no one? There
is no one. The flower. Is there no one?
But, the flower, is it no one?
—There is no one. It was the wind.—No one?

But, the wind, is it no one?—There
is no one. Illusion.—Is there no one?
And is illusion no one?

Translated by E. L. Turnbull

YELLOW SPRING

April had come, brimful
of yellow flowers:
the rivulet ran yellow
and yellow were the hedgerow and hillside,
the cemetery of the children,
that garden where love used to dwell.
The sun was anointing the world with yellow
from its dripping sunbeams;
alas, for the golden lilies,
the warm water of gold,
the yellow butterflies fluttering
over the yellow roses!
Garlands of yellow were entwined
in the trees, and the day
was a blessing perfumed with gold,
in a golden awakening of life.
Midst the bones of the dead,
God was opening his hand full of yellow.

E. L. T.

THE LAST JOURNEY

. . . I shall go away. And the birds will stay
still singing;
and my garden will remain, with its tree of green,
and its white well of water.
Every afternoon the sky will be blue and placid;
and the bells will chime as this afternoon
they are chiming,
the bells of the old belfry.

And those will die who once did love me;
the town will be made over new each year;
and in that corner of my whitewashed, blossoming garden,
my nostalgic spirit will wander . . .
   I shall go away; I shall be lonely without hearth
      and green tree,
without well of clear water,
without the sky so blue and placid . . .
and the birds will remain still singing.

E. L. T.

LOVE ·

   You have not died, no.
                     You are reborn,
   with the roses, each spring.
      Even as life, you have
   your withered petals;
   you have your snow,
   even as life . . .
                  But your soil,
   love, is sown with
   profound promises,
   which shall be redeemed even though
   in oblivion.
                  In vain is your not loving.
      The fresh breeze, one day, returns to your soul;
   upon a night of stars,
   love, you descend upon the senses,
   as chaste as the very first time.
      Since you are pure, you are
   eternal! Through the blue,
   the tender doves we thought were dead
   return to your presence, in flock of white . . .
   Your single flower opens with new petals . . .
   You gild with new tongues the immortal light . . .
      You are eternal, love,
   even as is the spring!

E. L. T.

FLEETING RETURN

What did she resemble, my God, tell me?
—Oh treacherous heart, oh irresolute mind!—
Was she most like the passing of the wind,
or like the flight of spring, my God, tell me?
    As light, as fickle, as fleeting was she
as thistledown of summer . . . Yes, I find
her vague smile within a laugh entwined . . .
a banner waving in air futilely.
    Oh banner, airy thistledown, caress
of smile and breeze, and wingèd flight of spring,
how mad, how sad your carnival, for lo,
    your change was bartered for nothing—oh sting
of memory, blind bee of bitterness!
I know not how you were, but that you were I know.

E. L. T.

WERE I REBORN

Were I reborn a stone,
even so I should love you, woman.

Were I reborn as wind,
even so I should love you, woman.

Were I reborn a wave,
even so I should love you, woman.

Were I reborn as fire,
even so I should love you, woman.

Were I reborn a man,
even so I should love you, woman.

E. L. T.

YOU LIGHT

Vertical light,
you, light;
golden light, you,
tall light;
vibrating light,
you, light.

And I, the black, the blind, the deaf, the dumb horizontal shadow.

E. L. T.

FORTUNATE BEING

Singing you go, and laughing through the water,
and through the air you go whistling and laughing,
a round of blue and gold, of green and silver,
so happy passing and repassing ever
amidst the first red blossoming of April,
the distinct form of instantaneous
equalities of light, of life, of color,
with us, kindled like river banks aflame!

What a happy being you are,
with universal and eternal happiness!
Happy, you break through the waves of the air,
you swim contrary to the waves of water!
Do you not have to eat, neither to sleep?
All the springtime, is it yours to enjoy?
All of the green, all of the blue,
the flowering all, is it yours?
There is no fear in your glory;
your fate is to return, return, return,
in rounds of green and silver, blue and gold,
through an eternity of eternities!

You give your hand to us in a moment
of possible affinity, of sudden love,
of radiant concession;
and with your warm contact,
in wild vibration of flesh and of soul,
we are enkindled with sweet harmony,
and we, made new, forget the usual,
we shine for an instant, happy with gold.
It seems that we too are going to be
perennial as you,
that we shall fly from ocean to the mountain,
that we shall leap from heaven to the sea,
and that we shall return, return, return
for an eternity of eternities.
We sing and we laugh through the air,
through the water we laugh and whistle.

But you must not forget yourself,
you are the casual, perpetual presence,
you are the fortunate creature,
the only magic being without shadow,
the one adored for warmth and grace,
the free, enraptured robber
that, in rounds of blue and gold, green and silver,
goes laughing, whistling through the air,
through the water singing and laughing!

E. L. T.

THE BEST THAT I HAVE

Green sea and grey sky and blue sky
and loving albatross upon the waves,
and in all, the sun, and thou in the sun,
observing desired and desiring god,
lighting with distinct golden rays my arrival;
the arrival of him that I am today,
of him that even yesterday I doubted
he could be in thee as I am.

What a changed man in me, desiring god,
from the being doubting the legend
of the god of the many glib speakers,
to be the firm believer
in the story I myself have created
all through my life for thee.

Now I come to this termination
of a year of my natural life,
in the depths of the air where I keep thee,
above this sea, these depths of water,
to this beautiful, blinding termination,
where thou art gradually entering me,
content to be thine, to be mine,
through the best that I have, my own expression.

E. L. T.

León Felipe

(1884-   )

León Felipe, whose real name was Camino y Galicia, was born in Zamora, lived in Salamanca, and studied in Santander and Madrid. He worked as a pharmacist, actor, hospital administrator in Africa, and teacher. In 1920 he published his first collection of poetry, *Verses and Prayers of the Traveler*. In 1923, helped by the famous Mexican writer, Alfonso Reyes, he gained entry into the intellectual circles of Mexico. The following year he married a professor of Spanish literature in the United States. He studied at Columbia University and taught briefly at Cornell. His second volume of *Verses and Prayers of the Traveler* appeared in 1929. The following year saw him once more in Mexico. He taught at the University of New Mexico in 1934 and alternated the next two years between Panama and Spain. His long poem, *The Insignia* (1937), in which he offers his blood to Spain in the cause of justice, marked the beginning of a new poetry of despair and bitterness from his pen. He claimed: "I have burned all rhetoric." From 1939 on he lived in exile in Mexico and in other Latin American countries.

Other poetry volumes of León Felipe include *Drop a Star* (1933); *The Spaniard of Exodus and Lamentation* (1939); *The Axe* (1939); *The Great Responsible One* (1940); *Call Me Publican* (1950); *You Will Earn the Light* (1953), his poetic autobiography; and *The Stag* (1958). He wrote a great deal of poetry for literary reviews and magazines, as well as ten dramas. Before his eightieth birthday he wrote that he wanted to destroy much of his published poetry. Poetry, for him, meant personal and human sadness, prayer, and beauty, especially that of humble things. He transcended all schools and poetic generations, although he wrote under many labels. He sang of Spain and the Civil War, but he also concentrated on universal tragedy and human anguish, often existential in tone. He sought spiritual satisfaction, peace, and plenty for mankind. Like Unamuno he wanted immortality, but whereas Unamuno stressed salvation and survival of the soul, Felipe was more aware of the social aspects of the Christian message. In his search for God he utilized the Bible in which, he said, "I have searched for myself . . . and found my tracks in all its corners." He felt that he was a solitary wanderer in an absurd world. He rejected absolute values, in his search for being and God, in an irrational world where humanity dragged out its miserable existence. The poet sobbed out his anguish for himself and for his fellow men who, he hoped, through suffering might achieve salvation.

The Spanish Civil War and Spain meant much to León Felipe, but humanity, which he criticized and for which he felt responsible, meant even more. His prophecies on the problems of the spirit, in simple sober style, do not disguise a deeply original human poet.

All selections are complete. The first three poems are from the first volume of *Verses and Prayers of the Traveler.* "Drop a Star" is from the volume by that name. The other selections are from *The Spaniard of Exodus and Lamentation.*

LITTLE PROLOGUES

Nobody went yesterday,
nor is going today,
nor will go tomorrow
toward God
along this same road
that I travel.
The sun for each man
keeps a new ray of light
and a virgin road
God.

*Translated by
K. Schwartz*

[*Undo that verse . . .*]

Undo that verse.
Remove the false fringes of rhyme,
the meter, the cadence
and even the idea itself . . .
Winnow the words . . .
and if afterwards something still remains
that

will be poetry.
What
does it matter
that the star
be remote
and
the rose
destroyed? . . .
We shall still have
the light and the aroma.

K. S.

WHAT A PITY

What a pity
that I cannot sing in the fashion
of this time as the poets of today sing!
What a pity
that I cannot intone with a choking voice
those brilliant romances
to the glories of my country!
What a pity
that I have no country!
I know that history is the same, always the same, that it goes
from one land to another land, from one race
to another race
as pass
those summer storms from one region to another.
What a pity
that I have no region,
native hearth, provincial land!
I should have been born in the entrails
of the Castilian steppe,
but I was born in a town of which I have no remembrance:
I spent the blue days of my infancy in Salamanca,
and my youth, a somber youth, in la Montaña.
Afterwards . . . I never again cast anchor,
and none of these lands elevates me

nor exalts me
to sing always in the same key
to the same river which passes
surrounding the same waters,
to the same sky, to the same field and in the same house.
What a pity
that I have no house!
An ancestral heraldic house
a house
in which I might keep
with other precious keepsakes
an old armchair of leather, a moth-eaten table . . .
and the portrait of a grandfather who had won
a battle.
What a pity
that I have no grandfather who won
a battle,
painted with a hand crossed
on his chest, and the other hand on his sword hilt!
And, what a pity
that I don't even own a sword!
Because . . ., what shall I sing if I have no country,
nor provincial land,
nor house
ancestral and heraldic,
nor the portrait of my grandfather who won
a battle,
nor an old armchair of leather, nor a table, nor a sword?
What shall I sing if I am a pariah
who scarcely owns a cape?
And yet . . .
          in this land of Spain
and in a town of Alcarria
there is a house
in which I lodge
and where I have, lent,
a pine table and a straw chair.
A book also I possess. And all my furniture is found
in a room
very large
and very white
which is in the lowest

and freshest part of the house.
It holds a most clear light
this room
so large
and white . . .
A very clear light
which enters through a window
facing a very wide street.
And to the light of this window
I come every morning.
Here I sit on my straw chair
and I while away the weary hours
reading in my book and watching,
through my windowpane, the people pass.
Things of small moment
a book and a windowpane
in a town of Alcarria,
and, yet, it suffices
to feel all life's rhythm in my soul.
For the whole rhythm of the world passes by these panes
when there pass
the goatherd following his goats
with an enormous crook,
that burdened woman
with a load
of wood on her shoulder,
those beggars who come dragging their miseries, from Pastrana,[1]
and that girl who so unwillingly goes to school.
Oh, that girl! She stops at my window
always glued to the windowpanes
as if she were an engraving.
How funny
her face
plastered on the pane
with its little chin sunk and its flattened nose!
I laugh a lot watching her
and I tell her that she is a pretty little thing . . .
She calls me
foolish, and marches off.
Poor girl. She no longer passes

---

1. A municipality in the Province of Guadalajara. (*Editor's note.*)

by this street so wide
traveling toward school so unwillingly,
nor does she stop
at my window
plastered against the pane
as if she were an etching.
For one day she became ill,
very ill,
and the next day the death bells tolled for her.
And on a very clear day,
along this street so wide,
through the window,
I saw how they carried her
in a very white box . . .
In a box
very white
which had on top a little crystal pane.
Through that pane one saw her face
just as it was when
plastered against my windowpane . . .
the windowpane
which now always recalls the little pane on that box
so white.
All the rhythm of life passes
by my windowpane . . .
And death also passes!
What a pity
that not being able to sing of other deeds,
because I have no country,
nor provincial land,
nor house
ancestral and heraldic,
nor the portrait of my grandfather who won
a battle,
nor an old chair of leather, nor a table, nor a sword,
and I am a pariah
who scarcely owns a cape . . .
I am forced to sing of things of such slight importance!

K. S.

DROP A STAR

Where is the star of mangers?
The prancing earth has paused in the wind.
And sailors' eyes fail to see
That fish—follow him!—
There rises, dancing,
the polar star.

The world is a slot machine,
with a slit in the forehead of the sky,
on the headboard of the sea.
(The machine has stopped,
the spring has broken.)
The world is something that functions
like the player piano of a bar.
(the spring has broken,
the machine has stopped . . .)
                    Sailor,
you have a star in your pocket . . .
          Drop a star!
Light with your hand the new music of the world,
the sea song of morning,
the coming hymn of man . . .
          Drop a star!
Cast off again this stranded boat, sailor.
You have a star in your pocket . . .
a new magnetic star of palladium and phosphorus.

                                        K. S.

QUERY

Am I a demagogue?
For dictators in the plaza have I ever given a cheer?
Not I! I've merely said,
And asked over and over:
"Who's been throwing sand in the motor around here?"

                        Translated by Willis K. Jones

WHERE IS GOD?

Three lessons and a Catechism
    with a One Act Play.
        "Oh, would that some one could tell me
        Where I shall be able to find him!
        I only know where he is not,
        And I know he is not with you."

To the Memory of Antonio Machado

W. K. J.

FIRST LESSON

God has existed always, children dear,
Long ere
The Phalanxes in various manners
Stamped Him there
Upon their uniforms and banners:
Before
The Legions ever started to baptize
With His own Holy name, the troops
And trimotors that sail the skies;
Before
They ever nailed His image above the door
Of all their barracks
And prisons where their victims rot;
Before 'twas worn on holy relics around the necks
Of archbishops
And prostitutes, best forgot,
And generals, brothers to Iscariot;
Before
It was considered on the Exchange, smart business
To pronounce His name.
God has existed always and for all the world,
For rich and poor the same,

Just as the earth existed centuries
Ere crooks partitioned it, as their fair game.
Then God
Belonged to all of you
As water, light, and wind were common property;
But now, like gold, He is possessed by just a few.
No longer does He bless the just;
He blesses rapine and deceit,
And those who have the mightiest fleet;
And there is one in Rome
Who does not hesitate these blessings to repeat.
Come, listen well, my children,
Listen well to me.
No instructor in hate am I;
I'd rather be
Professor of Love and Charity.
I do not know if you
Are children of the Carpenter of Galilee,
Or of the dictator; I only know
That you are God's own sons, all you who hark to me;
And so I say to you—
To bring my lesson to an end—
I say in simple words, and without rancor,
Not as a demagogue, but as a friend,
That yesterday some men
Stole from the rest of us everything:
Our strength, our song, the land we trod,
And
Now today
These same men, my children,
Have robbed us of our God.

W. K. J.

I KNOW WHERE HE IS

God, who knows everything,
Is cleverer than most men know.
Now by some outlaw archbishops
He has been kidnapped, and the crafty gang

Has made Him broadcast on the radio:
"Hello, I'm here with them. Hello!"

That doesn't mean He's on their side
But that He's there within their prison wall.
He tells us where He is, that's all,
So we may go,
A rescue party for the God we know.

W. K. J.

THERE IS NO GOD!

A One Act Play in twenty-four short lines.
Scene: Back stage.

CHARACTERS

> The audience
> The Director of the Revue
> García, the prompter
> The voice of the Wardrobe Mistress
> The voice of a Stage Hand
> Chorus of Players
>   and
> God, who does not appear.

What does the audience want? Why do they yell?
What is the reason for the loud to-do?
(That is the wrathy question at the prompter hurled
   By the Director of the great Revue.)
They are demanding God. They want Him out.
Well, send Him out and let Him take a bow.
It's not yet time to give His entrance cue.
Then cut the show, and send Him out right now!
O. K. Hey, God! Hey, God, go on the stage!
(The fat Director shouts in voice so grim)
Hey, God! Where's God? Has anyone seen God:
García, go and look for Him!
There is no God,

(The Wardrobe Mistress calls it out)
There is no God!
(A burly Stage Hand adds his shout)
You say there is no God?
(Surprised, the actors say)
No God? No God!
(Purple with rage the Prompter stops the play)
The theatrical God with all His trappery
By Franco's gang was spirited away!

W. K. J.

BUT WHO IS THE BISHOP?

It shall explain it all
Quite otherwise.
The bishop is the man
Who gives to Tragedy a gay disguise,
The man full of deceit.
The poet is the man who strips it bare;
The poet is one who waits for gloom
And then accepts it there.
The bishop says:
"On that tomorrow when you leave this earth,
You'll travel to a better land,
Where of wine and bread and butter there's no dearth."
The poet says:
"Man must be always battering a door,
A wall, a shed,
With his heart
And with his head."
I know, I know your sympathies
Are not with poets, but with bishops instead.

W. K. J.

Pedro Salinas

(1892-1951)

Born in Madrid, he studied law, philosophy, and literature there. A scholar and teacher as well as a poet, he taught at Seville, Murcia, Paris, Cambridge, and Madrid. Luis Cernuda, a famous poet in his own right and one of Salinas' students at Seville, viewed him as the guiding force of an entire generation of poets. At the end of the Spanish Civil War Salinas went to the United States. He taught at Wellesley, the University of California, and for many years at Johns Hopkins. Among his many critical works on literature are *Spanish Literature of the Twentieth Century* (1941), *Jorge Manrique* (1948), and *The Poetry of Rubén Darío* (1948). He also wrote short stories, a novel, and more than a dozen plays.

The central theme of most of his poetry concerns the meaning of reality. He viewed the modern material world with suspicion and sought for the essence hiding behind this apparent and deceptive reality. The interior world, he felt, contained a more significant reality where one might find life and love. The outer material world made the poet realize his own tragic solitude and limitations. His refined and intellectualized verse resembles that of Juan Ramón Jiménez for whom he had great admiration. His delicate imagery may stem partly from an early interest in, and love for, painting. In his later poetry, especially that written in the United States, the poet stresses more the concept of charity and belief in humanity. His final conclusion appears to be that art means little unless humanity survives.

His poetry collections include *Presages* (1923), nature meditations, full of the joy of love, living, and interior reality; *Certain Hazard* (1929), a view of the material world; *Fable and Sign* (1931), a contrast of poetic reality with objective certainty; *My Voice Stems From You* (1933), a return to the interior world of his beloved who gives the only meaning and reality possible in the poet's life and with whom he maintains a lyrical monologue; *Reason of Love* (1936), where he still seeks happiness but realizes the anguish of the world; *The Contemplated* (1946), about the Puerto Rican sea and its fascination; and finally *All Most Clear* (1949), his most anguished work. Man, he finally realized, to discover life had to find eternal vision, seek divine guidance and try to face the materialism of the modern world, as he meditated on the possibility of total destruction and approaching nothingness.

226

All the selections are complete poems. "On dry land" is from *Presages;* "Distant Sea," from *Fable and Sign;* "Do you not hear," from *My Voice Stems From You;* and the last two poems, from *Reason of Love.*

ON DRY LAND

On dry land
the soul of the wind
gave me news of the sea
with the tremulous lips
of the poplars of summer.
Breaths of the ocean
and longings for the voyage,
keel, prow and wake,
Circe and Golden Fleece,
of all did they whisper
the wise poplar trees
of the dry land.
And a white cloud
(a white sail)
on the horizon,
with gestures of canvas,
boasted of flight
in desired directions,
on that sea without wind
of that empty sky
of that dry land
by poplars of summer.

Translated by E. L. Turnbull

DISTANT SEA

This is not the sea, this is its image,
its impression, its reflection in the heavens.

This is not the sea, this is its tenuous
voice,

across the wide world,
in a loud speaker, through the air.

This is not the sea, this is its name
in a language without lips,
without nation,
without any words save this:
sea.

This is not the sea, this is its flaming
idea, unfathomable, limpid;
and I,
burning, extinguishing myself in it.

E. L. T.

DO YOU NOT HEAR . . .

Do you not hear how they ask for reality,
these, the dishevelled ones, these, the untamed ones,
the shadows we invent, you and I,
on this immense plain of distances?
Weary now of the infinite, weary
of time without measure, of namelessness,
and sick with longing for the material,
they ask for boundaries, days and names.
No longer
can they live like this, they are on the border
of the death of shadows, which is nothingness.
Come with me to the rescue.
Stretch out your hands to them, offer your body.
Together we shall seek for them
a color, a time, a breast, a sun.
Let them find their rest in you, be you their flesh.
Their great desire for roving shall grow calm,
while we clasp them
eagerly to our breast,
where they may find their pasture and repose.
They shall fall asleep at last folded close
in our dream, embracing. And thus afterwards,

when we shall part, to be nourished only
on shadows, from afar,
they
shall have their memories, shall have a past
of flesh and blood,
the time when they lived in us.
And their eager, wistful dream
of shadows, once more, shall be the return
to this mortal existence of roseate flesh
where love invents its infinity.

E. L. T.

IF THE VOICE WERE PERCEIVED . . .

If the voice were perceived with the eyes,
ah, how I should see you!
Your voice has a light that illumines me,
light of the hearing.
When you speak
space is aglow with the sound,
the great darkness which is silence
is broken. Your word
has gleams of dawn, of young aurora,
each day, as it comes to me afresh.
When you say yes,
a zenith of joy, a full midday
reigns, without the art of the eyes.
There is no night if you speak to me in the night;
neither solitude, here alone in my room,
if your voice reaches me, lightly thus, without body.
For your voice creates its body. There are born
in empty space innumerable
delicate and possible forms
of the body of your voice. Almost are deceived
the lips and the arms that seek you.
And phantom lips, and phantom arms
search round them, for your voice
brings to birth divine beings,
invention of your speech.

And in the light of hearing, in those confines
that the eyes do not see, all radiant,
they kiss for us,
the two lovers that have no more
day and no more night
than your starry voice, or your sun.

E. L .T.

I AM SO SURE . . .

I am so sure that your presence
shines through all that makes up my life.
sure that the light, rain and sky
are forms in which you escape from yourself,
a vague something between yourself and yourself,
that I am never alone
while the day seems to me your spirit,
or when the stars being kindled,
speak to me of your thoughts.
This tiny drop of rain
which falls on my paper
is no chance purple spot of flowery vegetation,
but the delicate scattered violet
that you send me from the April you are living.

And when the contacts of the night,
mass of darkness, solid mass,
wind, sounds reach me and touch me,
with boundless amazement
I see that the arm
I stretch out to you does not embrace you,
and that you persist in
withholding the all of yourself,
thus near to me though you are, back of all.
And only because your body is not seen,
though you pulsate in that which is nearest me,
I am forced to believe
the vague fiction of being alone.

E. L. T.

Jorge Guillén

(1893-   )

Guillén, born in Valladolid, has been a professor most of his life. He taught Spanish literature at Paris, Oxford, and Seville in Europe and for some twenty years at Wellesley College in the United States. He started publishing poetry about 1920 in literary reviews usch as *Litoral*. He became a follower of Paul Valéry and his theories about pure poetry, and he was considered its outstanding exponent in Spain. In 1961 he won the International Prize for Poetry. He has also published several essays on literary criticism.

Guillén's major work, *Canticle,* first published in 1928, went through several editions, in each of which he added a number of new poems. The first version contained seventy-five poems; the fourth edition (1950) had 332. *Canticle,* a song of praise to and faith in the world around him, overflows with the sheer joy of being alive. Nevertheless, his short, clean outbursts were considered by some critics to be cold, intellectual, dehumanized, and mathematical in their support of an ordered universe. Others viewed the formal beauty as merely an outer shell, which held poetic fire within. Characteristics of his poems are: vitality, optimism, freshness, formal perfection, color, clarity, animism, joy, and the exaltation of life over death. In spite of his view of reality, from time to time, the poet realizes that man's world is neither perfect nor happy, but life continues to be beautiful simply because it is life.

Among his later works are *Living and Other Poems* (1958), *Natural History* (1960), and *The Temptations of Anthony* (1962); but his second great poetic achievement, after *Canticle,* was *Clamor,* divided into three sections or volumes: *Maremagnum* (1957), *Which Wind to the Sea* (1960), and *At the Height of Circumstances* (1963). If *Canticle* showed faith in life, *Clamor* documented time and history. In this second period Guillén explains his hopes for humanity. Man needs rebirth, identification with nature, and an existential discovery of his essence. One still finds joy of being in his poetry, but it is tempered by a restrained despair, for the noise of the world cannot be shut out. As the poet realizes his end is approaching, that his future has been limited by the onslaughts of time, he hopes for courage to enjoy what remains to him.

All the selections, complete poems, are from *Canticle.* The first two are from the first section of the volume known as "Faith in Life"; "Slender Spring" is from the second section, "The Situated Hours"; the last two poems are from the third part, "The Bird in the Hand."

ADVENT

Moon of the April night,
How ample and sweet the air!
All will come back to me,
All I have lost with the birds.

Yes, with the morning birds
Chirping in chorus at dawn,
Twittering, warbling and singing,
Bringing unconscious blessing.

The moon is now very near us,
Quiet and calm in our presence.
That which I was awaits me,
Buried beneath my thoughts.

The nightingale shall sing
On the very tip of desire.
Flush of dawn, flush of dawn
Midst gentle breezes of heaven!

And was it gone, the time
I lost? The turning hand,
A nimble god, disposes
Of this moon so ageless.

Translated by E. L. Turnbull

ECSTASY OF BLISS

Oh ecstasy of bliss!
All things are winged for flight.

That which is close soars upward
Dissolved into the distance.

What host of slender forces!
What youthful animation
Above in the airy space,
With reality filled!

Like a mirror, the world
Gives back guileless reflections:
The most limpid distances
Dream of the true, the real.

Oh the sweetness of years
Irretrievable! Nuptials
Too late, with the life that
I liked not day by day!

More, more and yet more!
Towards the sun, in swift flight,
The fulness makes its escape.
Now I am only song!

E. L. T.

SLENDER SPRING

When infinite space, without outline, sums
  Up in a cloud
Its vast indecision, so lightly drifting,
  Where is its shore?
While the river upon its winding way
  Continues flowing,
Seeking slantwise, crosswise, most cunning draughtsman,
  Its own solution,
While the water, tinged a harsh, vivid green,
  Conceals its fishes
Under the deep and uncertain reflection
  Of a vibrant air . . .

When the morning gently leads its avenues
   Of tall, slim poplars,
Thanks to the shimmering, quivering wake
   Between their leafage,
With the aid of the sinuous progression
   Which harmonizes
The gentle undulation of the sky
   Above the wind
With the swiftly moving pace of the splendors
   That briskly sail . . .
Then spring, slender spring comes between the oars
   Of the rowers!

E. L. T.

THE NIGHTINGALE

The nightingale, fluent songster,
A very peacock of trilling,
Is sending forth his petition
Over the bend of the river,
Far, far away, to a day
Held suspended at noontide,
Where a bird of glowing crimson,
Zenith of a perfect spring,
The completely rounded sphere,
Never, never answers: yes.

E. L. T.

PERFECTION

The firmament, a dense blue,
Is overarching the day.
'Tis the rounding out of splendor,
Midday. All is curving dome.

At the centre lies, unwilling,
The rose, subject to a sun
At its zenith. And the present
So yields itself up that the
Foot that is moving now feels
The completeness of the planet.

E. L. T.

Federico García Lorca

(1898-1936)

Born in Fuentevaqueros, a small town near Granada, Lorca moved to that city with his parents. His mother was a school teacher, and Lorca once said that he had inherited the passion of his father and the intelligence of his mother. At an early age he showed great talent in art, music, and painting. Manuel de Falla, for a time, was his music instructor. García Lorca studied at the University of Granada and obtained his degree there. In 1919 he became a member of the Residencia de Estudiantes in Madrid, where he won acclaim for his recitals of poetry. In 1929 he visited New York and was appalled at what a materialistic society could do to man. In 1931 in Spain he directed a student theater, which toured the provinces and gave classic dramas for unsophisticated but appreciative audiences. He visited Buenos Aires in 1933 and was wildly acclaimed. In 1936 he was executed, under circumstances which have not been fully clarified to this day, by Falangist forces which supported Franco.

His first published book of poetry was *Book of Poems* (1921), full of warmth, religious and nature symbols, and including a series of dialogues in the style of the Middle Ages. The somewhat naïve and sentimental poems reveal the influence of Juan Ramón Jiménez. Other poetry volumes are *Songs* (1927); *Poem of the Deep Song* (1931), on Andalusian folklore; *Lament for the Death of Ignacio Sánchez Mejías* (1935), perhaps the greatest elegy in modern Spanish literature; and *The Diván of Tamarit* (Diván being a collection and Tamarit a place name near Granada) (1936), full of pagan and sensual love themes, Andalusian and Arabic folklore, and death themes, never absent from Lorca's poetry.

His poetic drama combines the same double imagery of the real and the unreal, tragedy and comedy, popular and sophisticated elements, and the rich and surprising imagery of his poetry. As early as 1920 he wrote a theatrical piece, *The Spell of the Butterfly*, the first published evidence of a long interest in the drama. In other dramas he dealt with a heroine of Granada who fought for the cause of liberty (*Mariana Pineda*, 1927); several semigrotesque farces in 1930 and 1931, which deal with the power of sex and love; and two surrealistic dramas, *When Five Years Pass* (1931), a study of time, frustration, and love, with

236

weird, shocking and yet appealing dreamlike sequences, and *The Public* (1933). In 1935 he again studied frustration and love in *Doña Rosita the Spinster* about a woman who grows old waiting for a lover she knows will never return.

Lorca's best known dramas, which form a kind of rural trilogy, are *Blood Wedding* (1933), based on the Spanish concept of honor, family rivalries, and the force of sexual passion; *Yerma or Wasteland* (1934), a study of a frustrated woman, bound by a rigid honor code, whose husband cannot give her the child she desperately wants and needs; and *The House of Bernarda Alba,* first performed in 1945 and published the following year, about an intransigent mother, her five daughters, and the concept of virginity.

García Lorca combines folklore and tradition and employs symbols such as the moon, the bull, the clock, the knife, and other sharp objects to convey the omnipresent idea of an imminent death, against a background of color, music, and flowers. In most of his dramas women are the principal characters. They usually die or are the cause of death in a world of passion and human fatality, a Spain that clings to an outworn code, which promotes the frustration and destruction of the unloved.

Lorca's two masterpieces are *Gypsy Ballads* (1928) and *Poet in New York,* not published until 1940. The first collection, filled with unusual imagery, shows us that death is everywhere, especially represented by the moon whose waxing and waning reflects the life and death of man. Blood, which marks the passage from life to death, solitude, pain, colors, flowers, and animals are other components of the work. *Poet in New York* stemmed from his visit to that city in 1929. He views primitive man, especially the Negro, as the victim of the evil civilized world. The poetry takes on a nightmarish and surrealistic tone as the poet mourns the loss of his innocence, searches for his identity, and protests against injustice.

Probably with Antonio Machado one of the two greatest poets of the century, he sought to unify his poetic world with the real one. He loved the primitive, the frustrated, the weak, the helpless, and, in general, all victims of the materialistic world. In his love of the natural, with a sensual and living passion, he animated common everyday objects to project fantastic symbolism in odd sensory combinations. He saw life and death with an almost childhood candor at times, but he revealed, also, the anguish of a man who had suffered and thus understood the sufferings of others. In his reflections on the Dionysian and Apollonian forces in man, Lorca plays with illusion and reality, as he reveals his knowledge of the dark forces which hem us in on all sides. In his fusion of popular and cultural elements, the old and the new, Lorca created a new poetic language and an almost unique imagery.

The first two selections, given in entirety, are from *Gypsy Ballads.* "Spilled Blood" is the second of four sections of *Lament for the Death of Ignacio Sónchez Mejías.*

BALLAD WALKING IN SLEEP

Green, oh I want you green.
Green wind and green the branches.
The ship upon the sea
and the horse on the mountain.
With shade at her girdle,
she dreams at her railing,
green her flesh, green her hair,
and her eyes of cold silver.
Green, oh I want you green.
Under the gipsy moon,
things are gazing at her,
she cannot gaze at them.

Green, oh I want you green.
Shining stars of white frost
come with the fish of shadow
opening the way of dawn.
The fig tree rubs its wind
with rough bark of its branches,
the mountain, thieving cat,
stretches out its sharp cactus.
But who will come? From where . . .?
She is still at her railing,
green her flesh, green her hair,
dreaming of bitter sea.

—My father, I would exchange
my good horse for her house,
my saddle for her mirror,
my sharp knife for her blanket.
My father, I come bleeding
from the passes of Cabra.
—Were I able, young fellow,
this deal here would be settled.
But I am I no longer,
nor is my house now mine.
—My father, I would die

decently in my bed.
Of steel, if it may be,
with the sheets of fine linen.
Do you not see the wound
from my breast to my neck?
—Three hundred dark red roses
are on your snow white shirt,
the warm blood oozes out
round the swathes of your sash.
But I am I no longer,
nor is my house now mine.
—Let me at least go up
as far as the high railings;
let me, let me go up,
as far as the green railings.
Balustrades of the moon
through which water resounds.

Now the two comrades climb
up towards the high railings.
Leaving a trail of blood.
Leaving a trail of tears.
On the roof tops were trembling
little lanterns of tin.
Tambourines of crystal by
thousands wounded the dawn.

Green, oh I want you green,
green wind and green the branches.
The two comrades climbed up.
The long, long wind was leaving
in the mouth a strange taste
of gall, mint and sweet basil.
—My father, tell me where,
where is your bitter daughter?
—How often she waited for you!
Oh, how often had she waited,
fresh young face and black hair,
standing at this green railing!

Above the cistern's surface
the gipsy girl was swaying.

Green her flesh, green her hair
and her eyes of cold silver.
An icicle of the moon
upheld her on the water.
Then the night became homely
as a little town square.
The drunken civil guards
were knocking at the door.
Green, oh I want you green.
Green wind and green the branches.
The ship upon the sea,
and the horse on the mountain.

Translated by E. L. Turnbull

BALLAD OF THE SPANISH
CIVIL GUARD

Black, all black are their horses
and black also their horseshoes.
Over their dark cloaks glisten
spots of ink and of wax.
Their skulls are skulls of lead,
for this they cannot weep.
With soul of patent leather
down the road they come riding.
Hunchbacked and nocturnal,
where they move they evoke
silences of dark rubber
and dread fears of fine sand.
They pass, if pass they will,
and hidden in their noddles
is a misty astronomy
of immaterial pistols.

Oh city of the gipsies!
At the corners are banners.
The pumpkin and the moon
with preserved mazard berries.
Oh city of the gipsies!

City of grief and musk,
with tall towers of cinnamon.
When the night was approaching,
night, the night that was darksome,
the gipsies in their founderies
were forging suns and arrows.
Badly wounded, a horse
at all the gates was knocking.
Cocks of crystal were crowing
at Jerez of the wine cellars.
The naked wind is turning
the corner of surprise
on the night, silver night,
night, the night that is darksome.

The Virgin and Saint Joseph
have lost their castanets,
and they look for the gipsies
to see if they can find them.
The Virgin comes dressed in
the gown of a mayor's wife,
made of glittering tinsel,
with a necklace of almonds.
Saint Joseph struts past pompously,
wearing a cloak of silk
Behind walks Pedro Domecq
(the great merchant of wines),
with three sultans of Persia.
The crescent moon was dreaming
of an ecstasy of storks.
Banners and lanterns deck
the flat roofs of the houses.
Dancers, slender and hipless,
wander sobbing through mirrors.
Nought but water and shadow
at Jerez of the wine cellars.

Oh city of the gipsies!
At the corners are banners.
Put out all your green lights,
for the worthy guard comes.
Oh city of the gipsies!

Who saw you and can forget?
Leave her far from the sea,
without combs for her tresses.

They advance two abreast
on the holiday city.
A sound of everlastings
invades the cartridge boxes.
They advance two abreast.
Double nocturne of cloth.
For them the sky with stars
is a show-case of spurs.

The city, free of fear,
was multiplying its gates.
The Civil Guard, forty strong,
through them enters to plunder.
Clocks and watches all stopped,
and the brandy in bottles
masked itself as November
not to arouse suspicion.
Then a flight of long howls
rose in the weathercocks.
Sabers slash through the breezes
that hoofs crush under foot.
Through the shadowy streets
the ancient gipsies flee
leading their sleepy horses,
in their hands jars of money.
Up the steep, narrow streets
climb the sinister cloaks,
leaving back in their wake
myriads of whirling scissors.

Now the gipsies are gathered
around Bethlehem's gate.
Saint Joseph, full of wounds,
wraps a girl in a shroud.
Sounds of sharp rifle shots
are heard all the night long.
The Virgin heals the children
with the spittle of stars.

But now the Civil Guard
advances spreading fires
where the youthful and naked
imagination burns.
Rosa Camborios groans
seated outside her door,
both of her breasts cut off
and laid out on a tray.
And other girls were running
their braids pursuing after,
where in the air are exploding
rosettes of black gun-powder.
When all the low roofs were
but furrows on the ground,
then the dawn shrugged its shoulders
on a long outline of stone.

Oh city of the gipsies!
The Civil Guard moves off
through a tunnel of silence
while the flames surround you.

Oh city of the gipsies!
Who saw you and can forget?
Let them seek you in my forehead,
You, sport of moon and of sand.

E. L. T.

LAMENT FOR THE DEATH OF
IGNACIO SÁNCHEZ MEJÍAS

II

Spilled Blood

No, I don't want to see it!

Tell the moon to come,
I don't want to see the blood
of Ignatius on the sand.

No, I don't want to see it!
The moon fully rounded.
Horse of the quiet clouds,
and the grey ring of sleep
with willows round the fences.
No, I don't want to see it!
My memory is burning.
Warn the jessamine flowers
with their delicate whiteness.

No, I don't want to see it!

The cow of the ancient world
was passing her joyless tongue
over a muzzle of blood
spilled on the sand of the ring,
and the bulls of Guisando,
near to death, almost stone,
were bellowing like two centuries
tired of treading the earth.
No.

No, I don't want to see it!

Up the steps came Ignatius
with all his death on his shoulders.
He was searching for the dawn,
and the dawn was not.
He is seeking his firm profile,
and in sleep he has lost it.
He sought his beautiful body
and he found his flowing blood.
Do not ask me to see it!
I do not wish to perceive
its flowing each time with less
force; that oozing stream that tinges
the rows of seats and is spilling
over the plush and leather
of the thirsting multitude.
Who calls to me that I come!
Do not ask me to see it!

His fearless eyes did not close
when he saw the horns near him,
but they, the terrible mothers,
lifted up their heads.
And across the cattle ranches
blew a wind of secret voices,
they cried out to the bulls of heaven,
the herdsmen of pallid mist.
There was no prince in Seville
that could be compared to him,
nor was there sword like his sword,
nor ever a heart so true.
Like to a river of lions,
such was his marvellous strength,
like to a torso of marble
such was his prudence portrayed.
His head was gilded with the
air of a Rome Andalusian,
and his laugh was a tuberose
of salt and of understanding.
In the bull-ring what a fighter!
On the mountain what a climber!
How gentle with spears of wheat!
How firm he was with the spurs
and how tender with the dew!
How dazzling, he, at the fair!
How terrible with the final
darts of darkness for the bull!

But now he sleeps without end.
Already the moss and grass
open with their skilful fingers
the flower of his skull.
Already the blood comes singing,
singing through marshes and meadows,
slipping through horns stiff with cold,
vacillating soulless through the mist,
meeting with cloven feet by the thousands
like a long, sorrowful tongue,
to form a dark pool of agony
near the river Guadalquivir of the stars.

Oh white wall of Spain!
Oh black bull of sorrow!
Oh cruel blood of Ignatius!
Oh nightingale of his veins!
No.

No, I don't want to see it!
There is no chalice that may hold it,
there are no swallows that may drink it,
there is no white frost that may cool it,
there is no song nor deluge of lilies,
no crystal that may plate it with silver.
No.
No, I don't want to see it!!

E. L. T.

Vicente Aleixandre

(1898-   )

Born in Seville, he spent a good part of his youth in Málaga, and southern cities and the sea were to play a large part in his poetry. He moved to Madrid. Raised in a well-to-do merchant family, he did not have to work, but he studied commerce and law. In 1917, while spending the summer in a little town near Avila, he was introduced to the poetry of Rubén Darío by Dámaso Alonso, and soon thereafter he studied the poetry of Antonio Machado and other outstanding poets. His future career had now become clear to him. In 1925 Aleixandre suffered a severe kidney disease, and in 1932 an almost fatal siege of illness left him with debilities from which he has never fully recovered. In 1933 he won the National Prize for Literature for the then as yet unpublished *Destruction or Love*. He is currently a member of the Spanish Royal Academy.

Aleixandre's difficult poetry combines surrealistic, Freudian, and existentialist themes and imagery. The poet's universal constants are love and death, for life is but a fleeting thing; through sensuality the physical may become spiritual, and in the final analysis love and death are viewed as the same thing. Aleixandre also establishes an inverse hierarchy in which nonliving things triumph over living things, the mineral over the vegetable, the vegetable over the animal, and the animal over man. In his latest poetry Aleixandre enhances the role of man as all-important, but he continues to believe that the substance of all things is one. He seems to be searching, at times, for a lost innocence, but his alienation from nature and from the world leads him to desire a fusion with the primeval whole.

His first poetry was published in literary reviews. His published volumes include *Ambito* (1928), *Swords Like Lips* (1932), *Destruction or Love* (1935), and *Passion in the Earth* (1935). *Shadow of Paradise, Final Birth,* and *The Heart's History* are later collections. Critics differ as to whether Aleixandre should be called a surrealist, a romantic, or an existentialist. He, himself, was never able to give an adequate explanation of his poetry. He once defined it as an "instrument of a fire which we would have to call telluric," but on another occasion he claimed: "I do not know what poetry is and I have profound doubts of all judgments about what is eternally inexplainable."

All of the selections, given in entirety, are from *Destruction or Love*.

COME ALWAYS, COME

Do not draw near. Your forehead, your passionate burning brow,
the traces of kisses,
that radiance that even by day is felt if you draw near,
that contagious radiance that is left in my hands,
that luminous river in which I plunge my arms,
of which I scarce dare drink, for fear afterwards of the cruel life of
brightness.

I would not have you live in me as lives the light,
with that isolation of a star that unites with its light,
to whom love is denied across the cruel blue space
which separates and does not unite,
where each inaccessible star
is a solitude that, groaning, sends forth its sadness.

Solitude sparkles in the world without love.
Life is a brilliant bark,
a rough immovable skin
where man cannot find his repose,
however he may apply his dream against a spent star.

But do not draw near. Your sparkling forehead, a glowing coal that
snatches me from my own conscience,
flashing sorrow in which suddenly I feel the temptation to die,
to scorch my lips with your ineffaceable friction,
to feel my flesh consume itself against your burning diamond.

Do not draw near, because your kiss is prolonged like the impossible
clash of the stars,
like space that suddenly breaks into flame,
generating ether where the destruction of worlds
is a single heart that consumes itself wholly.

Come, come, come like the burnt-out coal that imprisons death;
come like the blind night that brings your face near me;
come like two lips marked with red, by that long line that fuses
metals.

Come, come, my love; come sealèd brow, roundness almost
    revolving
that glows like an orb that is going to die in my arms;
come like two eyes or two deep solitudes,
two imperious calls from a depth unknown to me.

Come, come, death, love; come quickly, I destroy you;
come, for I would kill or love or die or give you all;
come, for you roll like a fickle stone,
bewildered as a moon that asks of me my rays!

Translated by E. L. Turnbull

COME, COME THOU

There where the sea does not pulsate,
where sorrow shakes its mane of glass,
where the breath gently exhaled
is not a butterfly of metal, but an air.

A soft gentle air
where words murmur as at an ear.
Where echo a few feeble feathers
that in the rosy ear are the love that insists.

Who loves me? Who says that love is a strong axe,
a weariness that cleaves the body through the centre,
a sorrowful arch through which passes the light
lightly without ever touching anyone?

The trees of the forest sing as if they were birds.
An immense arm encircles the wood as if it were a body.
A bird made golden by the lingering light
seeks ever for lips through which to escape from his prison.

But the sea does not beat as does a heart,
neither do the glass, nor the tresses of a far off stone
do more than attract all the brightness of the sun without giving it
    forth,

nor are the numberless fish that live in other heavens
more than the slowest waters of a distant eye.

Then this forest, this drop of blood,
this bird that escapes from the breast,
this breath that exhales from half open lips,
this pair of butterflies that at any point are going to make love . . .

This near-by ear that listens to my words,
this flesh that I caress with my lips of air,
this body that I clasp as if it were a name,
this rain that falls on my stretched out body,
this freshness of heaven in which some teeth are smiling,
where arms stretch out, where a sun is rising,
where a universal music sings invading all,
whilst the cardboard, the cords, the false fabrics,
the sad sackcloth, the rejected world,
draws back as a sea that roars without destiny.

                                                        E. L. T

DEATH

Ah, it is you, it is you, eternal name without date,
wild struggle of the sea with thirst,
steep rock all of water that threatens to crumble
over my flat form, a surface without remembrance.

It is you, shade of the powerful sea,
genial green grudge where all the fish are like stones in the air
depression or affliction that threatens my life
like a love that ends with death.

Kill me if you will, sea of merciless lead,
mighty drop that holds the earth,
destructive fire of my life without inspiration
here on the beach where the light is creeping.

Kill me as if with a dagger, a golden or shining sun,
a sharp glance from an inviolable eye,

a most powerful arm whose nakedness might be the cold,
a lightning flash that might seek my breast or its destiny . . .

Ah, soon, soon; I would die facing you, sea,
facing you, vertical sea whose foam touches the sky,
you, whose heavenly fish among the clouds
are like forgotten birds of the depths!

Let them come to me, your crystalline foaming waves,
let the green arms come toppling over,
let suffocation come when the body contracts
overcome beneath the black lips that collapse.

May the purple sun shine on uniform death.
May total death come on the beach that I uphold,
on this earthly beach that rests on my breast
by which it seems that light feet are escaping.

I like rose color or life,
I like red or its frantic yellow,
I like that tunnel where color dissolves
into the treacherous black which is the laugh on the lips of death.

I would kiss the ivory of the penultimate silence,
when the sea in great haste recedes,
when on the sand only some shells are left,
some cold scales of a few fish that make love.

Death like a handful of sand,
like water that is left alone in the hollow,
like the sea-gull that in the middle of the night
is tinged the color of blood above a sea that is not.

                                        E. L. T.

Rafael Alberti

(1902-   )

Born in Cadiz, as he says, into a Catholic and bourgeois family, Andalusia
and his childhood sea became constant notes in his poetry. He studied
in a Jesuit school in Cadiz. After his family moved to Madrid in 1917
he studied painting and even held an exhibition, but ill health forced
him to abandon that career. In 1931 he traveled through Europe and
later lived in the Soviet Union for three months. He became a member
of the Communist party but quarreled with its members, and was
expelled. He was an ardent supporter of the Spanish Republic and
defended Madrid during the battle for that city. He escaped to France,
where he was ill treated by the Vichy regime, and eventually he made
his way to Argentina where he has lived for more than a quarter of a
century.

His first published volume, which shared the National Prize for
Literature in 1925, was *Sailor on Land*. The poet feels imprisoned by
the earth and longs for an escape to the living and innocent sea of his
youth. *The Lover* (1926), about Nature and the sea; *The Dawn of the
Gillyflower* (1927), semi-Gongoristic verse; and *Lime and Song* (1928),
exotic Gongoristic poetry, could not equal *Concerning Angels* (1929)
in excellence. The latter collection, together with *Sailor on Land*, constitute his most important work. Reminiscent of Eliot's *The Waste
Land*, it is a surrealistic search for a lost religious faith in a destroyed
and destructive world that has lost its values. The poet finally achieves
a measure of happiness in an imperfect world. Some committed revolutionary war poetry such as *The Poet in The Street* (1931-36), and
his elegy to Ignacio Sánchez Mejías, in whose retinue he once fought in
a bullfight, are among other works he produced during his remaining
years in Spain. The elegy, *To See You and Not to See You*, while not
as moving as Lorca's, reflects Alberti's passion for bulls and bullfighting,
a theme in much of his poetry.

In America, *Between the Carnation and the Sword* (1941) summed
up Alberti's ambivalence about arms and letters. The sword represented
the struggle for Spain; the carnation, love and poetic imagination. Among
his other American works are *To Painting* (1945), sonnets and odes to
famous painters; *Returns of the Living Distance* (1953), full of passionate elegies and anguished longing for Spain; and *Ballads and Songs
of the Paraná* (1954).

Alberti, like most of his generation, sought meaning in Spanish cultural and popular traditions. In his use of the popular motif he especially resembles García Lorca, although he is more intellectual than the Granadine poet. In his exuberant happiness of life, he recalls Guillén. An experimenter in meters, Alberti has been baroque, popular, surrealistic, and even romantic, but above all a master of grace and form.

"The sea, the sea" and "Street Cry Under Sea" are from *Sailor on Land;* the three angel poems are from *Concerning Angels;* "Elegy for Garcilaso" is from *Sermons and Dwellings* (1930). The poems are given in their entirety.

THE SEA, THE SEA . . .

The sea, the sea,
the sea, only the sea!

Father, oh why to the city
did you drag me?

Why, oh why, did you pull me
out of the sea?

In dreams, the swell of the sea
tugs at the strings of my heart,
and away with it would flee.

Father, why did you drag me
here from the sea?

> *Translated by*
> *E. L. Turnbull*

STREET CRY UNDER SEA

How happy now would I be
with you, my fair young gardener,
in a garden under sea!

In a cart of cockle-shell,
drawn by a trout, oh what glee
for me, love, your wares to sell
under the salty blue sea!

—Fresh seaweed here from the sea,
seaweed, seaweed!

E. L. T.

THE GOOD ANGEL

One year, asleep already,
someone I wasn't expecting
stopped in front of my window.

—Awake! Then to my eyes
appeared feathers and sword blades.

Behind us we left mountains
and seas, clouds, peaks and wings,
setting suns and auroras.

—See her yonder! Her dream
is suspended from the nothing.

—Oh longing, oh firm marble,
steady light, steady moving
waters of my soul!

One said: Awake! And I
found myself in your dwelling.

E. L. T.

THE ANGEL OF NUMERALS

Virgins with T-squares
and compasses, guarding
celestial blackboards.

And the angel of numerals
pensively flying
from 1 to 2, from 2
to 3, from 3 to 4.

Dull chalk and wet sponges
erased and crossed out
the light of spaces.

Neither sun, moon, nor stars,
nor the sudden green
of the flash of lightning,
nor air. Only mist.

Virgins without squares
and compasses, weeping.

And on the blurred blackboards
the angel of numerals,
lifeless, shrouded, lying
on 1 and on 2,
on 3 and on 4.

E. L. T.

DEAD ANGELS

Look, yes, look for them:
in the insomnia of forgotten water-pipes,
in ditches choked by the silence of refuse.
Not far from puddles too small to reflect a cloud,
or lost eyes,
a broken ring,
or a trampled star.

Because I have seen them:
in that debris which appears for a moment in the mist.
Because I have touched them:
in the banishment of a broken brick,

come to naught, fallen from a tower or a cart.
Never far from chimneys that are crumbling,
nor from those clinging leaves that imprint themselves on the sole of
a shoe.

In all this.
But also in those scattered bits of wood that consume themselves
without fire,
in those collapsed absences which rickety furniture suffers,
not very far from the names and signs that grow cold on walls.

Look, yes, look for them:
under the drop of wax which buries the word in a book,
or the signature on one of those corners of letters
which blow around in the dust.
Near the broken fragments of a discarded bottle,
an old shoe lost in the snow,
and a razor thrown away on the edge of a precipice.

E. L. T.

ELEGY FOR GARCILASO

> . . . *before his time and almost in*
> *the flower of his youth cut off* . . .
> *Garcilaso de la Vega.*

You might have seen the ivy weeping blood when the saddest water
passed the night keeping guard over a soulless helmet,
a helmet dying on a rose that was born in the vapor that brings sleep
to the castles' mirrors
at that hour when withered tube-roses are recalling their past lives
seeing that dead violets forsake their sheaths
and lutes are silent having lulled themselves to rest.
It is true that phantoms and dream were the invention of the castle's
moat.
I do not know what it is on the battlements that watches that empty
motionless armor.

How is it there are lights that so soon decree the agony of swords
when they think that a lily is guarded by sword-blades that long
    outlive it?
To live a short time weeping is the fate of the snow which mistakes
    its way.
In the south, a bird of cold climes is always cut off almost in the
    flower of its youth.

                                    E. L. T.

Luis Cernuda

(1904-1963)

Born in Seville, he studied under Pedro Salinas at the University of that city. He took his law degree, but he never practiced. He taught briefly in France. During the Spanish Civil War he served and fought for the Spanish Republic. After the War he lived as an exile in Scotland, England, and later in Mexico.

Profile of the Air (1927), his first published work, deals with love and nature. The influence of Juan Ramón Jiménez and Jorge Guillén, to be noted in this volume, later gave way to surrealistic, despairing, and existential themes. The influence of Bécquer, whom Cernuda greatly admired, is also felt in the intangible, immaterial poetry. Although Cernuda wrote a great number of volumes, following the example of Guillén, he wrote one master work, *Reality and Desire* (1936), which went through a number of different editions. Some of the previous poetry collected in this volume includes the surrealistic *A River, A Love* (1929), the love poems of *Prohibited Pleasures* (1931), and the more sensual ones of *Where Forgetfulness Resides* (1935). Other titles are *The Young Sailor* (1936); *The Clouds* (1937), whose themes are religion, war, and death; *As One Who Awaits the Dawn* (1943), on man and his alienation from society; and *Ocnos* (1942), semilyrical confessions about Spanish poetry. Cernuda also wrote a great number of critical studies on Spanish and foreign literatures.

Cernuda is one of the most important surrealistic writers of modern Spain; and his major work, *Reality and Desire,* with its intellectual, romantic, sensual, religious and existential themes, should survive the rigors of time.

All selections, given in their entirety, are from *Reality and Desire.* "The Case of the Murdered Bird" is from Section III, "A River, A Love"; "Like the Light Sound" is from *Prohibited Pleasures,* Section IV; "Spanish Elegy," the first of two such poems by the same name, is from *The Clouds,* Section VII. The latest edition of *Reality and Desire* contains poems written between 1924 and 1956.

THE CASE OF THE MURDERED BIRD

We shall never know, never,
For what reason one day
Those lights were trembling gently.
It was a mournful foam,
A stronger breeze, perhaps nothing.
Only the waves know really.

Therefore to-day they show disdainfully
The color of their glances,
The color ignorant still, though a memory
Sings to it something very gently.

It was a bird perhaps murdered;
No one knows. By no one
Or by someone, sad perhaps, on the stones,
On the walls of the sky.

But of that to-day nothing is known.
Only a trembling of lights very gently,
A color of glances in the waves or in the breeze;
Also, perhaps, a fear.
All is uncertain, truly.

Translated by E. L. Turnbull

LIKE THE LIGHT SOUND

Like the light sound
Of a leaf that grazes a pane,
Water that caresses pebbles,
Rain that kisses a young forehead;

Like a swift caress,
A bare foot on the pathway,
Fingers that essay first love,
Warm sheets on a lonely body;

Like fleeting desire,
Brilliant silk in the light,
Slender adolescent just glimpsed,
Tears wept for being more than a man;

Like this life that is not mine
And nevertheless is mine;
Like this eagerness without name
That does not belong to me and yet is myself;

Like all that which near or far
Touches me, kisses me, wounds me,
Your presence is with me without and within,
Is my life itself and is not my life,
Thus like a leaf and another leaf,
They are the semblance of the wind that bears them away.

E. L. T.

SPANISH ELEGY

Tell me, speak to me,
You mysterious essence
Of our race
After so many centuries,
Creating breath
Of men now living,
Whom I see moved by hatred
Even to offer up their souls
To death, the deepest mother land.

When the ancient springtime
Returns to weave its enchantment
Over your vast body,
Which bird will find a nest
And what sap a branch
Where to put forth with green impulse?
What ray of joyous light,
What cloud over lonely field,

Will find water, the mirror of home at peace
Where to reflect its rainbow-hued movement?

Speak to me, Mother;
And calling you thus, I say
That never was woman to anyone
Such a mother as you are to me.
Speak to me, say but
One word to me in these sluggish days,
In these formless days
That seem to wield before you
A bitter knife
In the hands of your very own sons.

Do not draw away, absorbed in thought
Under your long veils the color of ashes
That deny to us your beautiful wide eyes.
Those fallen flowers,
Their petals torn midst blood and mire,
In your hands were shining eternally
Centuries back, when my life
Was a dream in the mind of the gods.

It is you, your eyes that he seeks,
He who calls you struggling with death,
You, distant and enigmatical
Mother of so many departed souls
That bequeathed to you, with the flash of a clear stone,
Their longing for eternity, founded on beauty.

But you are not only
Mistress of dead longings;
You have been tender and loving with our living longing,
Merciful with the misfortunes of our short lives.
Did you know perchance if we were worthy of you?

Now look through your tears:
See how many are the traitors,
See how many are the cowards,
Far from you in shameful flight,
Denying your name and your bosom,
When at your feet, during the long waiting,

If from the ground we lift our eyes to you,
Your sons dimly foresee
The reward of these prophetic hours.

He does not know what life is
Who never drew breath in battle.
The war soars above us with dark wings,
I hear its icy whistle,
And I see the sudden dead
Fall on the scorched grass,
While my body
Suffers and struggles with some in front of those others.

I do not know what trembles and dies within me
At seeing you thus grieved and lonely,
In ruins the fair gifts
Of your sons, across the ages;
For much have I loved your past,
Victorious radiance between darkness and oblivion.

You are your past
And at the same time you are
The dawn that as yet does not illumine our fields.
Alone you survive
Even though death may come;
Only in you lies the power
To make us await the future blindly.

For in spite of these and those dead
And in spite of these and those living that fight,
Something makes known that you suffer with all.
And their hatred, their cruelty, their struggle,
Before you are vain as are their lives,
For you are eternal
And you created them only
For the peace and the glory of their lineage.

                                        E. L. T.

Miguel Hernández

(1910-1942)

Born into a poor peasant family in Orihuela, he earned his living as a goatherd and by selling milk. He studied in public school and then with the Jesuits. He became an ardent Catholic. At the age of sixteen he began writing poetry and contributed to various literary reviews. When Juan Ramón Jiménez met him, he was amazed at the young poet's ability and called him that "surprising boy from Orihuela." Hernández married Josefina Manresa Marluenda, the daughter of a member of the Civil Guard, and she became the inspiration for some of his poetry. During the Civil War he fought for the Republic, and when his side lost he was imprisoned. The authorities denied him adequate medical care and food, and as a result of his sufferings he died at the age of thirty-two in a Franco prison. He wrote his last words on the prison walls, taking leave of his brothers, comrades, and wife, as well as of the sun and the wheat, symbols of the nature he loved so much. For Hernández was typically a telluric poet, and his physical work with the earth and animals never ceased to be one of his most important poetic inspirations.

In addition to a few dramas, Hernández wrote the following published works: *Moon Connoisseur* (1933), dehumanized and Gongoristic poetry influenced somewhat by that of Jorge Guillén and Rafael Alberti; *The Never Ceasing Lightning* (1936), sonnets on love and death, containing pantheistic and existentialistic themes; *Winds of the People* (1937), which won him a share of the National Prize for Poetry, on the horrors of war in general and the Spanish Civil War in particular; *The Man in Ambush* (1939), full of painful reflections on the victims of the Spanish Civil War, and on the tragic destiny of man; *Song and Ballad Book of Absences* (1938-41), poetry written in jail and showing the despair of a man near death who longs for his family and thinks of the approaching end. Hernández also wrote many uncollected poems, whose themes were those of sadness, solitude, and unrequited love. His "Fatal Summons" was the third twentieth-century elegy dedicated to Ignacio Sánchez Mejías, the great bullfighter.

Hernández was a deep poet who sang of love and nature, at times almost with a mystical fervor. Like most other good Spanish poets of the twentieth century, he represents a fusion of popular and cultural elements. Unlike some, he felt that poetry, in addition, should attempt to uplift the people and fix their eyes on far and perhaps utopian horizons. His unfortunate death ended the career of one whose poetic gifts might have enabled him to equal the greatest names in Spanish literature.

"Moon Connoisseur" is from the book by that same name. "The Never Ceasing Lightning" and "My name is clay" come from *The Never Ceasing Lightning*. "Winds of the People" is from the volume by that name. "The Lullaby of the Onion" is from *Song and Ballad Book of Absences*. All the selections, except "Winds of the People," are given in their entirety.

MOON CONNOISSEUR

To glory, to glory, bullfighters!
It is almost the time of my quarter moon,
Brash emulators of the lizard
Magnificent in your shining colors.
Through the arch, against the picadors
I go like an arrow of horns.
To your glory, rake of the arena, if I do not
anchor you first on my gilded horns.

Translated by Kessel Schwartz

THE NEVER CEASING LIGHTNING

A hungry knife
its sharp wing sweet and deadly
flies a circle of brilliance
around my life.

A lightning bolt
of contorted metal
pecks at my side,
fashioning there a nest of sadness.

My temple, that florid balcony
of my early years,
is now black—and my heart,
my heart is white with age.

So great is the strength
of this ever circling pain,
that I go by night to meet my youth
as the stealthy moon entering the village.

I pick with my eyelashes,
salt of the soul and salt of the eye,
and flowers, from the web of my sadness
I pick.

Where could I go
that I would not look for damnation?
Your destiny is the shore,
mine is the sea.

That I should rest from this labor
of hurricane, love or hell,
is not possible—and pain itself
will shape me, to my unending grief.

But at the end
it is I who will conquer
oh bird and lightning ray of life, and you, my heart,
for no one will make me doubt of death.

Go on, then, go on knife,
flying and stabbing. Some day
time will grow yellow
on my photograph.

K. S.

My name is clay . . .

My name is clay though they call me Michael.
Clay is my profession and my destiny,
which spots with its tongue whatever it licks.

I am a sad instrument of the road.
I am a sweetly infamous tongue
spread out at the feet I idolize.

Like a nocturnal, fallow water ox
who wants to be an idolized creature,
I charge at your shoes and all around you,
and made of rugs and of kisses
I kiss and sow with flowers the heel which injures me.

I place reliquaries of my kind
at your biting heel, at your footstep,
and I always anticipate that step
so that your unfeeling foot may scorn
all the love which I lift up to you.

When the glass woolly with ice bleats,
When winter closes your window,
I place beneath your feet a winged hawk,
stained with clay and heart of earth,
wetter than the face of my tears.
Under your feet a melted comb
of humble honey, trampled and alone,
a scorned and fallen heart
like seaweed in a dying wave.

Clay, vainly I invest myself with poppy,
clay, vainly I stretch out my arms,
clay, in vain I bite your heels,
giving you badly wounded flapping
toads like convulsed hearts.

Scarcely have you tread, barely have you placed on me
the image of your heel,
then it breaks and shatters the armor
of bipartite syrup which girdles my mouth
with pure and lively flesh,
asking, fragmented, that it may be pressed
always by your foot of free, mad, hare.

Its taciturn froth clusters,
sobs agitate the branches
of cerebral wool under your step.
And you walk by, and the winter wax
is set on fire by the setting sun,
martyr, jewel and pasture of the wheels,

glutted with submitting to the
circular daggers of the cart and the sharp hoof.
Beware, for clay may bear animals
of corrosive skin and vengeful claw.

Fear that the clay may suddenly grow,
fear that it increase and climb and cover tenderly,
tenderly and jealously
your reed ankle, my torment,
fear that it may inundate the tuberose of your leg
and grow and ascend your forehead.

Fear that it rise with hurricane force
from the bland winter earth
and shatter and thunder and fall in floods,
strong and tender, on your blood.

Fear an assault of offended foam
and fear a loving cataclysm.

Before the drought consumes it,
the clay will have engulfed you.

K. S.

WINDS OF THE PEOPLE

Winds of the people pull me,
winds of the people drag me,
winds of the people,
scatter my heart,
winnow my throat.

Oxen when beaten
drop their heads
pitiably meek,
but the lions lift their heads,
bring death with their deadly claws.

I am not of the people of oxen,
but I am the son of that people
all fierce like lions,
son of that people
whose mountain crags
are with eagles filled,
whose meadows are watched over
by the proud and fearless bull.

Never did the oxen fare
in the desolate meseta of Spain.
What black mind would put the yoke
to the necks of heroes?
Who shall ever harness the hurricane?
Who imprison the thunderbolt?
Asturians of braveries,
Basques of armored stone,
Valencians of laughter,
Castilians wrought of the soil,
from the earth rising on wings,
Andalusians, hot as lightning,
swift torrent, river of tears,
born of the guitar and the anvil.
Men of Estremadura,
bodies the color of rye,
Galicians of rain and peace,
Catalonians, the steady,
Aragonese of noble ancestors,
Murcians of dynamite
fruitfully exploding,
Leonese, Navarrese, masters all,
masters of hunger, sweat, and the ax,
kings of the deep mines,
lords of the turned fields,
men like trees whose proud deep roots
go from life to death,
from nothing to nothing.
Yokes they would hang on us,
these tyrants of madness,
yokes you will break on their heads.

If I die, let me die
with my head upraised,

dead, twenty times dead,
with my mouth to the grama grass.

Singing, I await death,
for above the rattle of the machine guns,
above the din of the battle lines—
listen—the nightingales sing!

Translated by Willard Maas

THE LULLABY OF THE ONION[1]

The onion is cold
never-ending poverty.
Cold as your days are cold,
Cold as my nights.
Hunger and onions
Black ice of hunger, and frost
large and round.

In a cradle of hunger
my child lay.
On the blood of the onion
he sucked.
So your blood, my son
is a frosting of sugar
and onion and hunger.

A dark woman
dissolved in moonlight
pours herself drop by drop
over the cradle.
Laugh, child,
that the moon is yours to swallow
when you have need.

---

1. Hernández wrote this poem upon receiving his wife's letter in which she said the child had only bread and onions to eat. He dedicated the poem to his son. (*Editor's note.*)

Laugh and laugh again,
Lark of my house!
Your laughter is to my eyes
the light of the world.
Laugh, loudly and long,
that my soul, on hearing you,
will fly free.

Your laughter frees me—it gives me
wings—it takes away
loneliness—it tears me
from my prison
Oh little mouth that flies to me!
Oh heart that on your lips bursts!

Your laughter is
a victorious sword,
conqueror of flowers
and larks.
Rival of the sun
Future of my body
and my love.

Warm new flesh fluttering with life,
Bright questioning eyes,
A picture that had never been painted.
How many bright birds
will flutter and soar
from your body!

I awoke from innocence.
You must never wake up.
Sadness' taste is in my mouth.
You must always laugh.
Always, from your cradle, little bird.
Defend your laughter
feather by feather.

Your flight is high,
my newborn son,
and so vast,
it merges with the heavens.

If only I too
could soar
to the source of your life.

On the eighth month of your life you laugh at me
With five orange blossoms in your mouth.
With five small
ferocities,
with five teeth,
with five blooming
jasmines.

They shall grow to be the guardian and strength
of tomorrow's kisses,
when you feel them
to be a weapon of love.
And someday you will feel the fire that begins there
And flows down and down, searching for
the very center of your being.

Fly my son, to the two moons
of the breast.
You will be satisfied.
It will help the sadness of the onion.
Do not crumble away.
Do not try to know what's wrong
nor what is happening.

                                        K. S.

José Hierro

(1922-   )

Although he spent the greater part of his life in Santander, he now lives in Madrid. He published his first works in the review *Proel,* which he directed. His volume *Joy* (1947) won the coveted Adonais prize, and his poetic anthology, published in 1953, won the National Prize for Literature. His first collection, *Land Without Us* (1947), gives us the notes to be found throughout his work. He writes tender poems of love, joy and sadness, solitude, death, and the passing of time, and although some critics, and the poet himself, have occasionally reflected adversely on his poetic style, his ear for rhythm, his simplicity and depth of thought, existential themes, and social interests make him one of the most important contemporary poets. Hierro considers himself a documentary poet. "If some poem of mine is read, by chance, a hundred years from now, it will not be for its poetic value but for its documental value."

In spite of his direct poetry and his disdain for esthetic concern, he believes in formal beauty which fits the modern need. Although much of his poetry involves a reporting of events, he also writes poetry he calls "hallucinations," more emotional and more poetic, in the historical sense of that word, but he continues to reject isolated beauty unless it reflects humanity and human problems in some way. Although many call him an existential poet, he refuses to agonize and despair because even in the darkest moments life offers its beautiful colors. Many have seen in his work a constant criticism of the contemporary Spanish situation and government, but he always offers a note of optimism and hope.

Among his other collections are: *With the Stones, With the Wind* (1950), on love and life and the passing of time; *As Much as I Know of Me* (1957); and *Collected Poetry* (1962).

All the poems are given in their entirety. "Farewell to the Sea" and "First Morning" are both from *Land Without Us.* "The Sun Sinks" is from *Book of Hallucinations,* part of Hierro's *Collected Poetry.*

FAREWELL TO THE SEA

No matter how I try at leave-taking
to keep you completely in my corner
of solitude, no matter how much I want
to drink your infinite eyes,
your long silvery afternoons
your vast gesture, gray and cold,
I know that on returning to your shores
we shall feel differently.
Never again shall I see you
with these eyes that look at you today.

That apple perfume,
whence does it come? Oh dream of mine,
sea of mine! Fuse me, remove
my flesh, my mortal dress!
Forget me in the sand
and let me also be one more son,
a treasure of calm water
which returns to you, to your saline
birth, to live your life
like the saddest of rivers!
Fresh branches of foam . . .
Dreaming, vague boats . . . Children
gleaning the setting honey
of the sun . . . What a new, fresh, clean
world! It is born daily
from the sea, and travels the roads
which surround my soul, and runs
to hide beneath the shade,
lugubrious oil of night,
returning to its origin and beginning.
And Oh, I now must leave you
to travel another road! . . .

No matter how I try on parting
to carry your image, sea, with me;
no matter how I wish to transfix you,
to fix you, exactly, in my senses;

no matter how I seek your chains
to deny myself my destiny,
I know that soon your gray mesh
of tenuous threads will break.
Never again shall I see you
with these eyes which view you today.

Translated by K. Schwartz

FIRST MORNING

How alone, earth, without us!
It is possible that it is the soul,
vagabond along your slope,
which feels alone.
Today it is my foot which travels you.
Step by step it disenchants you.
More than one hundred years of your dream
reclining on the seas.
More than one hundred years without us,
chained to other dawns.
We walked through your memory
as though reflected in your image.
When we tried to seize your stone
in our hands, it liquefied.
When we tried to smell your grass,
hear your wind among the reeds,
bite the bread of your autumns,
drink the wine of your vines,
when we tried to feel ourselves, earth,
crying children in your skirt,
other autumns, other winds,
other waves awoke us
from our silent evening
and our tragic morning.

I look. I see you as always:
newly disenchanted.
Today it is my foot which travels you,
my own voice which calls you

among the reeds, between the apple trees,
between the ruins of ships
like skeletons of whales
who died on your beaches.

How sad, land without us!
It is possible that it is the vagabond soul,
along your slope,
which feels alone.

K. S.

THE SUN SINKS

Pardon me. It will not occur again.
Now I should like
to meditate, gather myself, forget: be
a leaf of forgetfulness and solitude.
There would have been need of the wind
which scatters the scales of autumn
with noise and color.
The wind would have been needed.

I speak with humility,
with disillusion, the gratitude
of one who lived from the alms of life.
With the sadness of one who seeks
a poor truth on which to lean and rest.
Beautiful alms—beings, dreams, events, love—
gratuitous gift, because I deserved nothing.

And the truth! And the truth!
Sought sporadically, in beings,
wounding them and wounding me;
stirred up in words;
dug from the depth of deeds
minimum, gigantic, what difference does it make:
after all, nobody knows
what is small and what is large;
a cherry may be called large
("today cherries fall alone,"

they told me one day, and I know why it was),
a mountain may be small,
the universe and love—.

I have forgotten something
that had happened.
Something of which I repented
or, perhaps, I bragged.
Something that must have been different.
Something that was important
because it belonged to my life: it was my life.
(Pardon me if I consider my life important:
it is all that I have, that I had;
I must have lived it a long time ago
in darkness, without tongue, ears or hands,
hanging in the void,
without hope.)

But history (nostalgia)
has been erased
and I have no projects
for tomorrow, nor even believe
that that morrow exists (hope).
I walk through the present
and I do not live the present
(plenitude in sorrow and joy).
I seem an exile
who has forgotten even his country's name,
his exact situation, the roads
which lead to it.
Pardon me for needing
to ascertain its exact site.

And when I know where I lost it,
I want to offer you my exile, which is worth
as much as life for me, which is its meaning.
And then sad, but firm,
pardon me, I shall offer you a life
now with neither demon nor hallucinations.

                                        K. S.

PART III

Essay

Miguel De Unamuno*

(1864-1936)

Unamuno lived a life of struggle and doubt, at war with himself constantly. From an ardent Catholic family, he experienced a religious
crisis in 1897 in an attempt to re-create his youthful faith, which insisted
that immortailty of the soul was his even as his reason denied it. He
sought that immortality through his creative works, especially his poetry,
through his children, through religious faith, and in the flesh. This quest,
along with a great love for Spain, were the key threads in almost all his
essays. These covered a wide range of topics in social, political, philosophical, and religious areas, for Unamuno was the most cultured and
well-read member of the Generation of '98. He conveyed his thoughts in
a personal, almost conversational, style, often filled with contradictions.
He explained away these contradictions as he claimed: "My undertaking
has been, is and will be, that those who read me think and meditate on
fundamental things, and it has never been to offer them ready made
solutions." His constant search for truth led him to make many im-
passioned statements, for, as he said, "I do not give ideas nor propose
doctrines. I give pieces of my heart."

Among his principal essays are: *About Purity* (1895), *Life of Don
Quijote and Sancho* (1905), *My Religion and Other Essays* (1910),
Soliloquies and Conversations (1911), *Of the Tragic Sense of Life in
Man and in Peoples* (1913), *Essays* (7 volumes) (1917-18), and *The
Agony of Christianity*, written first in French in 1925 and published in
Spanish in 1931.

About Purity concerns Unamuno's spiritual and historical evaluation
of the Castilian and eternal tradition. He coined the expression "intrahistory" to explain his concept of acceptance of the world of present
exterior reality as but a temporal fragment of an eternal inner day-by-day
history of the soul, a kind of sedimentation and eternalization of a series
of "presents" already past, which represented the sum total of the efforts
and souls of all previous Spaniards. He sought a new interpretation of
the Spanish spirit, rejecting science and modern technology as solutions
to Spain's problems, and in spite of Spain's backwardness in certain areas,
he attempted always to emphasize positive Spanish values and traditions.
Thus, he tried to define the essence of national culture and art, as he

---

* See pp. 55-56 and p. 189.

279

examined the role of language, traditionalism, social thought, will, and the need for the rejuvenation of Spain.

The *Life of Don Quixote and Sancho* interprets the characters of Cervantes' novel as symbols of the Spanish soul and offers a profession of faith in the Quixotic purpose, which Unamuno associates with Christ, survival, and immortality.

Unamuno's major essay is *The Tragic Sense of Life*, a kind of personal confession, which examines the conflict between time and eternity, faith and knowledge, materialism and idealism, as the author agonizes about the impossibility of immortality of both the spirit and the flesh. Through love and compassion giving rise to faith, Unamuno hopes existentially through will and action to resolve the contradictions inherent in the problem and to achieve immortality through his hunger for eternity. He acknowledges the problem of the man of flesh and blood who is born to die and who must come to terms with extinction and nothingness. His immortality will be one of struggle, not of absorption, peace or appeasement. His reason may insist there is no proof of the beyond, but his heart will always tell him there must be something after this earthly life.

The selection given is the entire first chapter of *The Tragic Sense of Life*.

The Tragic Sense of Life

CHAPTER 1

THE MAN OF FLESH AND BONE

Homo sum; nihil humani a me alienum puto, said the Latin playwright. And I would rather say, *Nullum hominem a me alienum puto:* I am a man; no other man do I deem a stranger. For to me the adjective *humanus* is no less suspect than its abstract substantive *humanitas,* humanity. Neither "the human" nor "humanity," neither the simple adjective nor the substantivized adjective, but the concrete substantive—man. The man of flesh and bone; the man who is born, suffers, and dies—above all, who dies; the man who eats and drinks and plays and sleeps and thinks and wills; the man who is seen and heard; the brother, the real brother.

For there is another thing which is also called man, and he is the subject of not a few lucubrations, more or less scientific. He is the legendary featherless biped, the ζῷον πολιτικόν[1] of Aristotle, the social contractor of Rousseau, the *homo economicus* of the Manchester school, the *homo sapiens* of Linnæus, or, if you like, the vertical mammal. A man neither of here nor there, neither of this age nor of another, who has neither sex nor country, who is, in brief, merely an idea. That.is to say, a no-man.

The man we have to do with is the man of flesh and bone—I, you, reader of mine, the other man yonder, all of us who walk solidly on the earth.

And this concrete man, this man of flesh and bone, is at once the subject and the supreme object of all philosophy, whether certain self-styled philosophers like it or not.

In most of the histories of philosophy that I know, philosophic systems are presented to us as if growing out of one another spontaneously, and their authors, the philosophers, appear only as mere pretexts. The inner biography of the philosophers, of the men who philosophized, occupies a secondary place. And yet it is precisely this inner biography that explains for us most things.

It behooves us to say, before all, that philosophy lies closer to poetry than to science. All philosophic systems which have been constructed as a supreme concord of the final results of the individual sciences have in every age possessed much less consistency and life than those which expressed the integral spiritual yearning of their authors.

And, though they concern us so greatly, and are, indeed, indispensable for our life and thought, the sciences are in a certain sense more foreign to us than philosophy. They fulfil a more objective end—that is to say, an end more external to ourselves. They are fundamentally a matter of economics. A new scientific discovery, of the kind called theoretical, is, like a mechanical discovery— that of the steam-engine, the telephone, the phonograph, or the aeroplane—a thing which is useful for something else. Thus the telephone may be useful to us in enabling us to communicate at a distance with the woman we love. But she, wherefore is she useful to us? A man takes an electric tram to go to hear an opera, and asks himself, Which, in this case, is the more useful, the tram or the opera?

Philosophy answers to our need of forming a complete and unitary conception of the world and of life, and as a result of this conception, a feeling which gives birth to an inward attitude and

---

1. Political man. (*Editor's note.*)

even to outward action. But the fact is that this feeling, instead of
being a consequence of this conception, is the cause of it. Our
philosophy—that is, our mode of understanding or not understanding the world and life—springs from our feeling towards life itself.
And life, like everything affective, has roots in subconsciousness,
perhaps in unconsciousness.

It is not usually our ideas that make us optimists or pessimists,
but it is our optimism or our pessimism, of physiological or perhaps
pathological origin, as much the one as the other, that makes our
ideas.

Man is said to be a reasoning animal. I do not know why he
has not been defined as an affective or feeling animal. Perhaps
that which differentiates him from other animals is feeling rather
than reason. More often I have seen a cat reason than laugh or
weep. Perhaps it weeps or laughs inwardly—but then perhaps, also
inwardly, the crab resolves equations of the second degree.

And thus, in a philosopher, what must needs most concern us
is the man.

Take Kant, the man Immanuel Kant, who was born and lived
at Königsberg, in the latter part of the eighteenth century and the
beginning of the nineteenth. In the philosophy of this man Kant,
a man of heart and head—that is to say, a man—there is a significant
somersault, as Kierkegaard, another man—and what a man!—would
have said, the somersault from the *Critique of Pure Reason* to the
Critique of Practical Reason. He reconstructs in the latter what he
destroyed in the former, in spite of what those may say who do
not see the man himself. After having examined and pulverized
with his analysis the traditional proofs of the existence of God, of
the Aristotelian God, who is the God corresponding to the ζῷον
πολιτικόν, the abstract God, the unmoved prime Mover, he reconstructs God anew; but the God of the conscience, the Author
of the moral order—the Lutheran God, in short. This transition of
Kant exists already in embryo in the Lutheran notion of faith.

The first God, the rational God, is the projection to the outward
infinite of man as he is by defintion—that is to say, of the abstract
man, of the man no-man; the other God, the God of feeling and
volition, is the projection to the inward infinite of man as he is by
life, of the concrete man, the man of flesh and bone.

Kant reconstructed with the heart that which with the head he
had overthrown. And we know, from the testimony of those who
knew him and from his testimony in his letters and private declara-
tions, that the man Kant, the more or less selfish old bachelor who

professed philosophy at Königsberg at the end of the century of the Encyclopedia and the goddess of Reason, was a man much pre-occupied with the problem—I mean with the only real vital prob-lem, the problem that strikes at the very root of our being, the problem of our individual and personal destiny, of the immortality of the soul. The man Kant was not resigned to die utterly. And because he was not resigned to die utterly he made that leap, that immortal somersault,[1] from the one Critique to the other.

Whosoever reads the *Critique of Practical Reason* carefully and without blinkers will see that, in strict fact, the existence of God is therein deduced from the immortality of the soul, and not the immortality of the soul from the existence of God. The categorical imperative leads us to a moral postulate which necessitates in its turn, in the teleological or rather eschatological order, the im-mortality of the soul, and in order to sustain this immortality God is introduced. All the rest is the jugglery of the professional of philosophy.

The man Kant felt that morality was the basis of eschatology, but the professor of philosophy inverted the terms.

Another professor, the professor and man William James, has somewhere said that for the generality of men God is the provider of immortality. Yes, for the generality of men, including the man Kant, the man James, and the man who writes these lines which you, reader, are reading.

Talking to a peasant one day, I proposed to him the hypothesis that there might indeed be a God who governs heaven and earth, a Consciousness[2] of the Universe, but that for all that the soul of every man may not be immortal in the traditional and concrete sense. He replied: "Then wherefore God?" So answered, in the secret tribunal of their consciousness, the man Kant and the man James. Only in their capacity as professors they were compelled to justify rationally an attitude in itself so little rational. Which does not mean, of course, that the attitude is absurd.

Hegel made famous his aphorism that all the rational is real and all the real rational; but there are many of us who, unconvinced by Hegel, continue to believe that the real, the really real, is irra-

---

1. *"Salto inmortal."* There is a play here upon the term *salto mortal,* used to denote the dangerous aerial somersault of the acrobat, which cannot be rendered in English.—J. E. C. F.

2. *"Conciencia."* The same word is used in Spanish to denote both consciousness and conscience. If the latter is specifically intended, the qualifying adjective *"moral"* or *"religiosa"* is commonly added.—J. E. C. F.

tional, that reason builds upon irrationalities. Hegel, a great framer of definitions, attempted with definitions to reconstruct the universe, like that artillery sergeant who said that cannon were made by taking a hole and enclosing it with steel.

Another man, the man Joseph Butler, the Anglican bishop who lived at the beginning of the eighteenth century and who Cardinal Newman declared to be the greatest man in the Anglican Church, wrote, at the conclusion of the first chapter of his great work, *The Analogy of Religion,* the chapter which treats of a future life, these pregnant words: "This credibility of a future life, which has been here insisted upon, how little soever it may satisfy our curiosity, seems to answer all the purposes of religion, in like manner as a demonstrative proof would. Indeed a proof, even a demonstrative one, of a future life, would not be a proof of religion. For, that we are to live hereafter, is just as reconcilable with the scheme of atheism, and as well to be accounted for by it, as that we are now alive is: and therefore nothing can be more absurd than to argue from that scheme that there can be no future state."

The man Butler, whose works were perhaps known to the man Kant, wished to save the belief in the immortality of the soul, and with this object he made it independent of belief in God. The first chapter of his *Analogy* treats, as I have said, of the future life, and the second of the government of God by rewards and punishments. And the fact is that, fundamentally, the good Anglican bishop deduces the existence of God from the immortality of the soul. And as this deduction was the good Anglican bishop's starting-point, he had not to make that somersault which at the close of the same century the good Lutheran philosopher had to make. Butler, the bishop, was one man and Kant, the professor, another man.

To be a man is to be something concrete, unitary, and substantive; it is to be a thing—*res.* Now we know what another man, the man Benedict Spinoza, that Portuguese Jew who was born and lived in Holland in the middle of the seventeenth century, wrote about the nature of things. The sixth proposition of Part III. of his *Ethic* states: *unaquæque res, quatenus in se est, in suo esse perseverare conatur*—that is, Everything, in so far as it is in itself, endeavours to persist in its own being. Everything in so far as it is in itself—that is to say, in so far as it is substance, for according to him substance is *id quod in se est et per se concipitur*—that which is in itself and is conceived by itself. And in the following proposition, the seventh, of the same part, he adds: *conatus, quo unaquæ-*

que res in suo esse perseverare conatur, nihil est præter ispsius rei actualem essentiam—that is, the endeavour wherewith everything endeavours to persist in its own being is nothing but the actual essence of the thing itself. This means that your essence, reader, mine, that of the man Spinoza, that of the man Butler, of the man Kant, and of every man who is a man, is nothing but the endeavour, the effort, which he makes to continue to be a man, not to die. And the other proposition which follows these two, the eighth, says: *conatus, quo unaquæque res in suo esse perseverare conatur, nullum tempus finitum, sed indefinitum involvit*—that is, The endeavour whereby each individual thing endeavours to persist involves no finite time but indefinite time. That is to say that you, I, and Spinoza wish never to die and that this longing of ours never to die is our actual essence. Nevertheless, this poor Portuguese Jew, exiled in the mists of Holland, could never attain to believing in his own personal immortality, and all his philosophy was but a consolation which he contrived for his lack of faith. Just as other men have a pain in hand or foot, heart-ache or head-ache, so he had God-ache. Unhappy man! And unhappy fellow-men!

And man, this thing, is he a thing? How absurd soever the question may appear, there are some who have propounded it. Not long ago there went abroad a certain doctrine called Positivism, which did much good and much ill. And among other ills that it wrought was the introduction of a method of analysis whereby facts were pulverized, reduced to a dust of facts. Most of the facts labelled as such by Positivism were really only fragments of facts. In psychology its action was harmful. There were even scholastics meddling in literature—I will not say philosophers meddling in poetry, because poet and philosopher are twin brothers, if not even one and the same—who carried this Positivist psychological analysis into the novel and the drama, where the main business is to give act and motion to concrete men, men of flesh and bone, and by dint of studying states of consciousness, consciousness itself disappeared. The same thing happened to them which is said often to happen in the examination and testing of certain complicated, organic, living chemical compounds, when the reagents destroy the very body which it was proposed to examine and all that is obtained is the products of its decomposition.

Taking as their starting-point the evident fact that contradictory states pass through our consciousness, they did not succeed in envisaging consciousness itself, the "I." To ask a man about his

"I" is like asking him about his body. And note that in speaking of the "I," I speak of the concrete and personal "I," not of the "I" of Fichte, but of Fichte himself, the man Fichte.

That which determines a man, that which makes him one man, one and not another, the man he is and not the man he is not, is a principle of unity and a principle of continuity. A principle of unity firstly in space, thanks to the body, and next in action and intention. When we walk, one foot does not go forward and the other backward, nor, when we look, if we are normal, does one eye look towards the north and the other towards the south. In each moment of our life we entertain some purpose, and to this purpose the synergy of our actions is directed. Notwithstanding the next moment we may change our purpose. And in a certain sense a man is so much the more a man the more unitary his action. Some there are who throughout their whole life follow but one single purpose, be it what it may.

Also a principle of continuity in time. Without entering upon a discussion—an unprofitable discussion—as to whether I am or am not he who I was twenty years ago, it appears to me to be indisputable that he who I am to-day derives, by a continuous series of states of consciousness, from him who was in my body twenty years ago. Memory is the basis of individual personality, just as tradition is the basis of the collective personality of a people. We live in memory and by memory, and our spiritual life is at bottom simply the effort of our memory to persist, to transform itself into hope, the effort of our past to transform itself into our future.

All this, I know well, is sheer platitude; but in going about in the world one meets men who seem to have no feeling of their own personality. One of my best friends with whom I have walked and talked every day for many years, whenever I spoke to him of this sense of one's own personality, used to say: "But I have no sense of myself; I don't know what that is."

On a certain occasion this friend remarked to me: "I should like to be So-and so" (naming someone), and I said: "That is what I shall never be able to understand—that one should want to be someone else. To want to be someone else is to want to cease to be he who one is. I understand that one should wish to have what someone else has, his wealth or his knowledge; but to be someone else, that is a thing I cannot comprehend." It has often been said that every man who has suffered misfortunes prefers to be himself, even with his misfortunes, rather than to be someone else without them. For unfortunate men, when they preserve their normality in their misfortune—that is to say, when they endeavour to persist in their own being—prefer misfortune to non-existence. For myself I can say that as a youth, and even as a child, I remained unmoved when shown the most moving pictures of hell, for even then nothing appeared to me quite so horrible as nothingness itself. It was a furious hunger of being that possessed me, an appetite for divinity, as one of our ascetics has put it.[1]

To propose to a man that he should be someone else, that he should become someone else, is to propose to him that he should cease to be himself. Everyone defends his own personality, and only consents to a change in his mode of thinking or of feeling in so far as this change is able to enter into the unity of his spirit and become involved in its continuity; in so far as this change can harmonize and integrate itself with all the rest of his mode of being, thinking and feeling, and can at the same time knit itself with his memories. Neither of a man nor of a people—which is, in a certain sense, also a man—can a change be demanded which breaks the unity and continuity of the person. A man can change greatly, almost completely even, but the change must take place within his continuity.

It is true that in certain individuals there occur what are called changes of personality; but these are pathological cases, and as such are studied by alienists. In these changes of personality, memory, the basis of consciousness, is completely destroyed, and all that is left to the sufferer as the substratum of his individual continuity, which has now ceased to be personal, is the physical organism. For the subject who suffers it, such an infirmity is equivalent to death—it is not equivalent to death only for those who expect to inherit his fortune, if he possesses one! And this infirmity is nothing less than revolution, a veritable revolution.

A disease is, in a certain sense, an organic dissociation; it is a rebellion of some element or organ of the living body which breaks the vital synergy and seeks an end distinct from that which the other elements coordinated with it seek. Its end, considered in itself— that is to say, in the abstract—may be more elevated, more noble, more anything you like; but it is different. To fly and breathe in the air may be better than to swim and breathe in the water; but if the fins of a fish aimed at converting themselves into wings, the fish, as a fish, would perish. And it is useless to say that it would end by becoming a bird, if in this becoming there was not a process

---

1. San Juan de los Angeles.

of continuity. I do not precisely know, but perhaps it may be possible for a fish to engender a bird, or another fish more akin to a bird than itself; but a fish, this fish, cannot itself and during its own lifetime become a bird.

Everything in me that conspires to break the unity and continuity of my life conspires to destroy me and consequently to destroy itself. Every individual in a people who conspires to break the spiritual unity and continuity of that people tends to destroy it and to destroy himself as a part of that people. What if some other people is better than our own? Very possibly, although perhaps we do not clearly understand what is meant by better or worse. Richer? Granted. More cultured? Granted likewise. Happier? Well, happiness . . . but still, let it pass! A conquering people (or what is called conquering) while we are conquered? Well and good. All this is good—but it is something different. And that is enough. Because for me the becoming other than I am, the breaking of the unity and continuity of my life, is to cease to be he who I am—that is to say, it is simply to cease to be. And that—no! Anything rather than that!

Another, you say, might play the part that I play as well or better? Another might fulfil my function in society? Yes, but it would not be I.

"I, I, I, always I!" some reader will exclaim; "and who are you?" I might reply in the words of Obermann, that tremendous man Obermann:[1] "For the universe, nothing—for myself, everything"; but no, I would rather remind him of a doctrine of the man Kant— to wit, that we ought to think of our fellow-men not as means but as ends. For the question does not touch me alone, it touches you also, grumbling reader, it touches each and all. Singular judgments have the value of universal judgments, the logicians say. The singular is not particular, it is universal.

Man is an end, not a means. All civilization addresses itself to man, to each man, to each I. What is that idol, call it Humanity or call it what you like, to which all men and each individual man must be sacrificed? For I sacrifice myself for my neighbours, for my fellow-countrymen, for my children, and these sacrifice themselves in their turn for theirs, and theirs again for those that come after them, and so on in a never-ending series of generations. And who receives the fruit of this sacrifice?

---

1. A somber, philosophical novel written by Etienne Pivert de Sénancour (1770-1846). (*Editor's note.*)

Those who talk to us about this fantastic sacrifice, this dedication without an object, are wont to talk to us also about the right to live. What is this right to live? They tell me I am here to realize I know not what social end; but I feel that I, like each one of my fellows, am here to realize myself, to live.

Yes, yes, I see it all!—an enormous social activity, a mighty civilization, a profuseness of science, of art, of industry, of morality, and afterwards, when we have filled the world with industrial marvels, with great factories, with roads, museums, and libraries, we shall fall exhausted at the foot of it all, and it will subsist—for whom? Was man made for science or was science made for man?

"Why!" the reader will exclaim again, "we are coming back to what the Catechism says: 'Q. For whom did God create the world? A. For man.'" Well, why not?—so ought the man who is a man to reply. The ant, if it took account of these matters and were a person, would reply "For the ant," and it would reply rightly. The world is made for consciousness, for each consciousness.

A human soul is worth all the universe, someone—I know not whom—has said and said magnificently. A human soul, mind you! Not a human life. Not this life. And it happens that the less a man believes in the soul—that is to say in his conscious immortality, personal and concrete—the more he will exaggerate the worth of this poor transitory life. This is the source from which springs all that effeminate, sentimental ebullition against war. True, a man ought not to wish to die, but the death to be renounced is the death of the soul. "Whosoever will save his life shall lose it," says the Gospel; but it does not say "whosoever will save his soul," the immortal soul—or, at any rate, which we believe and wish to be immortal.

And what all the objectives do not see, or rather do not wish to see, is that when a man affirms his "I," his personal consciousness, he affirms man, man concrete and real, affirms the true humanism —the humanism of man, not of the things of man—and in affirming man he affirms consciousness. For the only consciousness of which we have consciousness is that of man.

The world is for consciousness. Or rather this *for,* this notion of finality, and feeling rather than notion, this teleological feeling, is born only where there is consciousness. Consciousness and finality are fundamentally the same thing.

If the sun possessed consciousness it would think, no doubt, that it lived in order to give light to the worlds; but it would also and above all think that the worlds existed in order that it might

give them light and enjoy itself in giving them light and so live.
And it would think well.

And all this tragic fight of man to save himself, this immortal
craving for immortality which caused the man Kant to make that
immortal leap of which I have spoken, all this is simply a fight
for consciousness. If consciousness is, as some inhuman thinker
has said, nothing more than a flash of light between two eternities
of darkness, then there is nothing more execrable than existence.

Some may espy a fundamental contradiction in everything that
I am saying, now expressing a longing for unending life, now affirming that this earthly life does not possess the value that is given to it.
Contradiction? To be sure! The contradiction of my heart that says
Yes and of my head that says No! Of course there is contradiction.
Who does not recollect those words of the Gospel, "Lord, I believe,
help thou my unbelief"? Contradiction! Of course! Since we only
live in and by contradictions, since life is tragedy and the tragedy
is perpetual struggle, without victory or the hope of victory, life
is contradiction.

The values we are discussing are, as you see, values of the
heart, and against values of the heart reasons do not avail. For
reasons are only reasons—that is to say, they are not even truths.
There is a class of pedantic label-mongers, pedants by nature and
by grace, who remind me of that man who, purposing to console
a father whose son has suddenly died in the flower of his years,
says to him, "Patience, my friend, we all must die!" Would you
think it strange if this father were offended at such an impertinence?
For it is an impertinence. There are times when even an axiom
can become an impertinence. How many times may it not be said—

> *Para pensar cual tú, sólo es preciso*
> *no tener nada mas que inteligencia.*[1]

There are, in fact, people who appear to think only with the
brain, or with whatever may be the specific thinking organ; while
others think with all the body and all the soul, with the blood, with
the marrow of the bones, with the heart, with the lungs, with the
belly, with the life. And the people who think only with the brain
develop into definition-mongers; they become the professionals of
thought. And you know what a professional is? You know what a
product of the differentiation of labour is?

---

1. To be lacking in everything but intelligence is the necessary qualification for thinking like you.

Take a professional boxer. He has learnt to hit with such economy of effort that, while concentrating all his strength in the blow, he only brings into play just those muscles that are required for the immediate and definite object of his action—to knock out his opponent. A blow given by a non-professional will not have so much immediate, objective efficiency; but it will more greatly vitalize the striker, causing him to bring into play almost the whole of his body. The one is the blow of a boxer, the other that of a man. And it is notorious that the Hercules of the circus, the athletes of the ring, are not, as a rule, healthy. They knock out their opponents, they lift enormous weights, but they die of phthisis or dyspepsia.

If a philosopher is not a man, he is anything but a philosopher; he is above all a pedant, and a pedant is a caricature of a man. The cultivation of any branch of science—of chemistry, of physics, of geometry, of philology—may be a work of differentiated specialization, and even so only within very narrow limits and restrictions; but philosophy, like poetry, is a work of integration and synthesis, or else it is merely pseudo-philosophical erudition.

All knowledge has an ultimate object. Knowledge for the sake of knowledge is, say what you will, nothing but a dismal begging of the question. We learn something either for an immediate practical end, or in order to complete the rest of our knowledge. Even the knowledge that appears to us to be most theoretical—that is to say, of least immediate application to the non-intellectual necessities of life—answers to a necessity which is no less real because it is intellectual, to a reason of economy in thinking, to a principle of unity and continuity of consciousness. But just as a scientific fact has its finality in the rest of knowledge, so the philosophy that we would make our own has also its extrinsic object—it refers to our whole destiny, to our attitude in face of life and the universe. And the most tragic problem of philosophy is to reconcile intellectual necessities with the necessities of the heart and the will. For it is on this rock that every philosophy that pretends to resolve the eternal and tragic contradiction, the basis of our existence, breaks to pieces. But do all men face this contradiction squarely?

Little can be hoped from a ruler, for example, who has not at some time or other been preoccupied, even if only confusedly, with the first beginning and the ultimate end of all things, and above all of man, with the "why" of his origin and the "wherefore" of his destiny.

And this supreme preoccupation cannot be purely rational, it must involve the heart. It is not enough to think about our destiny: it must be felt. And the would-be leader of men who affirms and proclaims that he pays no heed to the things of the spirit, is not worthy to lead them. By which I do not mean, of course, that any ready-made solution is to be required of him. Solution? Is there indeed any?

So far as I am concerned, I will never willingly yield myself, nor entrust my confidence, to any popular leader who is not penetrated with the feeling that he who orders a people orders men, men of flesh and bone, men who are born, suffer, and, although they do not wish to die, die; men who are ends in themselves, not merely means; men who must be themselves and not others; men, in fine, who seek that which we call happiness. It is inhuman, for example, to sacrifice one generation of men to the generation which follows, without having any feeling for the destiny of those who are sacrificed, without having any regard, not for their memory, not for their names, but for them themselves.

All this talk of a man surviving in his children, or in his works, or in the universal consciousness, is but vague verbiage which satisfies only those who suffer from affective stupidity, and who, for the rest, may be persons of a certain cerebral distinction. For it is possible to possess great talent, or what we call great talent, and yet to be stupid as regards the feelings and even morally imbecile. There have been instances.

These clever-witted, affectively stupid persons are wont to say that it is useless to seek to delve in the unknowable or to kick against the pricks. It is as if one should say to a man whose leg has had to be amputated that it does not help him at all to think about it. And we all lack something; only some of us feel the lack and others do not. Or they pretend not to feel the lack, and then they are hypocrites.

A pedant who beheld Solon weeping for the death of a son said to him, "Why do you weep thus, if weeping avails nothing?" And the sage answered him, "Precisely for that reason—because it does not avail." It is manifest that weeping avails something, even if only the alleviation of distress; but the deep sense of Solon's reply to the impertinent questioner is plainly seen. And I am convinced that we should solve many things if we all went out into the streets and uncovered our griefs, which perhaps would prove to be but one sole common grief, and joined together in beweeping them and crying aloud to the heavens and calling upon God. And this, even though God should hear us not; but He would hear us. The chiefest sanctity of a temple is that it is a place to which men go to weep in common. A *miserere* sung in common by a multitude tormented by destiny has as much value as a philosophy. It is not enough to cure the plague: we must learn to weep for it. Yes, we must learn to weep! Perhaps that is the supreme wisdom. Why? Ask Solon.

There is something which, for lack of a better name, we will call the tragic sense of life, which carries with it a whole conception of life itself and of the universe, a whole philosophy more or less formulated, more or less conscious. And this sense may be possessed, and is possessed, not only by individual men but by whole peoples. And this sense does not so much flow from ideas as determine them, even though afterwards, as is manifest, these ideas react upon it and confirm it. Sometimes it may originate in a chance illness—dyspepsia, for example; but at other times it is constitutional. And it is useless to speak, as we shall see, of men who are healthy and men who are not healthy. Apart from the fact there is no normal standard of health, nobody has proved that man is necessarily cheerful by nature. And further, man, by the very fact of being man, of possessing consciousness, is, in comparison with the ass or the crab, a diseased animal. Consciousness is a disease.

Among men of flesh and bone there have been typical examples of those who possess this tragic sense of life. I recall now Marcus Aurelius, St. Augustine, Pascal, Rousseau, *René, Obermann,* Thomson,[1] Leopardi, Vigny, Lenau, Kleist, Amiel, Quental, Kierkegaard —men burdened with wisdom rather than with knowledge.

And there are, I believe, peoples who possess this tragic sense of life also.

It is to this that we must now turn our attention, beginning with this matter of health and disease.

Translated by J. E. Crawford Flitch

---

1. James Thomson, author of *The City of Dreadful Night.*

José Martínez Ruiz

(1873-1967)

Azorín, as he is known throughout the Spanish-speaking world, was the oldest of nine children. He was born in Monóvar, for him the "peaceful city," and he studied for eight years in a Piarist school in Yecla. These two cities form an important part of his novels, almost all somewhat autobiographical and involving long descriptions of the countryside. He studied law in various universities. In his early life he was a radical anarchist; he later became a reactionary conservative. He indulged actively in politics bewteen 1907 and 1919, but after that year he devoted himself largely to literature. It was Azorín who first coined the phrase "Generation of ninety-eight." He became a member of the Royal Academy in 1924.

Author of almost a hundred volumes of essays, plays, novels, and short stories, Azorín published his first complete work, *The Castilian Soul,* in 1900. He first used the pseudonym Azorín in *Will* (1902). Among his novels are *Will, Antonio Azorín* (1903), *The Confessions of a Little Philosopher* (1904), *Don Juan* (1922), *Dona Inés* (1925), and *Félix Vargas* (1928). His essays include *The Route of Don Quixote* (1905); *Spanish Readings* (1912); *Castile* (1912); *Classics and Moderns* (1913); *On the Margin of the Classics* (1915); *Rivas and Larra* (1916); *An Hour of Spain* (1924), his entrance speech to the Academy; and *The Oasis of the Classics* (1952). *Old Spain* (1926) and *Comedia del Arte* (1927) are two of his well-known plays. *Brandy, Much Brandy* and *Angelita* are samples of surrealistic dramas, a phase he went through in the late twenties and early thirties.

All of Azorín's works are lyric, delicate, introspective, evocative descriptions of Spanish history, literature, and nature. Like Unamuno he cultivates Spanish "intrahistory," for he feels that whereas great events come and go, human nature and the small details of life remain the same in their eternal significance. Because of this insistence on details he has been called the "apostle of Castilian minutiae." One critic called his essays "little albums of Spanish life." Another said they resembled an "archaic melody played on a clavichord." Ortega y Gasset claimed that Azorín sought to petrify esthetically the commonplace and the insignificant but that he was a "sensitive of history." Included in the impressionistic re-creations built up out of details about old ruins, cities, and

294

cathedrals are special nostalgic literary re-creations of the classics, which make the reader feel the events are taking place before his eyes rather than in the remote past.

In addition to his insistence on microscopic descriptions of the countryside in which he reveals himself as a master of words, Azorín shows a continued preoccupation with time. His philosophy is that "to live is to see return." Also, if time can be slowed down, our fleeting existence, which leads but to death, may be prolonged.

An Hour of Spain was read to the Royal Academy on October 26, 1924. Azorín's entrance speech was later published in book form, of which we have selected Chapters 19, 40, and 41 in their entirety.

An Hour of Spain
Between 1560 and 1590

CHAPTER 19

CASTLES IN SPAIN

In Spain there are many castles. They are almost all in ruins, they are to be seen here and there all over the country. In the sixteenth century many of these castles had already fallen into decay. In *Las Partidas*[1] there is minute mention of the castles. The whole of *título* XVIII in the second *Partida* (*título* composed of thirty-two laws), is taken up with the castles. This solicitude shows the importance of the castles in Spain. The prose of the venerable Code is contemporary with the foundation of many of those castles which we see in ruins. Reading it, we feel as if we were penetrating into some fortress of the thirteenth century. There are castles which dominate the plains from the heights; others are "set," as in jewellery, in the walls of the cities; we come upon one fronting the sea, lording it over that blue immensity, blue, green, or blackening gray. . . . They are rough, strong, huge, the castles of Spain. They sound fantastic, but their existence is beyond doubt. In them princes and dynasties were imprisoned, kings were born and died;

---

1. Las Siete Partidas, the laws of Castile, compiled by King Alphonso the Tenth, in the thirteenth century.

in them were raised the banners of child-kings; by means of them bloody rebellions were perpetuated. In that of Medina del Campo an uhappy queen lived and the greatest queen of Spain died; from the round tower of another,—that of Alaejos—doña Juana, spouse of Enrique IV, was let down in a basket one night, in 1468; Montiel, in 1369, witnessed the terrible struggle between the King Don Pedro and his brother Don Enrique; in Monzón Jaime I passed his infancy; Escalona was restored by Don Alvaro de Luna and was reputed the most perfect in Spain; in splendid Olite were celebrated the nuptials of the Prince of Viano and doña Inez of Cleves; in Pedraza in 1526, Henry and Francis, sons of Francis I, were imprisoned and during four years kept as hostages; in Arévalo was confined William of Nassau, Prince of Orange; in Javier was born one of the most meritorious of Spanish saints; Pamplona was the prison of Quintana; in Bellver, in Palma de Mallorca, Jovellanos was confined; and in that castle of which we spoke, fronting the sea, certain artillery men were imprisoned in 1873, who, united with those of all Spain, originated the fall of a throne.

All these castles speak to us of turbulence, factions, revolts, tumults. Loyalty and fidelity have been sheltered within their walls too. They heroically resisted the fury of sieges. In the heterogeneity and effervescence of Spain all these castles—in towns and in open country—are as it were the sensitive points of the national organism. It is expected in *Las Partidas* that the castles be sufficiently supplied with provisions. Water must least of all run short. "They must not forget salt, nor oil, nor vegetables." The most efficient protectors of the castles are the archers. The archers should know their duties well, and be able to make and mend their bows. "Whereas: the sentinels and the second sentinels, called *montarazes*, and the patrols outside at the foot of the castle, and the look-out guards placed on the towers by day, and the listening sentries by night; the warden. should care for them all as far as he possibly can, to preserve their loyalty, treating them well, and not reducing that which they ought to receive. And he should change them often, that they may not stay too long in one place." Our imagination conjures up the life in those castles, it hearkens all the sounds and sees the lights and shadows. It hears the sonorous noise of the footsteps, intermixed with clinking of spurs, under the resounding vaults; the neigh of the horses; the clamour of the soldiers and servants; the sharp call of the trumpets and the barking of the packs of hounds. It watches the splendour of the torches throwing fantastic shadows on the walls, the dense smoke of the fires kindled in the courtyards, the vivid colours of the trappings and uniforms—gold, red, green, silver—standing out against the blackened ramparts. Perchance we descry a wanderer mounting the slope towards the castle. He is coming nearer. He walks supported by a high staff; a wide *sombrero* covers his head; a mane of hair, tossed back, falls over his shoulders. When he gets near, we see that his eyes are blue and his hair golden. The wanderer comes from distant lands. Perhaps he came to Spain, in 1212, accompanying some lord—Teobaldo Blasón or Arnaldo de Narbona—to help in the battle of Las Navas.[1] Since then he has journeyed wandering, from castle to castle. On arriving before the gateway of the fortress, face to face with the archers who appear on the walls, he lifts his head, takes off his hat with a noble gesture, and in sweet melancholy voice intones a prayer to the Virgin:

> *Vera vergena María,*
> *Vera vida, vera fes,*
> *Vera vertatz, vera vía. . . .*

Of that castle to which we referred, fronting the sea, nothing remains but the outside walls. The building of its first fortifications was begun about 1194 in the times of Sancho *el Fuerte*. The mighty fabric rises on a ridge; on the one hand lies the city—at the foot of the slope—and on the other we see the sea. Looking towards the castle from beyond the sea, are France and England—our historical rivals—the nearest coast of France can be discerned on the right with the naked eye. On the left, far off, we see three tiers of mountains: the first, green and reddish, with small white specks of houses; the second, blue, dim, blurred; the third made up of peaks, sharp, fine, delicate, almost invisible in the mistiness of the surrounding air. Those remote, ethereal mountains are the mountains of ancient and noble Cantabria. The strong battlemented wall of the castle remains intact. Appearing above the ramparts, we see the walls of a big house. The castle ramparts are black, the walls of the house are yellow. The interior of the house has been demolished; from the field, through the empty window spaces, we can see the sky. A complete study of plant life could be pursued on the declivities of the castle, in the moats and fortifications. Ferns, thistles, nettles, herbage, grass, mallow, bramble, fill both

---

1. Las Navas de Tolosa or Navas de San Juan in Jaén, Spain, where the kings of Castile and Navarre defeated the Moors in an important battle and checked their advance into Andalusia. (*Editor's note.*)

fortress and declivities with verdure. On the topmost edge of the
high wall grows fennel; against the background of deep blue it
outlines its little sprays, fine and erect. There are growths in the
joints of the blocks of stone, on the merlons, in the escutcheons
which project above the gateway. The yellow-coloured flowerets of
the mouse-ear (*oreja de ratón*) alternate with the small forest
pinks—*dianthus caryophyllus,* of Linnæus—so graceful and bright.
Those little woodland pinks enamel the slopes; they peep out from
among the ferns and brambles, the children gather them when
they climb up to the castle in the afternoon. The pink is the flower
of Spain. "This is the favourite flower of the Spaniards"—say D.
Claudio and D. Esteban Boutelou in their *Tratado de las flores*
1804--; "we cultivate none other with so much care and diligence,
and indeed it is true that it possesses every quality that can recommend a flower, uniting the characteristics of brilliancy, glow and
variety of hue, with fragrance and sweetness of scent; which
things are the most valuable and the most to be desired in flowers."
Those forest pinks, aflame and fragrant, growing on the frontiers,
seem the vanguard of the flowers of Spain. The flowers of Spain
luxuriate in colour and vitality, they are not the bland, delicate
flowers of other nations. They are well represented by the forest
pinks; inland, all over Spain, the traveller will come upon small
pinks, serrated, opening out red, white, pied, all of brilliant hue
and penetrating perfume. On the castle slopes, in the moats, on the
walls themselves, pinks mingle with the purple flowers of the
mallow and with the white flowers of coriander and privet. Within
the fortress, in the principal hall, now roofless, sprigs of lent
gilliflowers cover the floor, and in April its velvet blossoms, mul-
berry coloured, form a close and lovely carpet. The grim square
stones of the walls are variegated with patches of black and
yellow lichen. From a merlon, a wild fig tree crooks its branches
over the moat. Ivy creeps up the wall to the height of the battlements, and rests there, displaying its broad green cloak. All these
plants have a free, luxurious life. The air, above the sea, 116
meters high, is fresh and pure. A fine haze veils the horizon. If
after a long stay in these parts we forsake the region of misty
horizons and go up to the central table land, our eyes drink in,
there, with avidity, the luminous distances and the high relief of
clear and firm terrestrial lines.

This castle fronting the ocean has seen—like the other castles
of Spain—both tragedies and wars. Hundreds of years ago the sea
began to reach up to the houses of the townspeople. Fire, all

down the centuries, has raged furiously against the city. Between 1266 and 1813 ten or twelve great conflagrations have swept away the population. The old castle has watched the flames blazing at its feet, has heard the crash of falling houses, the cries of the terrified people and the clang of the bells. In 1688, in this same castle, a thunderbolt exploded the powder magazine. It left the fortress in ruins. Now all is repose. The sea stretches out, immense. From below comes up the cry of the sea-gulls. The sea-gulls wheel slowly over the blue waters, or rest upon the waves—like small bits of white paper—and stay there motionless long at a time, borne and carried, lifted and sunk, softly, gently rocked.

CHAPTER 40

THE REAL ESPAÑOLA

The aged *señora* lives in the outskirts of the city; in a part called *Los Pradillos* (the Little Meadows); we reach this district after crossing a stream by way of the Roman bridge. Where now stands a flour factory, there stood, in 1860, the old slaughter-house. The slaughter-house was built on lands which had been occupied from 1640 to 1802 by the monastery of San Agustín. In 1570, before the time of the monastery, there arose on this spot a group of houses. Those dwellings went by the name of *the houses of Sancho Gil.* Sancho Gil was a bishop of the diocese; but it is not known whether the houses belonged to the bishop or to a Jewish banker of the same name. In 1880, a violent polemic was started between two local journals, one republican and the other conservative, on the subject of the demolition of the old slaughter-house. The house in which the *anciana* lived had a small entrance-hall; at the far end of it you saw a wooden staircase; a narrow balcony, also of wood, ran round the wall; a small door—the door of the *anciana's* apartment—opened on to this gallery. The aged *señora* leaves the house every evening at twilight and walks to the city. She crosses the bridge and climbs the *Cuesta de Trajineros* (the Waggoners' Slope). After that she directs her steps towards the cathedral. The *anciana* walks a little bit slowly; in one hand she carries a white crook, and in the other, hidden beneath her cloak, a cruet of oil. Everyone in the city knows this little old lady. Within the cathedral

a lamp is burning, in the chapel of Protection. The light in the
lamp has not been extinguished for a hundred years. Just in the
same way as this *anciana* empties her cruet into the cup of the
lamp, so her mother, and her mother's mother, emptied it before
her. The little light has never gone out. At the hour when the
señora penetrates into the cathedral, the great aisles lie in shadow.
The high windows are paling in the last splendours of evening.

Lope de Vega, in his comedy *El Molino* (The Mill), makes a
duchess, excited, angry, say to one of her ladies:

> . . . For fain with a sword alone
> And the fury of my breast,
> I would do a deed, Theodora,
> Worthy a woman of Spain.[1]

In another comedy by the same Lope, *La Moza de cantaro*
(The Pitcher Girl), doña María de Guzmán y Portocarrero (the
heroine disguised as a servant girl), kills a man who has insulted
her father. The *anciana* who is taking her way to the cathedral
has never gone to those extremes; but she has been a valiant woman
and a spirited. Now, she is wrinkled and bent; time was, she
captivated everyone with the grace of her figure and the beauty
of her face. No one is left to her in this world. Of the three sons
born to her, one died in Flanders; the second went out to the
Indies and there ended his days; the third met his death in a
pestilence which came upon the city. The *señora* bore with fortitude
all her adversities. Among them, that which shook her most deeply
was the unfaithfulness of her husband. There had been a moment
when she was on the point of doing the deed which Lope's duchess
would fain have done.

The true *española* is a lover of home. During part of the year
she likes to live in the country. She keeps her home spotless. She
nurses her children. She does white work. She embellishes the
mending with ingenious and quaint darning designs. She can make
preserves. She cares tenderly for the sick. She dresses simply. When
she has passed the age of thirty she is seen only in dark colours.
She neither wastes her substance nor stints that which is needful for
the comfort of the house. They could not say of her: "She throws

---

1. . . . *Que con una espada sola*
   Y la furia de ni pecho.
   Hiciera, Teodora, un hecho
   De verdadera española.

away the flour and saves the ashes." In her character, underneath
kindliness, underneath the most gracious courtesy, we come upon
a foundation of indomitable energy. And that impression of im-
petuosity—as we saw it in the severe and vigorous landscape—that
impression of fortitude allied with grace and with the most delicate
sensitiveness, is just what gives to the woman of Spain her insuper-
able attraction. She—impetuous and sensitive—is the *verdadera
española* of whom Lope de Vega speaks.

The *anciana* who lives in the houses of Sancho Gil—the bishop
or the banker—goes to the cathedral every evening. Unchanging is
her faith. Unchanging has been her love. She has been tender and
strong. Her hands, thin now and worn—what beautiful hands they
once were!—keep the little light shining bright in the lamp. One
evening, on entering the chapel, the *anciana* suddenly felt ill. On
the following day they came upon her, dead. The light of the lamp
had gone out.

CHAPTER 41

EPILOGUE BY THE SEA

Sempronio.—Has dicho?

Calixto.—Cuan brevemente pude.[1]

La Celestina, Acto I.

The dream is ended. We are in the same worldly drawing-room
where we were when we began to dream. Before us extends the
great sea. The night—blind and cold—has thrown its shadows over
the wide expanse of water. For a moment, our spirit was drawn
away from actual things. The surrounding reality ceased to exist
for us. We come back now to the present world. The stars are
shining in the black vault. We carried with us into our dream
somewhat of enthusiasm and affection.

Translated by Alice Raleigh

1. "Hast said?"
   "As briefly as I could."

Ramiro de Maeztu

(1875-1936)

Along with Baroja and Azorín he was one of the *enfants terribles* of the
"Generation of ninety-eight," perhaps the most revolutionary of them all.
Born of a Cuban father of Basque descent and an English mother, he
lived for a while in Paris, worked on his father's sugar plantation in
Cuba, and later worked as a journalist in Spain. He lived in England
for a time and served as a war correspondent during the First World
War. He started his political activity as a radical socialist and fought for
liberal causes from 1898 to about 1905, even spending some time in a
Bilbao prison for his activities. Influenced by the ideas of the Englishman,
T. E. Hulme, he became a militant Catholic, monarchist, and conservative. He was the only writer of his generation who immediately declared
for the dictator, Primo de Rivera. For his service to the state he was
named Ambassador to Argentina in 1928. In 1934 he became a member
of the Royal Academy. He helped organize the Spanish Action group of
extreme Catholic-Fascist orientation. He died as a result of his political
and war activities in a Madrid prison.

Toward Another Spain (1899) stressed that Spain's loss of the War
of 1898 and her decadence had come about because she had locked
herself away from the rest of Europe. He rejected these early ideas
vehemently in *Authority, Liberty and Function in the Light of War*
(1916), published in Spanish in 1919 as *The Crisis of Humanism*. In
this work he defended the State, order, discipline, and Catholic orthodoxy
as the means to Spain's revival. In other works he praised Spain's historical role as the defender of the faith, especially in *Defense of His-
panidad* (1934). He felt that Spain might create a new empire based
on the ideas of the sixteenth century about the State and Catholicism.
His most important literary criticism was *Don Quixote, Don Juan, and
the Celestina* (1926), where he viewed Quixote as a parody of the spirit
of chivalry and stressed the positive value of force, as embodied by Don
Juan. Maeztu was not a profound thinker, but he was a profoundly
patriotic Spaniard who promoted his ideas, distasteful as they were to
many, with great vigor.

The selection, the entire chapter titled "Death and Resurrection," is
from Part III of *Authority, Liberty and Function*. It is the antepenultimate
chapter of the volume.

302

Authority, Liberty, and Function

DEATH AND RESURRECTION

How can men be cured of the excessive value which they grant to their personality? The reactionaries and obscurantists say that by suppressing popular education the number of men who possess self-consciousness will disappear or diminish, and it will, therefore, be possible to make them live a life of obedience and faith. Perhaps the reactionaries are right; but it is also possible to cure with more culture the evil increased by culture. Why should it not be possible to sharpen our culture up to such a point that we may come to see ourselves with the same eyes as we see the others? When we judge the others we do not grant to them the same value as they grant to themselves. We know quite well that the proudest of men may lack any value. The positive value of a man is measured by what he produces, and his negative value by what he consumes; and there is no other objective measure of value. It won't do for me to believe myself to be the first of men. If what I produce is worth less than what I consume, my value is negative; by which I mean that the world would gain if I ceased to exist. But in this sacrifice of personality to objective values there remains an element of irrationality which we shall not be able to understand unless we realize at the same time the nature of heroism.

A few months ago the newspapers spoke of a French artillery officer who, mortally wounded on the battlefield, began to talk to his companion about the supreme beauty of dying for one's country, and who, when feeling the shadows of death upon his eyes, cried: "Vive la France!" and expired. I cannot tell what image of France crossed the mind of the dying man—perhaps the ascendant France of Joan of Arc and Rheims; perhaps the noon of France under Louis XIV and Napoleon; perhaps the sanguinary spectre of the French Departments devastated by the invader; perhaps the ironical recollection of a bourgeois, rationalist, and pacific France, satisfied with the Here and Now, but far away from that region of sacrifice, creation, and destruction which seems to be the central point of life. What is probable is that the officer died in the intuitive certainty that his life had not been lived in vain. He probably believed that his blood, in one form or another, would not be fruitless: either because the death of her sons immediately assures the continuity of France, or that the same spirit which to-day leads French soldiers to die for their country will tomorrow, perhaps, induce the women of the land to sacrifice their momentary selfishness on the altars of the survival of the Gallic blood. What is certain is that through the soul of this dying officer and of many other thousands of French heroes passed in the last moments the Themes of Death and Resurrection which, in their intermingling, form the fundamental mystery of nearly every religion.

One of the best modern English books I have read, "Themis: A Study of the Social Origins of Greek Religion," by Miss Jane Harrison, satisfactorily proves the thesis that the Olympic gods, with their athanasia or "eternity through not dying," achieved at the cost of life, were elaborated by the Hellenic spirit centuries after Dionysos and the other gods of Death and Resurrection—the symbols of the succession of the seasons of the year, of the permanence of the tribe amid the deaths of individuals, and of the universal palingenesis of Nature. From Miss Harrison's book we see that the gods of classic Greece gradually get rid of everything that, in primitive times, identified them with the cyclic pulsations of life; they expel from Olympus all the gods or daimons who still retain the feet of a goat or the body of a cow or serpent as if to indicate their earthly origin; and they end by turning themselves into mere negations of the "mystery-gods" of fertility.

"So far then," writes Miss Harrison, "our conception of the Olympian is mainly negative. He refuses the functions of the totemistic daimon, he sheds his animal or plant form. He will not be a daimon of Earth, nor yet even of the Sky; above all he refuses to be a year-daimon with his function of ceaseless toil. He will not die to rise again, but chooses instead a barren immortality. He withdraws himself from man and lives remote, a 'jealous god.'" "The Olympian has clear form, he is the 'principium individuationis' incarnate; he can be thought, hence his calm, his *sophrosyne*. The mystery-god is the life of the whole of things, he can only be felt —as soon as he is thought and individualized he passes, as Dionysos has to pass, into the thin, rare ether of the Olympian. The Olympians are of conscious thinking, divided, distinct, departmental; the mystery-god is the impulse of life through all things, perennial, indivisible."

What Miss Harrison has done with paganism can also be done, and with less labour, with the religion of Israel. Although it may be truly said that the religion of Israel and of the Old Testament is the only one that was never acquainted with mysteries or mythologies, a reading of the prophets is enough to convince one that among the Jews, too, the concept of God underwent an evolution analogous to that which, among the Greeks, changed Dionysos into Apollo. The God of Moses still remembers that other divinity which primitive Israel worshipped in the symbol of the Golden Calf. He was still an immanent, national, actual God who spoke directly through the mouth of the prophets. And the later prophets devoted themselves to little more than ridding the idea of God of those naturalistic traits which recalled, as did the Golden Calf, the periodical Death and Resurrection of Nature. The God of Israel was gradually outgrowing the confines of Israel and of the Earth until he made himself completely transcendental, unknowable, and unimaginable—a mere concept of righteousness and justice, even by the time of the Prophet Amos.

It is curious to note that this progressive rationalizing of the idea of God is always effected at the cost of Death and Resurrection. It is significant enough that the God of the Decalogue—who was still the God of Israel and not yet of the world—should have forgotten to include in his Commandments that of giving one's life for one's country in the hour of danger, and of perpetuating life in successive generations. The first prophet to speak of God as a God of Love was Hosea. Unhappy in his marriage with a frivolous woman, Hosea conceived the ambition of fanning her sparks of goodness into a pure flame. In this relation of the loving husband to the beloved, whom he wishes to save not only by tenderness, but also by discipline, Hosea saw a symbol of the relationship existing between the Creator and His creatures. It might be thought that this amorous conception of the deity would have made Hosea more indulgent to the rites which recalled the old gods of fertility. Not at all. No one mocked more bitterly the symbols of the Golden Calf; no one more strictly separated the cult of Nature from the cult of Divinity. Although the naturalistic rites had millennial traditions, Hosea saw in them only a corrupt and corrupting paganism of which Israel had to cleanse herself.

Even to-day it is characteristic of the upholders of a purely rationalist morality to dislike any standard of conduct which is based on the mystery of Death and Resurrection. It might be said that the morality which such people preach is purely spatial, in the sense that they wish to extend justice to all men and nations over the entire surface of the earth. This spatial morality, which is that of the cardinal virtues, may be called rationalistic, that is, selfish, because its results are immediately and pleasantly apparent, in the sense that if we behave with prudence, justice, fortitude, and temperance towards our fellow-men we thereby extend spatially the action of the moral sense, and thus free ourselves from the fear that our misconduct might make us the victims of revenge. But Mr. Benjamin Kidd has already told us that this spatial ethic is not enough. Mr. Kidd could not see the possibility of the permanence of a civilization unless by rooting it in an act of faith. Without the sacrifice of the present generation for the sake of the generations to come, humanity would die out even though it had succeeded in making social justice prevail in every corner of the globe. And this sacrifice of the visible to the invisible, of the present to the future, cannot be consciously achieved by the practice of the cardinal or rational virtues. It requires, in addition, the aid of the theological: Faith, the root; Hope, the flower; and Charity, the fruit.

When humanity is located in space, it is only logical that the ethical ideal should lead us to wish that the earth might be changed into an Olympus without cradles or graves inhabited by immortal gods. As this is impossible, many "spatial" moralists recommend the ideal of reducing, as far as possible, the number of births and deaths. Thus we may explain the pacifist and Malthusian ideas which have become so widespread in our days. The blind alley into which these ideas lead us was most candidly revealed by Mr. William Archer in an article in the *Daily News,* in which he affirmed the antithesis of "Fecundity versus Civilization"; for, if fecundity is the contrary of civilization, the civilization to which Mr. Archer aspires must be sterility.

In the struggle between societies or sections of society, heroic and religious, with societies so rationalistic and calculating that their members cannot decide either to defend them with arms or perpetuate them by maternity, there is no doubt that the latter must succumb. Some rationalists try to meet this danger by proposing measures which may induce calculating societies to perpetuate themselves. Mr. Bertrand Russell has recently devoted a lecture to this question. It is obvious that the intervention of society in these problems is just, because it is not right that good women should suffer the burdens and risks of maternity while the selfish women enjoy the privileges which their voluntary sterility grants them. That is why I am favourable to compulsory maternity, which naturally implies maternity grants. But this measure of justice does not relieve us of the need of a heroic morality. A State or a Guild of a thousand members which pays every year the cost of forty new children will have to sacrifice itself much more than another which only pays for ten more children every year. What happens here is that we have transferred to the corporation the cost that now falls upon the individual. This measure will be just because in consequence of it the bad individuals will also pay for the raising of future generations, while at present only the good do so. But the need of heroism and faith will always be the same.

Compared with this sterility of the "rationalizing reason," there is a spring breeze in the impulse which leads Miss Harrison to follow M. Bergson in his desire "to apprehend life as one, as indivisible, yet as perennial movement and change," and nevertheless to disown the dogmas and even the symbols through which the full life of Dionysos transforms itself into the empty abstraction of Apollo. If I had to choose between Mr. Archer and Miss Harrison, I should remain, naturally, with Miss Harrison. Between an absolute, teleological, iron monism, such as that of the religion of Israel, and an absolute meaningless and fluent pluralism, such as that of Dionysos and Cybele; between a sterile civilization and a fecundity without sense, I should rather give up the meaning than life; I would sacrifice the Commandments of Jehovah rather than those of Nature. For I may or may not be a man who lives conformably to the Law; but I cannot do otherwise than live conformably to Nature.

But I am not bound to choose. Every religion which has lasted in the world has necessarily had to be a mixture of the vital principle and of the rational principle; because the world, with all its creatures, is of precisely such a mixture. It was not for nothing that in the Temple of the Oracle at Delphi the year was divided into the rites sacred to Dionysos and those sacred to Apollo; for although it is impossible to think simultaneously of an immortal and of a god that dies and rises again, yet when our spirit passes from the world in space to the world in time, it finds that it can establish a profound affinity between its two pagan symbols, and can see in Apollo the projection of Dionysos in space, and in Dionysos the projection of Apollo into time—in Apollo a Dionysos visualized in plastic, and in Dionysos an Apollo fluent in music.

Thus, too, our Christianity. For "we preach Christ crucified, unto the Jews a stumbling-block, and unto the Greeks foolishness"

(I Cor. i. 23); the Jews and rationalists call us pagans and tell us that our God dies and rises again, like Dionysos. And why are we not to be called heathens? Heathens we are; heathens and Jews, both. By the side of the transcendent god who cannot be represented or thought, such as Jehovah or the Immovable Mover of Aristotle, we place a god who dies and rises again, and this god permits us to exclaim triumphantly, with St. Paul: "O death, where is thy sting? O grave, where is the victory?" (I Cor. xv. 55), and then we declare that there is only one god, and not two. We think of God as transcendent and immovable, or as immanent and vital, and then we say that His distinct and separate Persons form no more than one God. We admit that we cannot explain this mystery of the Trinity; but we add for the sceptical reader that this mystery of the divinity is no more mysterious than that of the first reality which presents itself to his eyes.

For it is characteristic of every reality, as, for instance, the piece of paper I am writing on, that everything in it flows and does not advance by leaps; that it is continuous and yet changes incessantly and that in the whole of Nature no particular change is exactly like another, but only more or less analogous. Everything is continuous and everything changes. These are the two principles of reality: it is continuous, because we cannot conceive of a reality which could be discontinuous; it is heterogeneous, because it is continually changing itself into something else, and change presupposes heterogeneity. And this unity of continuity and heterogeneity—a necessary postulate—is that which gives to reality its character of irrationality. As, in the smallest of its parts, reality is a continuous heterogeneity, its unity slips fatally away from our concepts. And not only vital reality, as M. Bergson says, but all reality, including the so-called inert matter.

Every reality is a continuous heterogeneity—heterogeneity is change; change, death; continuity, resurrection; every reality is something that survives, dies, and rises again, something of whose continuity and heterogeneity we cannot think at the same time, but in which we must suppose that there exists a unity of continuity and heterogeneity that is not rational. We cannot make reality rational except by artificially suppressing its heterogeneity, as in mathematics and physical science; or by suppressing its continuity and cutting it up arbitrarily into segments, as we do in history or the descriptive sciences. But the enthusiastic Bergsonism of Miss Harrison carries her too far when it leads her to see a danger, "an almost necessary disaster," in "each and every creed and dogma."

Are we to suppress in ourselves the tendency which leads us to theorize on our experiences, and, as this theorizing on our experiences is the basis of personality, are we also to suppress personality?

The fact that consciousness of personality is dangerous for societies, in so far as it isolates individuals, has induced some young Frenchmen to invent the "unanimist" ideal. Miss Harrison has published an apologia of "unanimisme" in England. Its credo consists in submerging the individual consciousness in the "blood" of the association or collectivity. But individual consciousness is, if not as an end, as an instrument, one of the highest values. It is not possible to suppress it without making all human culture disappear with it. To wish to suppress it is to wish to go back to savagery. What is good and positive in "unanimisme" is the acknowledgment that reason is not enough to make us heroic, and that heroism is necessary to maintain civilized societies. In societies that have lost the joy of battle for the sake of battle, and have learnt to enjoy love while being afraid of the burdens of the family, the supreme functions of maternity and of the defence of the country must be based on heroism. We are no longer sufficiently primitive, as Miss Harrison would like us to be, to trust to the instinct of the species; and reason will never find arguments convincing enough to persuade a soldier that he ought to die in a trench, or a selfish woman that she ought to bear a child. When we deal with these things reason must bow. Their perplexities can only be solved by heroism, and heroism must be founded on faith. In heroism, practical faith, and in faith, theoretical heroism, we find a unity superior to instinct and to reason, and which includes both in a mixture analogous to that of continuity and heterogeneity which constitutes every reality.

If we cannot conceive reality but as a continuous heterogeneity, how can we conceive of the God of this Reality but both as continuous or eternal and as heterogeneous or changing, that is, dying and rising again? What has Miss Harrison in her book but a dogma of Dionysos? What has Bergson in his "Evolution Créatrice" but a dogma of life? And why disaster in dogmas when dogmas, too, are heterogeneous continuities which die and rise again? No reader, on reading this chapter for the second time, will read in it what he read there for the first. Some of his ideas will have died, but others will have risen from the corruption of the letter. In all propositions and dogmas there is an element of truth or falsity, unalterable, eternal, and independent of our will and of life. But the knowledge and interpretation of propositions and dogmas die and rise again.

Eternity and mutability fuse together in propositions as in realities. The psychological moment is always death and resurrection. Eternity is extra-psychological.

And thus this war, a magnifying-glass, makes us live again, in the faith of a French artillery officer, the profound life of the dogma of Death and Resurrection. In times of peace we had almost forgotten that life is essentially a tragedy: the tragedy of Death and Resurrection. We had fallen into the ridiculous aspiration towards an athanasia far from the flux of life. The example of the heroes who die that their country may live will stimulate the nations to give up their dream of a Malthusian and pacifist Olympus; and thinkers to adjust, as far as possible, their theories to the mystery of life and reality: Death and Resurrection.

.   .   .   .   .

To sum up what I have written: The principle of function is a better base of societies than the principles of authority and liberty. It is better because it is more just. And when I say that it is more just I assert in the principle of function a quality independent of the wills of men. It is more just whether they like it or not. But in order to triumph it is necessary that men should like it—all men; or at any rate the most powerful and influential. How can they be made to like it? The way will be prepared by the historians who study the present war. I myself have no doubt that its horrors must be attributed to the fact that the world has fallen a prey to the two antagonistic and incompatible principles of authority and liberty. The war will have shown that the more unjust of these two principles—although the more efficient—is that of unlimited authority. It is the more unjust because no man has a subjective right to command others. It is the more efficient, provided that the authorities are not stupid, because it unifies the social forces in the direction prescribed by the authority, and because it implies a principle of order. The mere fact that a combination of half the world was necessary to defeat Germany is proof of its efficiency. The strength of the liberal principle lies in its respect for vocation. But in the liberal principle there is no efficiency, for there is no unity of direction. Nor is there justice in it, for it allows some individuals to invade the field of others. The idea of liberty leads men to act as if every letter printed in this article expanded right and left and tried to conquer the space occupied by the adjoining letters. The result of absolute liberty is universal confusion. But the reason why both these principles of authority and liberty should be rejected is the same for each: that both principles are founded on subjective rights. And these rights are false. Nobody has a subjective right to anything; neither rulers nor ruled.

This conclusion will be reached by historians and thinkers. But that is not enough. It is not enough for men to know that it is necessary to sacrifice all kinds of rights founded on personality in order to establish society on a firm basis of justice. Personality must be sacrificed. That is not only a theory but action. The critique may refute authority and liberty as bases of society. But to the conviction that our true life consists in being functionaries of absolute values we arrive only by an act of faith, in which we deny that our ego is the centre of the world, and we make of it a servant of the good. This act of faith is a kind of suicide, but it is a death followed immediately by resurrection. What we lose as personalities we reconquer, multiplied, as functionaries. The man who asks for money simply for himself cannot ask for it with the same moral confidence as he who asks for it in order to study a problem or to create social wealth. St. Paul says (I Cor. xv. 44) that in death "It is sown a natural body," but that in the resurrection "It is raised a spiritual body." The doctrine of Death and Resurrection opens also the way for the submission of man to higher things.

José Ortega y Gasset

(1883-1955)

Obtaining his doctorate at the University of Madrid in 1904, Ortega spent the next two years studying philosophy in Germany. He came to love German culture, to the detriment of his own Spanish heritage, but in his later years he changed many of his ideas about Spain and tried to put Spanish culture in its relationship to that of other countries into proper perspective. In 1910 Ortega became a Professor of Metaphysics at the University of Madrid, a position he held until 1936. He helped start the newspaper *The Sun* as well as the most important cultural journal of modern Spain, *Revista de Occidente*. From 1936 to 1945 he lived in various European countries and in Argentina. Once more in Spain, he founded the Institute of Humanities in Madrid in 1948.

Ortega belonged to the generation following that of the "ninety-eight" group, and he was more intellectual and less emotional than his predecessors. He rejected as unsystematic the ideas of Unamuno and sought to organize history as a system. Where Unamuno had worshiped Quixote, Ortega praised Cervantes. Ortega wrote essays on almost all branches of human knowledge including philosophy, metaphysics, ethics, art, music, literature, and sociology. He passed through periods of objectivism and perspectivism to arrive at an existentialist philosophy of vital reason. *Meditations on the Quixote* (1914) contains many existential ideas used much later by Heidegger. Other works among the many published by Ortega include *The Spectator*, in eight volumes (1916-34); *Invertebrate Spain* (1921), where Ortega claims that Spain has always been decadent because of the absence of a select minority and the lack of a German cultural heritage; *The Theme of Our Time* (1923), stressing the biological function of thought, which along with culture and art should be at the service of life; *Goethe From Within* (1933); *Ideas and Beliefs* (1940); *Studies on Love* (1940); and *History as a System* (1941).

Ortega's most influential work on literature was *The Dehumanization of Art and Ideas on the Novel* (1925). He stated that art should abandon human principles, avoid live forms, be art and nothing more than art, avoid all social meaning, be a game and, by stylizing, deform reality. The novel, he said, was a dying form without new themes or ideas. His most famous work outside of Spain was *The Revolt of the*

Masses (1930) in which he claims there are no longer protagonists in the world, only a chorus. Mass man crushes everything individual, superior, qualified, or select and refuses to recognize the concept of superior intellects. Fundamentally intolerant, mass man detests all distinction. He has been given instruments for existing, but he has not been educated. Although he lives in a civilized world, modern mass man lives as a primitive. Even specialists, including scientists, speak as mass men when they speak on subjects other than the tiny fragment of knowledge included in their specialty. Unless a change takes place and we return to a system of the rule of select minorities, along with the concept of a United States of Europe, mass man in the form of communism or fascism will triumph.

Ortega's primary philosophic concept was that of ratio-vitalism. Life must be the center of all thought and is something that we live here and now. Man is himself and his "circumstances," that is, things which surround us as we become aware of them. Human life is a continuous interplay between these circumstances and the individual, and thus life is a constant uncertainty. The ego must work with things to project its program, and at each moment it must determine what it is to become at the next moment. Only man has this freedom of choice.

Ortega, the most important Spanish figure of his generation, was claimed, in death, by the Spanish government as their own. In reality he was bitterly opposed to the Catholic Church as a political organ, and he had always reiterated his great dislike for the Franco regime.

The selections, including all of Chapter 12 and all but a page of Chapter 13, are from the First Part of *The Revolt of the Masses*.

The Revolt of the Masses

CHAPTER 12

THE BARBARISM OF "SPECIALISATION"

My thesis was that XIXth-Century civilisation has automatically produced the mass-man. It will be well not to close the general exposition without analysing, in a particular case, the mechanism of that production. In this way, by taking concrete form, the thesis gains in persuasive force.

This civilisation of the XIXth Century, I said may be summed up in the two great dimensions: liberal democracy and technicism. Let us take for the moment only the latter. Modern technicism springs from the union between capitalism and experimental science. Not all technicism is scientific. That which made the stone axe in the Chelian period was lacking in science, and yet a technique was created. China reached a high degree of technique without in the least suspecting the existence of physics. It is only modern European technique that has a scientific basis, from which it derives its specific character, its possibility of limitless progress. All other techniques—Mesopotamian, Egyptian, Greek, Roman, Oriental—reach up to a point of development beyond which they cannot proceed, and hardly do they reach it when they commence to display a lamentable retrogression.

This marvellous Western technique has made possible the proliferation of the European species. Recall the fact from which this essay took its departure and which, as I said, contains in germ all these present considerations. From the VIth Century to 1800, Europe never succeeds in reaching a population greater than 180 millions. From 1800 to 1914 it rises to more than 460 millions. The jump is unparalleled in our history. There can be no doubt that it is technicism—in combination with liberal democracy—which has engendered mass-man in the quantitative sense of the expression. But these pages have attempted to show that it is also responsible for the existence of mass-man in the qualitative and pejorative sense of the term.

By mass—as I pointed out at the start—is not to be specially understood the workers; it does not indicate a social class, but a kind of man to be found to-day in all social classes, who consequently represents our age, in which he is the predominant, ruling power. We are now about to find abundant evidence for this.

Who is it that exercises social power to-day? Who imposes the forms of his own mind on the period? Without a doubt, the man of the middle class. Which group, within that middle class, is considered the superior, the aristocracy of the present? Without a doubt, the technician: engineer, doctor, financier, teacher, and so on. Who, inside the group of technicians, represents it at its best and purest? Again, without a doubt, the man of science. If an astral personage were to visit Europe to-day and, for the purpose of forming judgment on it, inquire as to the type of man by which it would prefer to be judged, there is no doubt that Europe, pleasantly assured of a favourable judgment, would point to her men of science. Of course, our astral personage would not inquire for exceptional individuals, but would seek the generic type of "man of science," the high-point of European humanity.

And now it turns out that the actual scientific man is the proto-type of the mass-man. Not by chance, not through the individual failings of each particular man of science, but because science itself —the root of our civilisation—automatically converts him into mass-man, makes of him a primitive, a modern barbarian. The fact is well known; it has made itself clear over and over again; but only when fitted into its place in the organism of this thesis does it take on its full meaning and its evident seriousness.

Experimental science is initiated towards the end of the XVIth Century (Galileo), it is definitely constituted at the close of the XVIIth (Newton), and it begins to develop in the middle of the XVIIIth. The development of anything is not the same as its con-stitution; it is subject to different considerations. Thus, the consti-tution of physics, the collective name of the experimental sciences, rendered necessary an effort towards unification. Such was the work of Newton and other men of his time. But the development of physics introduced a task opposite in character to unification. In order to progress, science demanded specialisation, not in herself, but in men of science. Science is not specialist. If it were, it would *ipso facto* cease to be true. Not even empirical science, taken in its integrity, can be true if separated from mathematics, from logic, from philosophy. But scientific work does, necessarily, require to be specialised.

It would be of great interest, and of greater utility than at first sight appears, to draw up the history of physical and biological sciences, indicating the process of increasing specialisation in the work of investigators. It would then be seen how, generation after generation, the scientist has been gradually restricted and confined into narrower fields of mental occupation. But this is not the im-portant point that such a history would show, but rather the reverse side of the matter: how in each generation the scientist, through having to reduce the sphere of his labour, was progressively losing contact with other branches of science, with that integral inter-pretation of the universe which is the only thing deserving the names of science, culture, European civilisation.

Specialisation commences precisely at a period which gives to civilised man the title "encyclopaedic." The XIXth Century starts on its course under the direction of beings who lived "encyclo-paedically," though their production has already some tinge of specialism. In the following generation, the balance is upset and specialism begins to dislodge culture from the individual scientist. When by 1890 a third generation assumes intellectual command in Europe we meet with a type of scientist unparalleled in history. He is one who, out of all that has to be known in order to be a man of judgment, is only acquainted with one science, and even of that one only knows the small corner in which he is an active investigator. He even proclaims it as a virtue that he take no cognizance of what lies outside the narrow territory specially cultivated by himself, and gives the name of "dilettantism" to any curiosity for the general scheme of knowledge.

What happens is that, enclosed within the narrow limits of his visual field, he does actually succeed in discovering new facts and advancing the progress of the science which he hardly knows, and incidentally the encyclopedia of thought of which he is conscientiously ignorant. How has such a thing been possible, how is it still possible? For it is necessary to insist upon this extraordinary but undeniable fact: experimental science has progressed thanks in great part to the work of men astoundingly mediocre, and even less than mediocre. That is to say, modern science, the root and symbol of our actual civilisation, finds a place for the intellectually commonplace man and allows him to work therein with success. The reason of this lies in what is at the same time the great advantage and the gravest peril of the new science, and of the civilisation directed and represented by it, namely, mechanisation. A fair amount of the things that have to be done in physics or in biology is mechanical work of the mind which can be done by anyone, or almost anyone. For the purpose of innumerable investigations it is possible to divide science into small sections, to enclose oneself in one of these, and to leave out of consideration all the rest. The solidity and exactitude of the methods allow of this temporary but quite real disarticulation of knowledge. The work is done under one of these methods as with a machine, and in order to obtain quite abundant results it is not even necessary to have rigorous notions of their meaning and foundations. In this way the majority of scientists help the general advance of science while shut up in the narrow cell of their laboratory, like the bee in the cell of its hive, or the turnspit in its wheel.

But this creates an extraordinarily strange type of man. The investigator who has discovered a new fact of Nature must necessarily experience a feeling of power and self-assurance. With a certain apparent justice he will look upon himself as "a man who knows." And in fact there is in him a portion of something which, added to many other portions not existing in him, does really constitute knowledge. This is the true inner nature of the specialist, who in the first years of this century has reached the wildest stage of exaggeration. The specialist "knows" very well his own, tiny corner of the universe; he is radically ignorant of all the rest.

Here we have a precise example of this strange new man, whom I have attempted to define, from both of his two opposite aspects. I have said that he was a human product unparalleled in history. The specialist serves as a striking concrete example of the species, making clear to us the radical nature of the novelty. For, previously, men could be divided simply into the learned and the ignorant, those more or less the one, and those more or less the other. But your specialist cannot be brought in under either of these two categories. He is not learned, for he is formally ignorant of all that does not enter into his specialty; but neither is he ignorant, because he is "a scientist," and "knows" very well his own tiny portion of the universe. We shall have to say that he is a learned ignoramus, which is a very serious matter, as it implies that he is a person who is ignorant, not in the fashion of the ignorant man, but with all the petulance of one who is learned in his own special line.

And such in fact is the behaviour of the specialist. In politics, in art, in social usages, in the other sciences, he will adopt the attitude of primitive, ignorant man; but he will adopt them forcefully and with self-sufficiency, and will not admit of—this is the paradox—specialists in those matters. By specialising him, civilisation has made him hermetic and self-satisfied within his limitations; but this very inner feeling of dominance and worth will induce him to wish to predominate outside his specialty. The result is that even in this case, representing a maximum of qualification in man—specialisation—and therefore the thing most opposed to the mass-man, the result is that he will behave in almost all spheres of life as does the unqualified, the mass-man.

This is no mere wild statement. Anyone who wishes can observe the stupidity of thought, judgment, and action shown to-day in politics, art, religion, and the general problems of life and the world by the "men of science," and of course, behind them, the doctors, engineers, financiers, teachers, and so on. That state of "not listening," of not submitting to higher courts of appeal which I have repeatedly put forward as characteristic of the mass-man, reaches its height precisely in these partially qualified men. They symbolise, and to a great extent constitute, the actual dominion of the masses, and their barbarism is the most immediate cause of European demoralisation. Furthermore, they afford the clearest, most striking example of how the civilisation of the last century, *abandoned to its own devices,* has brought about this rebirth of primitivism and barbarism.

The most immediate result of this *unbalanced* specialisation has been that to-day, when there are more "scientists" than ever, there are much less "cultured" men than, for example, about 1750. And the worst is that with these turnspits of science not even the real progress of science itself is assured. For science needs from time to time, as a necessary regulator of its own advance, a labour of reconstitution, and, as I have said, this demands an effort towards unification, which grows more and more difficult, involving, as it does, ever-vaster regions of the world of knowledge. Newton was able to found his system of physics without knowing much philosophy, but Einstein needed to saturate himself with Kant and Mach before he could reach his own keen synthesis. Kant and Mach—the names are mere symbols of the enormous mass of philosophic and psychological thought which has influenced Einsten—have served to *liberate* the mind of the latter and leave the way open for his innovation. But Einstein is not sufficient. Physics is entering on the gravest crisis of its history, and can only be saved by a new "Encyclopaedia" more systematic than the first.

The specialisation, then, that has made possible the progress of experimental science during a century, is approaching a stage where it can no longer continue its advance unless a new generation undertakes to provide it with a more powerful form of turnspit.

But if the specialist is ignorant of the inner philosophy of the science he cultivates, he is much more radically ignorant of the historical conditions requisite for its continuation; that is to say: how society and the heart of man are to be organised in order that there may continue to be investigators. The decrease in scientific vocations noted in recent years, to which I have alluded, is an anxious symptom for anyone who has a clear idea of what civilisation is, an idea generally lacking to the typical "scientist," the highpoint of our present civilisation. He also believes that civilisation *is there* in just the same way as the earth's crust and the forest primeval.

CHAPTER 13

THE GREATEST DANGER, THE STATE

In a right ordering of public affairs, the mass is that part which does not act of itself. Such is its mission. It has come into the world in order to be directed, influenced, represented, organised—even in order to cease being mass, or at least to aspire to this. But it has not come into the world to do all this by itself. It needs to submit its life to a higher court, formed of the superior minorities. The question as to who are these superior individuals may be discussed *ad libitum,* but that without them, whoever they be, humanity would cease to preserve its essentials is something about which there can be no possible doubt, though Europe spend a century with its head under its wing, ostrich-fashion, trying if she can to avoid seeing such a plain truth. For we are not dealing with an opinion based on facts more or less frequent and probable, but on a law of social "physics," much more immovable than the laws of Newton's physics. The day when a genuine philosophy[1] once more holds sway in Europe—it is the one thing that can save her—that day she will once again realise that man, whether he like it or no, is a being forced by his nature to seek some higher authority. If he succeeds in finding it of himself, he is a superior man; if not, he is a mass-man and must receive it from his superiors.

For the mass to claim the right to act of itself is then a rebellion against its own destiny, and because that is what it is doing at present, I speak of the rebellion of the masses. For, after all, the one thing that can substantially and truthfully be called rebellion is that which consists in not accepting one's own destiny, in rebelling against one's self. The rebellion of the archangel Lucifer would not have been less if, instead of striving to be God—which was not his destiny—he had striven to be the lowest of the angels—equally

---

1. For philosophy to rule, it is not necessary that philosophers be the rulers—as Plato at first wished—nor even for rulers to be philosophers —as was his later, more modest, wish. Both these things are, strictly speaking, most fatal. For philosophy to rule, it is sufficient for it to exist; that is to say, for the philosophers to be philosophers. For nearly a century past, philosophers have been everything but that—politicians, pedagogues, men of letters, and men of science.

not his destiny. (If Lucifer had been a Russian, like Tolstoi, he would perhaps have preferred this latter form of rebellion, none the less against God than the other more famous one.)

When the mass acts on its own, it does so only in one way, for it has no other: it lynches. It is not altogether by chance that lynch law comes from America, for America is, in a fashion, the paradise of the masses. And it will cause less surprise, nowadays, when the masses triumph, that violence should triumph and be made the one *ratio*, the one doctrine. It is now some time since I called attention to this advance of violence as a normal condition.[1] To-day it has reached its full development, and this is a good symptom, because it means that automatically the descent is about to begin. To-day violence is the rhetoric of the period, the empty rhetorician has made it his own. When a reality of human existence has completed its historic course, has been shipwrecked and lies dead, the waves throw it up on the shores of rhetoric, where the corpse remains for a long time. Rhetoric is the cemetery of human realities, or at any rate a Home for the Aged. The reality itself is survived by its name, which, though only a word, is after all at least a word and preserves something of its magic power.

But though it is not impossible that the prestige of violence as a cynically established rule has entered on its decline, we shall still continue under that rule, though in another form. I refer to the gravest danger now threatening European civilisation. Like all other dangers that threaten it, this one is born of civilisation itself. More than that, it constitutes one of its glories: it is the State as we know it to-day. We are confronted with a replica of what we said in the previous chapter about science: the fertility of its principles brings about a fabulous progress, but this inevitably imposes specialisation, and specialisation threatens to strangle science.

The same thing is happening with the State. Call to mind what the State was at the end of the XVIIIth Century in all European nations. Quite a small affair! Early capitalism and its industrial organisations, in which the new, rationalised technique triumphs for the first time, had brought a commencement of increase in society. A new social class appeared, greater in numbers and power than the pre-existing: the middle class. This astute middle class possessed one thing, above and before all: talent, practical talent. It knew how to organise and discipline, how to give continuity and consistency to its efforts. In the midst of it,

---

1. Vide *España Invertebrada*, 1912.

as in an ocean, the "ship of State" sailed its hazardous course. The ship of State is a metaphor re-invented by the bourgeoisie, which felt itself oceanic, omnipotent, pregnant with storms. That ship was, as we said, a very small affair: it had hardly any soldiers, bureaucrats, or money. It had been built in the Middle Ages by a class of men very different from the bourgeois—the nobles, a class admirable for their courage, their gifts of leadership, their sense of responsibility. Without them the nations of Europe would not now be in existence. But with all those virtues of the heart, the nobles were, and always have been, lacking in virtues of the head. Of limited intelligence, sentimental, instinctive, intuitive—in a word, "irrational." Hence they were unable to develop any technique, a thing which demands rationalisation. They did not invent gunpowder. Incapable of inventing new arms, they allowed the bourgeois, who got it from the East or somewhere else, to utilise gunpowder and automatically to win the battle against the warrior noble, the "caballero," stupidly covered in iron so that he could hardly move in the fight, and who had never imagined that the eternal secret of warfare consists not so much in the methods of defence as in those of attack, a secret which was to be rediscovered by Napoleon.[1]

As the State is a matter of technique—of public order and administration—the "ancien régime" reaches the end of the XVIIth Century with a very weak State, harassed on all sides by a widespread social revolt. The disproportion between State power and social power at this time is such that, comparing the situation then with that of the time of Charlemagne, the XVIIIth-Century State appears degenerate. The Carolingian State was of course much less

---

1. We owe to Ranke this simple picture of the great historic change by which for the supremacy of the nobles is substituted the predominance of the bourgeois; but of course its symbolic geometric outlines require no little filling-in in order to be completely true. Gunpowder was known from time immemorial. The invention by which a tube was charged with it was due to someone in Lombardy. Even then it was not efficacious until the invention of the cast cannon-ball. The "nobles" used firearms to a small extent, but they were too dear for them. It was only the bourgeois armies, with their better economic organisation, that could employ them on a large scale. It remains, however, literally true that the nobles, represented by the medieval type of army of the Burgundians, were definitely defeated by the new army, not professional but bourgeois, formed by the Swiss. Their primary force lay in the new discipline and the new rationalism of tactics.

powerful than the State of Louis XVI, but, on the other hand, the society surrounding it was entirely lacking in strength.[1] The enormous disproportion between social strength and the strength of public power made possible the Revolution, the revolutions—up to 1848.

But with the Revolution the middle class took possession of public power and applied their undeniable qualities to the State, and in little more than a generation created a powerful State, which brought revolutions to an end. Since 1848, that is to say, since the beginning of the second generation of bourgeois governments, there have been no genuine revolutions in Europe. Not assuredly because there were no motives for them, but because there were no means. Public power was brought to the level of social power. *Good-bye for ever to Revolutions!* The only thing now possible in Europe is their opposite: the *coup d'état*. Everything which in following years tried to look like a revolution was only a *coup d'état* in disguise.

In our days the State has come to be a formidable machine which works in marvellous fashion; of wonderful efficiency by reason of the quantity and precision of its means. Once it is set up in the midst of society, it is enough to touch a button for its enormous levers to start working and exercise their overwhelming power on any portion whatever of the social framework.

The contemporary State is the easiest seen and best-known product of civilisation. And it is an interesting revelation when one takes note of the attitude that mass-man adopts before it. He sees it, admires it, knows that *there it is,* safeguarding his existence; but he is not conscious of the fact that it is a human creation invented by certain men and upheld by certain virtues and fundamental qualities which the men of yesterday had and which may vanish into air to-morrow. Furthermore, the mass-man sees in the State an

---

1. It would be worth while insisting on this point and making clear that the epoch of absolute monarchies in Europe has coincided with very weak States. How is this to be explained? Why, if the State was all-powerful, "absolute," did it not make itself stronger? One of the causes is that indicated, the incapacity—technical, organising, bureaucratic—of the aristocracies of blood. But this is not enough. Besides that, it also happened that the absolute State and those aristocracies *did not want to aggrandise the State at the expense of society in general.* Contrary to the common belief, the absolute State instinctively respects society much more than our democratic State, which is more intelligent but has less sense of historic responsibility.

anonymous power, and feeling himself, like it, anonymous, he believes that the State is something of his own. Suppose that in the public life of a country some difficulty, conflict, or problem presents itself, the mass-man will tend to demand that the State intervene immediately and undertake a solution directly with its immense and unassailable resources.

This is the gravest danger that to-day threatens civilisation: State intervention; the absorption of all spontaneous social effort by the State, that is to say, of spontaneous historical action, which in the long run sustains, nourishes, and impels human destinies. When the mass suffers any ill-fortune or simply feels some strong appetite, its great temptation is that permanent, sure possibility of obtaining everything—without effort, struggle, doubt, or risk—merely by touching a button and setting the mighty machine in motion. The mass says to itself, *"L'Etat, c'est moi,"* which is a complete mistake. The State is the mass only in the sense in which it can be said of two men that they are identical because neither of them is named John. The contemporary State and the mass coincide only in being anonymous. But the mass-man does in fact believe that he is the State, and he will tend more and more to set its machinery working on whatsoever pretext, to crush beneath it any creative minority which disturbs it—disturbs it in any order of things: in politics, in ideas, in industry.

The result of this tendency will be fatal. Spontaneous social action will be broken up over and over again by State intervention; no new seed will be able to fructify. Society will have to live *for* the State, man *for* the governmental machine. And as, after all, it is only a machine whose existence and maintenance depend on the vital supports around it, the State, after sucking out the very marrow of society, will be left bloodless, a skeleton, dead with that rusty death of machinery, more gruesome than the death of a living organism.

Such was the lamentable fate of ancient civilisation. No doubt the imperial State created by the Julii and the Claudii was an admirable machine, incomparably superior as a mere structure to the old republican State of the patrician families. But, by a curious coincidence, hardly had it reached full development when the social body began to decay.

Already in the times of the Antonines (IInd Century), the State overbears society with its anti-vital supremacy. Society begins to be enslaved, to be unable to live except *in the service of the State.* The whole of life is bureaucratised. What results?

INTRODUCTION TO SPANISH LITERATURE

The bureaucratisation of life brings about its absolute decay in all orders. Wealth diminishes, births are few. Then the State, in order to attend to its own needs, forces on still more the bureaucratisation of human existence. This bureaucratisation to the second power is the militarisation of society. The State's most urgent need is its apparatus of war, its army. Before all the State is the producer of security (that security, be it remembered, of which the mass-man is born). Hence, above all, an army. The Severi, of African origin, militarise the world. Vain task! Misery increases, women are every day less fruitful, even soldiers are lacking. After the time of the Severi, the army had to be recruited from foreigners.

Is the paradoxical, tragic process of Statism now realised? Society, that it may live better, creates the State as an instrument. Then the State gets the upper hand and society has to begin to live for the State.[1] But for all that the State is still composed of the members of that society. But soon these do not suffice to support it, and it has to call in foreigners: first Dalmatians, then Germans. These foreigners take possession of the State, and the rest of society, the former populace, has to live as their slaves—slaves of people with whom they have nothing in common. That is what State intervention leads to: the people are converted into fuel to feed the mere machine which is the State. The skeleton eats up the flesh around it. The scaffolding becomes the owner and tenant of the house.

When this is realized, it rather confounds one to hear Mussolini heralding as an astounding discovery just made in Italy, the formula: "All for the State; nothing outside the State; nothing against the State." This alone would suffice to reveal in Fascism a typical movement of mass-men. Mussolini found a State admirably built up—not by him, but precisely by the ideas and the forces he is combating: by liberal democracy. He confines himself to using it ruthlessly, and, without entering now into a detailed examination of his work, it is indisputable that the results obtained up to the present cannot be compared with those obtained in political and administrative working by the liberal State. If he has succeeded in anything it is so minute, so little visible, so lacking in substance as with difficulty to compensate

1. Recall the last words of Septimus Severus to his sons: "Remain united, pay the soldiers, and take no heed of the rest."

for the accumulation of the abnormal powers which enable him to make use of that machine to its full extent.

Statism is the higher form taken by violence and direct action when these are set up as standards. Through and by means of the State, the anonymous machine, the masses act for themselves. The nations of Europe have before them a period of great difficulties in their internal life, supremely arduous problems of law, economics, and public order. Can we help feeling that under the rule of the masses the State will endeavour to crush the independence of the individual and the group, and thus definitely spoil the harvest of the future? . . .

Translator anonymous by request

Julián Marías

(1914-)

Born in Valladolid, at the age of five he moved with his family to Madrid, where he has since lived as a typical Madrid citizen. In high school he showed a special fondness for science and philosophy, and he took his university degree in the latter subject at the University of Madrid where Ortega y Gasset was one of his many famous professors. During the Spanish Civil War he was drafted on the Republican side. In 1948 he helped Ortega found the Institute of Humanities in Madrid. In 1951 he visited the United States, for which he professes great admiration, and taught at Wellesley, Harvard, the University of California, and Yale. He became a member of the Royal Academy in 1964.

Marías has written on many subjects, but he is basically a philosopher and is a follower of Ortega's theory of vital reason. His first work, *History of Philosophy* (1941), translated into English, scorns chronological enumeration of philosophical systems and meditates on human problems, about which he is fairly optimistic. Many now consider him the foremost thinker of contemporary Spain. Among his many other volumes are *Miguel de Unamuno* (1943), also translated into English; *Introduction to Philosophy* (1947), translated into English under the title *Reason and Life; Ortega and the Idea of Vital Reason* (1948); *The Historical Method of Generations* (1949); *Ideas on Metaphysics* (1953); *Existentialism in Spain* (1953), where he claims that existential thinking has long been a part of Spanish thought; and *The United States in Profile* (1956), in which he compares American ways and institutions with those of Europe.

Reason and Life, which he began in 1945, seeks to define Western Man in the twentieth century and to analyze his need for philosophical direction. Like Ortega, Marías insists on the temporal aspects of philosophy, and he believes that man finds individual life in the process of fulfilling his living task. Marías examines the relationships of truth to history, reason, life and its vital problems, concluding that philosophy, unlike life, can advance only at the pace of its own self-evidence and self-justification.

The selections include portions of Chapter 7 and Chapter 12, the final chapter of the volume.

Reason and Life

CHAPTER 7

THE HORIZON OF VITAL PROBLEMS
The Vital Urgencies

To live is, in the first place, to find oneself in the world, i.e., *already* in the world; any idea of an "entrance" into life is subsequent to life itself and presupposes an inference; that is, it always presents itself as a construction or interpretation. The limitation of my memories and the beliefs which I find around me make me infer that there was a time when I began to live; but all such things occur *within my life,* a reality which for me is the primary one and precedes all the other realities I may encounter. Now though "being in the world" is given to me without my having had to do anything about it, in order to go on being there I am ineluctably compelled to do something. In the first place, as we saw, I must make a vital project which will articulate the elements of my surroundings into the form of a repertory of possibilities; in the second place, I must set those possibilities in motion in order actually to make my life, i.e., in order to live, in the sense of *to go on living.*

But at this point things begin to get more complicated. Above all, I find around me figures of life, modes of being human (in a word, vital projects) which I have not invented, but which are "there," in my social milieu; these projects have been created originally by other individual men or women, but to me they present themselves in the first place as something *given* and simply existing. The raw material out of which I make my personal figure of life is the repertory of those figures of life which already exist socially; but as there are always several of these —though their number may, as happens in primitive societies, be very small—I must choose from them, and this can only be done, as I showed before, in view of a minimum basic figure of life of my own, of which I am inescapably the author, and which is what we call *vocation* in the most exact sense of that word;

even in the hypothetical limiting case of my finding in my circumstance only a single figure of life, I should still have to decide to make it mine, and not even then would it strictly speaking be *given* to me.

Provided that I have this vital project, things offer themselves to me as possibilities—or, secondarily, as impossibilities; possibilities for living, I mean, giving the verb "live" the concrete sense which it only takes on when it denotes a definite and particular figure of life. In view of this project I choose from the concrete "doings" which present themselves to me as possible, and thus I execute my life, setting in motion the mechanism of my psychophysical activities; breathing, nourishing myself, moving about, manipulating things, dealing with my fellow men, remembering, imagining, thinking. But it sometimes happens that my circumstance does not allow some one of these activities; for example I cannot drink, because there is no water within my reach; or I cannot go to a certain place because a river intervenes between it and me; or else I cannot have dealings with my fellow men, because they flee from me, or persecute me. It must be noted that the situation in my circumstance only affects me because I have some particular project or intention; now, at this very moment, there is no water in my immediate surroundings; but as I do not intend to drink, the situation does not present any problem to me; and if I want to be alone, as the hermit does, men's dislike of me is no great obstacle, but perhaps the opposite. Consequently, the important thing is what I wish to do. When, on account of the situation in which I find myself, I cannot do what I wish, I do *something else;* that is, I stop wishing, in the strict sense, what I wished before—even though perhaps I may go on desiring it; I give up my original intention and reform it, convert it into another, replace it by another and different one. Always? That is the question.

If it were so, life would be simple and without problems; problems arise precisely when, for one reason or another, I cannot give up my intention; when I have to do something definite, which seems to me to be necessary. This is where we may speak of *vital urgencies*; and I prefer to designate them by this word, rather than "necessities," in order to emphasize their circumstantiality; for indeed it is not sufficient to say that I "need" to do something; because if that were all, if I simply had to do it "some time"—as Mohammedans have to make the pilgrimage to

Mecca—it would be a simple matter; what is serious is that I have to do it here and now, and that is why it is urgent, imperative, a *weighty* matter; that is why it is *grave, gravis.* I must eat, not "some time," but now, that is, today; I have to breathe at this moment, because if I do not, I die; I have to give first aid to this wounded person before he or she bleeds to death, because without him or her I do not wish to live.

This shows that there are two types of intention; one of them is to *live,* i.e., to go on living; I consider as urgencies in the strict sense the demands which must be satisfied if I am to remain alive; but it must be noted that the fact that I regard such urgencies or demands as forms of pressure exerted upon me, and passively borne by me, implies the assumption that I wish to go on living; because if I did not, there would be no such pressure; that is to say, it is I who exert pressure, it is I who urge and constrain the circumstance with my intention of living; it is this pressure of mine which "throws things into relief," so to speak, and makes some of them necessary; so that "necessary" does not mean that they oblige or compel me, but rather that I *need* them, that they are needed by me and therefore necessary to me; food and air lose their tremendous, compelling and "urgent" significance as soon as I give up eating or breathing, as soon as I decide not to demand them; *requisite* means, after all, something *required*; that is, required *by me,* and its indispensability depends on my intending or requiring.

But there is a second type of intention: those which are "internal" to our living. I mean by this that what is required to go on living is not the only "urgent" thing, because the sphere of urgencies extends far beyond the demands of "mere" survival. It sometimes happens that I "need" vitally things from the absence of which my death will not result; if I lose my fortune, or do not win a woman's love, or am deprived of liberty, these situations do not prevent me from living, as would a lack of air, or icy cold, or hunger; and yet I say that the former things are "necessary" or vitally urgent. What do I mean by this?

The matter becomes perfectly clear as soon as one realizes that *to live,* in the case of man, does not mean anything specific which is of general application. The verb "to live," when its subject is the sheep or the shark, means something highly concrete and precise: to breathe by means of lungs or gills, to feed on grass or animal life, to reproduce themselves, to move about on the green grass or in the sea water; as long as the sheep and the shark can do these things, they live; these things suffice for them; but if, on the contrary, they are without them, then they can do nothing else but die; the sheep without grass or without air perishes: the shark without his catch, or thrown on the sand with his belly to the sun, has no recourse but to die. But in the case of man, as living does not mean anything specific, if he cannot do one thing, he *does another*; that is the key to the fabulous efficiency of the human being: his aptitude for trying out new forms of life, in view of the circumstances; in principle—naturally, this must be taken with a grain of salt—man is . . . whatever he is able to be. But this has its limiting aspect; if we look at things from another angle, it turns out that man, as he chooses his life, does not have a repertory of fixed "requirements," as happens in animal life: you cannot say what a man "needs" in order to live, until you know what exactly he means by "living," that is, what he has decided to be—and therefore *to need*; because that is the important thing: man decides to need certain things— the expression is deliberately paradoxical—because he chooses a certain being which he has not got, which is not given to him, and which he therefore has to *make for himself*, with just those things. And when a man decides absolutely, when he attaches himself to a form of life and *makes it his*, then "living" means for him that alone, and what is necessary to him for that project or intention is automatically necessary to him, because he does not see any sense in living otherwise, and so not to live *like that* means for him to die. This happens when a man wills absolutely and without restriction to be loyal, to be a Christian, to be brave, to be rich, to be powerful, to be truthful, to be the lover of a particular woman. If in one sense man is *whatever he can be*, in another, and again within certain limits, he is *whatever he wants to be*.

This fact puts the significance of our vital urgencies in its proper perspective; they too depend on my vital project; in other words: like every vital reality, they are not pure "facts" but are derived from life, in the concrete sense which this possesses *qua human life*: that is to say, they are derived from some precise figure of life or vital intention. Even what is usually considered most "brutal" and factual, our necessities, are something which is constituted in life, and implies a reference to it; something which —to force the expression a little—man *must make*. Because, properly speaking, not even necessities are given to him; they too are proposed, I mean posited in view of his intention. The only thing that man is given is his life, and that as something-to-be-made; and everything in it that is *life* must be made by man himself.

CHAPTER 12

PHILOSOPHY

Reflexions on the Ground Covered

The introduction to philosophy—I said when summarizing its requisites—has for its mission *the discovery and the constitution, within our concrete circumstance, of the ambit of philosophical activity—also concrete—which that circumstance demands.* I believe that I have fulfilled the requirement which this book took as its starting-point, and that I have completed the introduction to philosophy, not of just *any* man, but of a European of the mid-twentieth century, who finds himself obliged to set himself a very definite horizon of problems as soon as he needs to *give an account* of the situation in which he actually finds himself, because he intends to live *authentically,* i.e., *in the truth.*

The philosophical problems have successively appeared in a nascent state; that is, not as a repertory of ignorances of contradictions, but as realities which appear in my life and prevent me from knowing what to hold by. These problems have no given, i.e., already valid or accepted, solution; nor do they belong to the domain of individual branches of knowledge, because they demand a radical certitude; in other words, they require that an account should be given of reality itself, underneath its interpretations. Accordingly, the method of philosophy must be historical and vital reason, because history is, as we have already seen, the *organon*[1] of the regression from interpretations to the reality interpreted, and reason is life itself, in its function of apprehending reality in its actual connexions.

I have attempted, then, to show the necessity of the intro-

---

1. Organon: A method for scientific or philosophic procedure or investigation. (*Editor's note.*)

duction of philosophy; but in order to understand the right meaning of this expression, the reader must recall what I pointed out
at the beginning of Chapter VII; for man, things are "necessary"
in the sense that they are *needed* by him, that man himself actively
needs them, requires them, in order to carry out a particular
intention; using a deliberately paradoxical expression, I said that
a man *decides to need* certain things, when he chooses a particular
figure of life. Only in this way does the introduction to philosophy
become necessary; but it then becomes absolutely necessary. I
mean that the present situation, which is characterized by a
profound crisis of all its existing norms and, within these, of
current beliefs, only tolerates life as authentic when it takes the
form of a search for a radical truth capable of giving an account
of the situation itself and of the beliefs, even of the truths to which
the man of our time holds, but which have to be articulated in
such a manner that they acquire the shape of a world. Consequently, the exposition of our real situation was not something
added on to or prior to the introduction to philosophy, but an
intrinsic part of it and the principle of its justification. Two things,
then, must be remembered: the first, that our situation—unlike
others—requires the introduction to philosophy if life as authenticity
is to be possible in it; the second, that the introduction to philosophy
requires, in its turn, to be set in movement and justified by our
situation itself.

But if the introduction is effective, this means that we move,
when it is over, in the very ambit of philosophy. And we may
ask ourselves: Since when? In other words: At what moment
did we secure access to philosophy? In my opinion, the reply
does not allow of the slightest doubt; strange as it may appear,
the reply is: From the very beginning. Why?

The reader will remember what the driving force behind this
Introduction to Philosophy is, or has been: the situation in which a
man finds himself, and which consists in not knowing what to
hold by in respect of it, and so in respect of reality. This real
and not fictitious situation obliges man, if he really wants to
know what to hold by, to know what he has to do, and therefore
to know for what reason and for what purpose he has to do it,
obliges him, I repeat, to seek a radical certitude; and as he finds
in his circumstance a historico-social reality called philosophy,
which traditionally claims to possess radical truth, and at the
same time he finds that the claim is not bound to be true, and
therefore he cannot remain in that belief, he must confront that

reality, in order to see how far it is capable of giving him the certitude he needs. And then, from the standpoint of his actual situation, of which he has to "take stock," he finds himself compelled to make the attempt to penetrate into that philosophy which exists in his circumstance; and this task is what is called the introduction to philosophy, and has been carried out from the first page of this book.

Now the task which consists in making for yourself a radical certitude, when this is lacking, and you cannot live without it— I mean, you cannot live the concrete and authentic life you intend to live—is what we expressly call *making a metaphysic*. Accordingly, from the moment when the need of that radical certitude which you lack is first felt in your life, and the search for it is undertaken, you are making a metaphysic. As soon, then, as you actually begin the task which we call the introduction to philosophy, then the making of a metaphysic, in its strictest form, also begins. Consequently, every authentic contact with philosophy *itself*, with philosophy in its selfhood, moves *already* in the ambit of philosophy, and situates us within it. In a word, the introduction to philosophy, which presents itself as something prior to philosophy (the latter being, at the outset, absolutely problematical), subsequently turns out to have consisted in the setting in motion and justifying of philosophy itself, i.e., in an essential ingredient of the latter. In other words, the introduction to philosophy is in all strictness a part of philosophy. For that reason, now that we have arrived at this point we can look back over what we have been doing since the beginning of this book, which turns out to be philosophy.

Characteristics of the Knowledge Required: Radicality, System, Circumstantiality

We find that when we attempted to make our way into philosophy, we were already making philosophy, that is, we were already within it; on the other hand, we can only see what it is like and study its characteristics, after having made it—I mean, after having begun to make it. But this is no more than a consequence of the *radicality* of philosophy. Metaphysics, I said before, because it *is* a method or path towards reality, constitutes itself in its own movement, consists in its own active self-constitution; it must itself discover each of its own characteristics. For this reason, philosophy implies the requirement that it should justify itself, that it should not lean on any other certitude but should, on the contrary, give an account of reality itself, underneath its interpretations, and so, also, of the supposed certitudes which I encounter.

If man had dealings only with *things*—that is, with particular things—he would have no cause to make philosophy. He would carry out his vital actions, spontaneous or imposed, he would make technique in order to produce what he needed and did not find "there," he would ask himself about the being of the things that failed him, and he would attempt to make science. But it happens that man, as we have seen at some length, finds himself *with* things *in* his life, and each one of his doings depends in the last resort on the totality of his life, as being the reality in which those things are rooted. Things set him problems, then, not on account of what they are *qua* things, but on account of the reality they possess; consequently each of them refers him to that life in which it is encountered and by its reference to which it acquires the character of something *real*. Philosophy, then, does not aim at the "manipulation" of things—not even at their mental manipulation, as do the natural sciences—and so does not pretend to teach us anything about things as such; but as man has to make his life, and has to make it with things, it is necessary to him that his whole life should take part in the apprehension of each thing *qua* reality; in other words, he needs to give an account of it and, for that purpose, to refer it to his life, which is the very organ of comprehension, reason itself in its most strict and rigorous sense.

In fact, man does this all the time, because to live is already to understand, to interpret; man only lives by understanding, because what there is is present to him as reality. When man finds himself in a true belief with respect to the reality which is his life, he does not need to make any special effort in order to live because that belief functions automatically, setting each thing in a coherent perspective for him, allowing him to know at each moment what to hold by in respect of what he has to do. But when man does not find himself in one sufficient and universal certitude, although he may have a great many certitudes, he does not know what to hold by, he does not know what to do; and as each one of us must make himself the person he has to be, the consequence of this ignorance is that he cannot be *himself*, that is to say his life is possible only as alienation, alteration and inauthenticity. Man, therefore, needs to be in a radical certitude in order to be able to be *himself;* and if he does not possess such a certitude there are only two authentic ways open to him: to receive one or to make one.

The first way does not lie within his power, though it may be within his power to *accept* a certitude when it is sufficiently offered to him, I mean, when in order not to find himself in it he has to resist, to resort to a certain distortion or falsification of himself. The second way, on the contrary, always lies within his power; I mean that he can adopt this way, and attempt to make a certitude for himself. But it should be noted that the mere attempt, when it is effective, consists in realizing that the situation in which you find yourself is one of incertitude; it is equivalent, then, to reaching *ipso facto* a certitude about the situation (the content of which is, precisely, incertitude) and to judge it to be an untenable one; one which accordingly compels you to undertake a particular task, which is the search for that necessary certitude. Philosophy, in its authentic and original form (it must not be forgotten that "deficient modes" are found in everything human), occurs as radicality, because it is one of the essential modes of the radicalization of human life.

But this is not enough. The understanding of anything as reality implies, as we have just seen, the referring of it to the radical truth about the entirety of our lives; consequently, no isolated truth has a philosophical character or is philosophically true; the structure of reality is, as has been shown in the course of this book, systematic; as the function of reason is to apprehend this reality in its con-nexions or *com-prehend* it, philosophy, which claims actually to give an account of reality, is, of inexorable necessity, a *system.* But it should be noted once again that it is not primarily a question of an extrinsic necessity, of a desideratum of philosophy, proceeding from the "idea" which one has of it as a form of cognition, but that this necessity is derived from the systematic structure of the very reality which is in question. Human life is systematic; for that reason, and only for that reason, philosophy must be system-atic; which means that it always *is* a system, in so far as it is philosophy, and that in so far as it lacks a systematic character it is a deficient philosophy. But we have spoken of this in greater detail in other parts of this book, and it is unnecessary to insist further.

This requirement has in fact been satisfied in the history of philosophy, at least in its full and successful forms, and its evident-ness has been increasingly accepted, especially since Hegel. But there is a third requirement, which it is necessary to insist upon emphatically, in the face of a great part of the philosophical tradition, which, although subject to it, has usually denied it: circumstantiality. Philosophy, indeed, has aspired to be a consideration of reality *sub specie aeternitatis,* automatically valid for every situation, exhaustively and exclusively true; an aspiration which appeared in an extreme form in the "absolute knowledge" of Hegel, but which has by no means been peculiar to Hegelianism. Now this intention, which attempts no less than to usurp the point of view of God, cannot possibly be realized, and not merely on account of any material difficulty, but also on account of the structure of reality, one of the ingredients of which, as we have seen, is the perspective —mine, yours, the other fellow's. The "absolutism of the intellect" is also a circumstantially determined perspective, but it is marred by two errors: the first consists in the fact that it is ignorant of its own circumstantiality, and therefore is doubly circumstantial, since it does not succeed in escaping from the limitation contained in its circumstantiality by means of historical knowledge, in which each perspective recognizes itself as such and, therefore, as something implying the rest and virtually enriched by them; the second error, more serious still, resides in the fact that in the name of its illusory and necessarily unsuccessful aspiration, this absolutism gives up its own irreplaceable point of view, and with it the merit of being a *real* vision of what there is. We might point out yet a third error which lies heavy on the forms of "absolutism of the intellect" which still occur in our age: and that is, that besides being circumstantial— which is not a fault—it belongs to another circumstance—which *is* one; in a word, it is anachronistic and therefore also in this case unreal.

Philosophy must be, then, a radical, systematic and circumstantial cognition of the very reality I encounter beneath all its interpretations.

Translated by Kenneth Reid and Edward Sarmiento

DATE DUE
